Six Circles, One Dewdrop

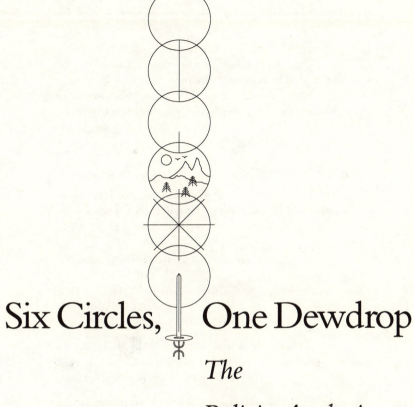

Six Circles, One Dewdrop

The

Religio-Aesthetic

World of

Komparu Zenchiku

Arthur H. Thornhill III

PRINCETON UNIVERSITY PRESS

PRINCETON, NEW JERSEY

Copyright © 1993 by Princeton University Press
Published by Princeton University Press, 41 William Street,
Princeton, New Jersey 08540
In the United Kingdom: Princeton University Press, Chichester,
West Sussex

Library of Congress Cataloging-in-Publication Data

Thornhill, Arthur H., 1951–
Six circles, one dewdrop : the religio-aesthetic world of Komparu
Zenchiku / Arthur H. Thornhill.
p. cm.
Includes bibliographical references and index.
ISBN 0-691-07352-X
1. Konparu, Zenchiku, b. 1405. Rokurin ichiro. 2. Nō. I. Title.
PN2924.5.N6T46   1993
895.6′22409—dc20   92-17863   CIP

Publication of this book has been aided by grants from the
Suntory Foundation and from the Japan Studies Endowment Fund
of the University of Hawaii at Manoa

This book has been composed in Linotron Bembo

Princeton University Press books are printed on acid-free paper,
and meet the guidelines for permanence and durability of the
Committee on Production Guidelines for Book Longevity of the
Council on Library Resources

Printed in the United States of America

I 2 3 4 5 6 7 8 9 10

For Lucy

Contents

List of Figures

Preface

THIS VOLUME is the outcome of a long fascination with the writings of Komparu Zenchiku that began during my undergraduate years at Princeton. During that period I worked under the guidance and generous encouragement of Karen Brazell, and I also consulted with William LaFleur, whose insights have continued to direct my later investigations. As a graduate student at Harvard, I was trained under the rigorous tutelege of Edwin Cranston in Japanese literature and Masatoshi Nagatomi in Buddhist studies. I am most grateful for this training, which enabled me to produce the present study.

Thanks go to the Japan Foundation and the Social Science Research Council, for grants that funded research in Japan; to the Japanese scholars Itō Masayoshi and Omote Akira, who kindly met with me and answered questions; to the estimable Kamikawa Rikuzō, who has tutored a generation of Japanologists; and to the many people who have read various versions of the manuscript and made suggestions, including Karen Brazell, Henry Smith, Peter Gregory, David Shaner, Rande Brown Ōuchi, Peter Lee, and Thomas Hare. Specific nuggets of information gleaned from David McCraw, Stephen Carter, Michael Saso, Robert Huey, and Royall Tyler, among others, have found their way into the text. It goes without saying that all errors are my own responsibility. Summer grants from the Japan Endowment Fund of the University of Hawaii—funded by a grant from the Japanese government—assisted me in the revision of the manuscript. I would also like to thank Dr. Hiroshi Motoyama, director of the Institute for Religious Psychology in Tokyo, for his insight and guidance. And a special debt is owed my wife, Lucy Lower, whose continued support and counsel, as both colleague and friend, have made this book possible.

The particulars of the text should be evident. Modified Hepburn romanization is used for Japanese, modified Wade-Giles for Chinese (which, while hardly perfect, seems more intelligible to the general reader than pinyin). Japanese names are given surname first; but, of course, many of the traditional names included here do not contain surnames at all, consisting of literary sobriquets, Buddhist names, professional names, and the like. The masculine pronoun is used in cases of indeterminate gender. Characters are included only where they seem crucial to the understanding of the passage; the character glossary provides key terms and names for those interested. For the sake of brevity, most titles of works are left untranslated, but English renditions, along with characters, are included in the bibliography. Ages are given by the traditional Japanese count: an individual is age 1 at birth, and the age increases at the time of the new year. (Since precise birthdates are seldom known, ages by the Western count cannot be determined accurately.)

Abbreviations

KKSS	*Komparu koden shūsei*
NKBT	*Nihon koten bungaku taikei*
NST	*Nihon shisō taikei*
SBCP	*A Source Book of Chinese Philosophy*
SKKS	*Shinkokinshū*
T	*Taishō daizōkyō*
ZS	*Zeami shū*
ZZ	*Zeami, Zenchiku*

Six Circles, One Dewdrop

Chapter One: Introduction

THE WESTERN fascination with noh drama is an enduring phenomenon of astonishing vitality and impressive pedigree. In a general sense, the interest falls into two broad categories. First there are those who examine the noh texts as works of Japanese literature. Drawing from incidents portrayed in such classics as the *Tales of Ise*, *Tale of Genji*, and *Tale of the Heike*, and replete with verse from both Chinese and Japanese sources, noh plays contain perhaps the greatest poetry of the "high medieval" age. The prototypical investigator of this persuasion is Ezra Pound, whose insights into the "unity of image" in the finest plays sparked new directions in modern poetry. In the other camp, there are those who study noh primarily as a dramatic form. Ostensibly ritualistic, abstract, and "symbolic," noh has been an inspiration for dramatists seeking alternate modes of theatrical expression that deviate from the norm of realism in the Western theater of the recent past. The most illustrious example is William Butler Yeats, who discovered in noh a congenial dramatic form that helped to shape his own plays based on Irish legend. Subsequently there have been many noh-inspired experiments in modern theater.

For investigators of both persuasions, the dominant figure in the tradition is Zeami Motokiyo (1363–1443). He is both the author of the finest plays in the repertoire and the stage performer who, with his father Kannami Kiyotsugu (1333–1384), synthesized the form of *sarugaku* that became so popular with the discriminating patrons of the day, the prototype of the stage art performed today as noh. In addition, Zeami was a prolific theoretician, leaving a group of treatises on the art of acting to be studied in secret by his heirs. To discern the qualities of his stage art, to appreciate his skill as a dramatist and performer, these works are invaluable. The continued interest in Zeami by all scholars of noh is entirely justified.

There are other reasons to study noh, however, and more particularly the genre of *nōgakuron*, or "treatises on the art of noh." Certainly, insofar as these works are repositories of performance wisdom, they can be explored, interpreted, and recast into language intelligible to artists of other dramatic traditions. But to the student of medieval Japanese culture, these works are valuable in quite a different way. They can be investigated as what Michel Foucault calls "monuments," the objects of study in his notion of the "archaeology of knowledge." That is, instead of investigating the artifacts of cultural discourse as "documents"—the veiled, incomplete record of the writer's initial thoughts, of a more coherent meaning to be extracted—the archaeologist respects the integrity of the monument as a discourse object with its own identity, its own volume. Thus the avowed goal is not to interpret, but rather "to define discourses in their specificity; to show in what way the set of rules that they put into operation is irreducible to any other; to follow them the whole length of their exterior ridges, in order to underline them the better."[1]

For the study of *nōgakuron*, this attitude suggests, first of all, that we should pay attention to the specific modes of expression. Some Western readers (and translators) wade through Zeami's writings to extract a practical meaning, a body of knowledge that can be transferred to another context. In the process, they marginalize an extremely important aspect of the original texts: their extensive allusion to literary and intellectual traditions current in medieval Japan. To the reader familiar with these traditions, Zeami is not merely a dramatist and performer who produces timeless art, he is a major participant in the ongoing intellectual and cultural discourse of his time. In other words, the metaphorical devices, the systematic typologies and allusions in his writings, are in no way secondary to the function of these works; on the contrary, to the dispassionate observer, they often emerge as the most fundamental, most manifest "meaning."

This "archaeological" approach is eminently suited to the theoretical writings of Komparu Zenchiku (1405–1468?), Zeami's son-in-law and legitimate artistic heir. The focus of the current study is a group of texts recorded by Zenchiku that feature a sequence of seven symbols, entitled "six circles and one dewdrop" (*rokurin ichiro*). These abstract categories are used to present a host of aesthetic, dramaturgical, and pedagogical principles that Zenchiku considered the essence of his art. Traditionally, noh scholars have viewed Zenchiku's writings with a combination of apprehension and disdain. Forever cast in the shadow of the illustrious Zeami, Zenchiku is criticized either as derivative and unoriginal or as excessively abstract and theoretical.[2] In fact there is considerable validity to these characterizations. Perhaps 90 percent of their "content"—that is, teaching on the art of performance—is based upon principles expounded

[1] Michel Foucault, *The Archaeology of Knowledge,* trans. A. M. Sheridan Smith (New York: Harper Colophon Books, 1976), 139.

[2] For example, see Nishio Minoru, *Dōgen to Zeami* (Tokyo: Iwanami shoten, 1965), 292, and Yasura Okakō, *Chūseiteki bungaku no tankyū* (Tokyo: Yūseidō, 1970), 251.

by Zeami. Furthermore, once the basic symbolic categories are established, they take on a life of their own. As Zenchiku's treatises evolve, they absorb an ever-increasing number of conceptual analogies whose relevance to dramatic performance is at times obscure. Yet these criticisms are relevant only if one is *looking for* transparency, pragmatic content, and inner consistency. What impresses first-time readers of these works is the very obscurity of his terse, cryptic categorizations and the formal elegance of his diagrams. Rather than considering this obscurity an impediment, a mere puzzle to be solved, the best approach is to excavate deeper to uncover the larger patterns of cultural discourse this facade of discontinuity represents, without yielding to a premature urge to clarify and paraphrase.

MICHI: THE WAY OF THE MEDIEVAL ARTS

In his study *Michi: chūsei no rinen*, Konishi Jin'ichi organizes his account of medieval Japanese literature and aesthetics around the concept of *michi* (or *dō*, C. *tao*), a term frequently used to indicate the "path" a student follows in learning such traditional arts as poetry, calligraphy, and tea (e.g., *kadō*, *shodō*, *chadō*). The term appears in such Heian period works as the *Genji monogatari*, indicating specialization and expertise in a given art. For example, *koto, fue no michi* refers to the pastime of playing the koto or flute; *michi no hito* denotes an accomplished artist.[3] Here *michi* represents the long "road" the devotee has traveled in learning his art, suggesting both continuity and the passage of time. As organized schools of poetry, calligraphy, and painting developed in the late Heian period, these two aspects of michi can be seen in the fixed styles the artist would practice in a prescribed manner, and in the transmission of the teachings that linked generations of artists. Konishi delineates three additional aspects of michi that emerged at this time: a standardization of technique and conception that encouraged conformity to a set ideal, rather than individual creativity and innovation; a notion of universality that implied that accomplished masters of various arts shared certain qualities of refinement and knowledge; and of course the social prestige and political influence enjoyed by the heads of the institutionalized schools.

In the Chinese intellectual tradition inherited by the Japanese, the term *tao* has many different uses, but these fall into two broad categories. In the texts of philosophical Taoism, it is the formless essence of the universe, the source of all things. In following the Tao, one must abandon all precon-

[3] Konishi Jin'ichi, *Michi: Chūsei no rinen* (Tokyo: Kōdansha, 1975), 13. These expressions are cited by Konishi. Many of the central themes of this work are summarized in his "Michi and Medieval Writing," in Earl Miner, ed., *Principles of Classical Japanese Literature* (Princeton: Princeton University Press, 1985), 181–208.

ceived notions of right and wrong, all externally imposed models. The Tao has no shape, so man should spontaneously follow the intuitions of an unfettered mind: "the Way that can be known is not the true Way." Conversely, Confucianists often described *tao* as the set manner in which civilization should function and man should behave. Emphasizing concrete manifestations of the Way, they devised codes of moral behavior to develop "humanity and righteousness." Chinese Buddhists in turn adopted the term *tao* to denote the traditional path of ascetic discipline and meditation followed by the renunciate.

Due to the overwhelming influence of Buddhism in the Heian period, the Way of the arts described above came to be associated with the path of spiritual cultivation taught by the Buddha. As a result, pursuits such as poetry and calligraphy assumed an attitude of high seriousness. On the one hand, artistic discipline became a vehicle for spiritual growth, and so the mastery of one's art was implicitly equated with the attainment of religious salvation or transcendental wisdom; conversely, self-cultivation was considered necessary for the highest levels of artistic attainment.[4] More than anything else, this developed conception of *michi* is responsible for the religious associations of the traditional Japanese arts. As the religious paradigm was more fully adopted by the artists and aestheticians of the Kamakura and Muromachi periods, the path of artistic discipline assumed a set pattern based on a characteristically Mahayana interpretation of spiritual development. In general terms, this is a three-stage process: (1) the careful study and disciplined practice of established styles or models, (2) the internalization of these models, and (3) a breakthrough into a new mode of unfettered creativity that transmits the inner essence of the established model.[5] In this fashion, externally imposed Confucian discipline gives way to Taoistic spontaneity and freedom.

The most visible artifact of this attitude toward artistic praxis is the genre of artistic treatises, found in many traditions, including poetry, noh, calligraphy, painting, and music. These works tend to be fragmentary; many times the most important material is to be orally transmitted, allegedly too precious to be written down. In this regard, they show the influence of esoteric Buddhism, where the mantras, mudras, and meditation practices are not only secret, but also ineffective without the personal initiation and empowerment of the disciple by his teacher. For this and other reasons, much of the tradition of artistic transmission is no longer

---

[4] The distinction between these two attitudes is discussed in Tu Wei-ming, "The Idea of the Human in Mencian Thought: An Approach to Chinese Aesthetics," in Susan Bush and Christian Murck, eds., *Theories of the Arts in China* (Princeton: Princeton University Press, 1983), 57.

[5] As described in Richard B. Pilgrim, "Zeami and the Way of Nō," *History of Religions* 12, 2 (November 1972), 138.

accessible. Still, these works are rewarding to study, for they possess their own inner logic, their own modes of knowledge. Their most consistent feature is the use of typologies: groupings of styles or principles that typify excellence and embody the inner essence of the art. This mode of representing practical and theoretical knowledge has a long history in the Chinese tradition, and as we study the individual typologies that appear in noh theory, strong resonances with other systems will occur.

Certainly poetry is the most prestigious of the michi arts, and for most of the medieval period it generates the major developments in aesthetics. An appropriate beginning for this study, then, is a cursory examination of the development of typologies in *waka* theory. For in a sense, Zenchiku's rokurin ichiro treatises are simply part of the larger discourse of the transmission of artistic practice.

In the early history of waka, the seminal text is the Kana Preface to the *Kokinshū*, composed in the early tenth century by Ki no Tsurayuki. Most of its critical terms and categories are borrowed from the Chinese poetic tradition. The best known of these is the dialectical pair of *kokoro*—the inner emotional "heart" of a poem, its content, meaning, conception—and *kotoba*, the outer "leaves of words," its diction, expression, style. Tsurayuki devotes even more attention, however, to the *rikugi*, a group of six Chinese terms that denote six styles or rhetorical modes of verse, illustrating each with example poems. To be sure, by Tsurayuki's time the precise meanings of these categories were obscure even to the Chinese, and they are of questionable relevance to *waka*.

The *Wakatai jisshu* (Ten styles of waka), traditionally attributed to Mibu no Tadamine (d. ca. 920), represents a significant advance in waka theory. Here there are ten styles, some derived from the rikugi. As before, there is a prototype for this typology in the Chinese poetic tradition, but now the categories seem to isolate significant qualities of native poetic expression. For example, one is the *kōjō-tai*, the "style of elevated emotion," most notable because its definition contains the first significant use of the term *yūgen*, the ideal of "mystery and depth" that is central to medieval aesthetics.

A major development occurs with the *Waka kuhon* (Nine varieties of waka) of Fujiwara Kintō (966–1041).[6] These nine categories are modeled on the "Nine Levels" of Rebirth in the Pure Land of Amida, nine distinct varieties of salvation attainable by believers in Amida's Original Vow; the level of rebirth is dependent upon the degree of accumulated merit. This

[6] For details, see Arthur H. Thornhill, "Typology in Traditional Japanese Poetics: The Reception of Chinese Buddhist Models," in Raymond A. Moody and Cornelia N. Moore, eds., *Comparative Literature East and West: Topics and Trends* (Honolulu: University of Hawaii Press, 1989), 1:177–83.

poetic treatise presents not merely descriptive categories, but a hierarchy of value. The nine styles are presented in the order of highest to lowest: when read in this fashion, the work can be seen as an evaluative ranking of poetic styles current in Kintō's time. Conversely, when the nine categories are read in reverse order, the treatise provides a normative model for the aspiring poet, who might begin with the lower styles and proceed to the more difficult. Furthermore, Kintō succinctly describes the qualities of each level. For the first time, we see three functions coming together in one typology: the enumerative, the descriptive, and the normative.

This new dimension of hierarchy is the direct result of the adoption of the Buddhist paradigm of the Nine Levels.[7] Absorbing the hierarchical mindset of the ranking systems of the governing beauracracy, Chinese Buddhism is replete with such typologies. The most famous of these is the Four Teachings associated with Chih-i (538–597), the de facto founder of the T'ien-t'ai School. The first of the p'an-chiao (evaluation of the teachings), this system imposes a sense of order upon the vast canon of Buddhist scripture imported from India by assigning each work to one of five periods and eight categories, which are then distilled into four categories: pitika (of the "lesser vehicle" only), shared, separate, and perfect. Inevitably, the intent of p'an-chiao is not merely to classify, but to present a hierarchy of value. In Chih-i's system, the Perfect teachings of the Lotus Sutra are supreme; in the similar fivefold division of the Hua-yen School, the highest truths are of course those of the Avataṃsaka Sūtra. At the same time, as expounded in the One Vehicle doctrine of the Lotus, and more generally through the notion of upāya, or "skillful means," the perfect teaching comprises all previous teachings, and conversely, there is an ultimate aspect to even the most provisional, incomplete teachings of the Buddha. These gradations of doctrine are often compared with the ten stages of a bodhisattva's spiritual progress, as expounded in the Daśabhūmika-sūtra.

In Japan, the first to develop his own set of p'an-chiao (J. hangyō) was Kūkai (774–835), the founder of the esoteric Shingon Sect. His Jūjūshin ron (Treatise on the ten stages of the development of mind) represents an important revolution within the Buddhist tradition, because it classifies not simply Buddhist teachings, but states of mind.[8] This is clearly implied in the title, and in the rankings, which include not just scriptures imported

---

[7] The Chinese practice of evaluating government officials by a similar nine-tiered grading system is discussed in John Timothy Wixted, "The Nature of Evaluation in the Shih-p'in (Gradings of Poets) by Chung Hung (A.D. 469–518)," in Bush and Murck, eds., Theories of the Arts in China, 225–64. It is clear, however, that Kintō's immediate inspiration is the Buddhist model.

[8] As discussed in Yuasa Yasuo, Kodaijin no seishin sekai (Kyoto: Minerva shobō, 1980), 221 ff.

from India, but also doctrines of indigenous Chinese schools of thought. They begin with the "outer writings" of Confucianism and Taoism and proceed through various doctrines of the "lesser vehicle," the Madhyāmika, the Yogācarā, and the Chinese schools of T'ien-t'ai and Hua-yen, before reaching the highest stage, the "secret treasury" of eso-teric practice as taught in Shingon. The strong presence of esoteric Bud-dhism in the religious and cultural mainstream clearly distinguishes the Japanese tradition from the Chinese. One result is an increasing emphasis on a hierarchy of experiential states in the discourse of artistic theory, and a more general emphasis on the primacy of the mind/heart—a phenome-non that this study will examine in both the artistic and intellectual tradi-tions. As noted earlier, the esoteric tradition is also responsible for the rhetoric of secrecy in the transmission from master artist to disciple.

It is no coincidence that the new hierachical dimension of poetic theory found in the *Waka kuhon* occurs in the early eleventh century, for this is precisely the period when the michi paradigm enters the arts. Now this sense of progression, of stages along the Way, becomes an important aspect of the typologies presented in literary and art theory. As the notion of michi develops in the medieval age, artists are increasingly constrained by convention and orthodoxy, yet at the same time artistic accomplish-ment implicitly has soteriological value.

The waka of the early medieval period illustrates these two complemen-tary outcomes. On the one hand, practitioners such as Fujiwara Shunzei (1114–1204) go to extraordinary lengths to justify poetry as an art of spiritual significance, and indeed the styles of poetry characteristic of the *Shinkokinshū* age are saturated with Buddhist influence. The poetic trea-tises of Shunzei's son Teika, featuring his own typology of Ten Styles (*jittei*), become the cornerstone of the later critical tradition; of the ten, the Style of Deep Feeling (*ushin-tei*), emblematic of sincere emotion, is consid-ered most fundamental. At the same time, however, one must not forget the continued strength of the conservative Nijō poets, whose implicit notion of michi emphasizes conformity to traditional diction and thematic treatment, rather than the inner depth that accrues from the practice of waka. For them, poetry is less a private, quasi-spiritual discipline than an endeavor of scholastic pedigree and political power.

Zeami's treatises on the art of noh contain many purely descriptive typologies that serve to identify and categorize accepted styles or princi-ples of performance. For example, he frequently discusses the *go'on*, five varieties of vocalization that accompany different compositions: con-gratulatory, yūgen, love, sorrow, and "the sublime" (*rangyoku*). At the same time, the hierachical mode of classification is eminently suited to his major theme, the training of the young actor. In the *Fūshi kaden*, an early work, he describes the cultivation of the Flower (*hana*) at different stages in a performer's career. The most poetic of Zeami's typologies, representative of his later views, is his Nine Ranks (*kyūi*). As with Kintō's Nine Varieties, the Nine Ranks represent specific artistic styles, ranked by absolute value. However, Zeami explicitly discusses the proper order of learning, which is *not* simply from lowest to highest. One starts at the middle, proceeds to master the highest levels, and only then descends to the lowest ranks. This process is explicitly based upon the paradigm of ascetic practice: the devotee begins at the level of the ordinary, practices until he attains a peak experience, a glimpse at the Absolute, and then descends from his enlightened position to affirm the nonduality of the highest and the lowest, and to save others.[9]

Zenchiku's "six circles and one dewdrop" is a symbolic construct whose form echoes all of the above, and many other relational models as well. As will be seen, it has no single, explicit prototype in either the artistic or religious/intellectual traditions, yet its creator and his contemporaries go to extraordinary lengths to align it to established typologies of dramaturgical and poetic theory, Buddhist doctrine, Confucian thought, and Shinto cosmology.

THE FORMATION OF THE *ROKURIN ICHIRO* TEXTS

The following chapters study the first two extant treatises composed by Zenchiku that deal with his "six circles and one dewdrop" system: *Rokurin ichiro no ki* (A record of six circles and one dewdrop) and *Rokurin ichiro no ki chū* (Commentary to "A record of six circles and one dewdrop"). Devised to represent a host of aesthetic, dramaturgical, and pedagogical principles Zenchiku received in training from his teacher Zeami, this symbolic typology of seven categories can be seen as a repository and also a reformulation of Zeami's teachings. Therefore, initially these categories are measured against the writings of Zeami, to demonstrate Zenchiku's own interpretation of Zeami's theories and his further development of certain teachings. The emphasis, however, is upon the dynamics of the rokurin ichiro typology itself: the six circles are analyzed as embodying a "centrifugal" progression, which delineates the generation of specific artistic effects, and also a "centripetal" process, by which the actor develops ever more profound levels of his art.

Perhaps the most extraordinary and valuable feature of these writings is

---

[9] Yasura Okakō states that Zeami's art and writings reflect this paradigm of religious training more completely than other medieval artists, who often adopted Buddhist paradigms merely for rhetorical purposes. Yasura, *Chūseiteki bungaku no tankyū*, 242. This is hard to judge, but it is true that—partly because they were "secret"—Zeami's writings are deeply personal, avoiding the flowery ornamentation prevalent in waka treatises.

the existence of two commentaries appended to the *Ki*, written by contemporaries of Zenchiku. The first is an analysis of the seven categories from a Buddhist perspective, composed by Shigyoku (1383–1463), abbot of the Kaidan-in at Tōdai-ji in Nara and an authority on the doctrines of the Kegon School. The second was written by Ichijō Kaneyoshi (or Kanera; 1402–1481), the famous scholar and court official. He responds with a primarily Confucian analysis that draws from the established Chinese classics, the newly imported writings of Neo-Confucianism, and also the native Shinto tradition. In the succeeding chapters, these commentaries are closely scrutinized.

It is important to savor fully the unique circumstances surrounding the creation of this document. Certainly, it is not unusual for a religious figure to engage in literary activity; there are many famous examples from Kūkai down through Myōe Shōnin and Ikkyū. And of course scholarship and poetry are both valued activities in the moral cultivation of the Confucianist. There is also the pattern of the professional poet who assumes the identity of a Buddhist renunciate as a convenient platform for his art: examples include Bishop Henjō and Saigyō. But the rokurin ichiro texts represent a different phenomenon. Here Shigyoku and Kaneyoshi act "professionally" as spokesmen for their respective intellectual/spiritual traditions, commenting on a treatise that expounds principles of artistic praxis. In his normal professional role, Shigyoku would compose a commentary on a sutra or a Chinese Buddhist work; similarly, Kaneyoshi might write a Confucian interpretation of passages from the *Great Learning* or Chu Hsi. But here both men are required to respond to *the same text*, one that is not explicitly allied to any single intellectual tradition. Zenchiku's seven categories are sufficiently abstract to accommodate contrasting statements from the respective commentators, statements that in other contexts might seem contradictory. Furthermore, in the succeeding drafts, Zenchiku himself responds to the remarks of these two learned authorities, assimilating their ideas and expanding the boundaries of his original conception. The result is an intimate intellectual and cultural dialogue among three minds more revealing than the orthodox pronouncements each might make in more formal, conventional surroundings.

The importance of this phenomenon is twofold. First, cognate Buddhist and Confucian metaphysical concepts are aligned, through their mutual application to Zenchiku's theoretical framework. Thus, the composite of Zenchiku's symbolic system and the two commentaries can be seen as a microcosm of the intellectual and cultural dialogue among the dominant creeds of the Muromachi period. At the same time, we are provided with a penetrating view of Buddhist and Confucian values and attitudes as they enter the realm of the arts. These commentaries illuminate not only the often-noted influence of Buddhism and Confucianism on the arts, but also how each tradition evaluates the role of artistic praxis in furthering its avowed goal of spiritual or moral cultivation.

ZENCHIKU AND THE *SARUGAKU* TRADITION

During Zeami's time, the Komparu troupe, earlier known as the Emai-za[10] (or Takeda-za), was considered the oldest of the Yamato *sarugaku* groups. It claimed direct descent from Hata no Kōkatsu (or Kawakatsu),[11] a minister to Shōtoku Taishi in the early seventh century and the founder of Kōryū-ji, a prominent Buddhist temple in the Uzumasa section of Kyoto. The Hata clan was of Chinese origin—the *Nihon shoki* indicates that they first immigrated during the reign of Emperor Ōjin (ca. A.D. 300)—and wielded influence at court in the early centuries of Japanese imperial rule. Zeami himself acknowledges the importance of Kōkatsu in this extraordinary passage from the *Fūshi kaden*:

> In our own country, during the reign of the Emperor Kinmei, on an occasion when the Hatsuse River in Yamato overflowed its banks, a jar floated down in the current. A high court official picked up the jar near the cedar gate of the Miwa shrine. Inside was a young child. His face was gentle, and he was like a jewel. Because the infant seemed to have descended from heaven, the incident was reported to the emperor at the imperial palace. That very night, the child appeared to the emperor in a dream and said, "I am the reborn spirit of the First Emperor of the Ch'in dynasty in China. My destiny has a connection with Japan, and I now appear to you." The emperor, thinking this occurrence a miracle, had the child brought to serve in court. When he grew to manhood, he came to be of surpassing talent and wisdom, and at the age of fifteen, he rose to the rank of minister. He was given the family name of Shin (C. Ch'in). Because

[10] The name Emai (or Enmai, or Enman-i) most likely derives from the name of a Buddhist temple, the Enman-ji, with which the troupe was once affiliated. A branch temple of Kōfuku-ji, it was probably located near Yakushi-ji in Nara. See Hirose Tamahiro, *Nō to Komparu* (Kyoto: Hatsune shobō, 1969), 134 ff., and P. G. O'Neill, *Early Nō Drama* (London: Lund Humphries, 1958), 12–13. Dōmoto Masaki speculates that the character *i* (well) in the name may denote a sacred water source on the temple grounds, one used in the Buddhist ritual *shunigatsu-e* (popularly known as *omizutori*) at Tōdai-ji, traditionally performed in the second month. Professional sarugaku entertainers were key participants in this annual observance, largely supplanting the roles of the *shushi* priests. See O'Neill, *Early Nō Drama*, 6. Furthermore, Dōmoto associates the name Komparu (golden spring) with a prayer still recited in the Nara region at the new year, "O first water of spring, bubbling up like gold." Dōmoto also summarizes many other theories for the origin of the name Komparu; it may be drawn from the poetic phrase "the coming spring (*komu haru*)." See Dōmoto Masaki, *Zeami* (Tokyo: Geki shobō, 1986), 590–91, n. 3.

[11] For a biography of Kōkatsu, see Imai Kei'ichi, *Hata no Kōkatsu* (Kyoto: Sōgeisha, 1968).

that Chinese character is pronounced "Hata" in Japanese, he was called Hata no Kōkatsu.[12]

Prince Shōtoku, at a time when there were disturbances in the land, asked this Hata no Kōkatsu to perform sixty-six dramatic pieces, following the precedents set down at the time of the gods and buddhas, and the prince himself made sixty-six masks for Hata no Kōkatsu's use. Kōkatsu performed these entertainments at the Shishinden Hall at the imperial palace at Tachibana.[13] The country soon became peaceful. Prince Shōtoku then passed this entertainment on for the benefit of future generations.[14]

This fanciful tale contains one verifiable fact: the existence of Kōkatsu's relationship with Shōtoku Taishi, which is recorded in the *Nihon shoki*.[15]

The second important figure in this lineage is Hata no Ujiyasu, an actor who performed at the court of Emperor Murakami (r. 946–967). Modern scholars acknowledge his existence and concede that he might have performed the art known as *sangaku*.[16] He also is mentioned in the *Fūshi kaden*, identified as the direct ancestor of a Komparu performer: "Mitsutarō and Komparu [Yasaburō] are descendents of Hata no Ujiyasu, [the latter] of the twenty-ninth generation. These performers are of the Emai troupe of the province of Yamato. This family possesses items handed down from Ujiyasu, including a demon mask carved by Prince Shōtoku, an image of the god of Kasuga Shrine, and a relic of the Buddha."[17]

This Mitsutarō was Zenchiku's great uncle, Yasaburō his father. The genealogy of the three generations preceding Zenchiku is shown in figure 1-1.[18] Dōmoto Masaki notes the unusual line of succession, shifting from

[12] The reading "Hada" was common in the medieval era and is provided in the original; the first character in the personal name Kōkatsu (or Kawakatsu) means "river" and is thus related to the legend recounted here.

[13] Shōtoku Taishi is believed to have been born in the vicinity of Tachibana-dera, but there is no evidence that the palace was located there.

[14] Text in Omote Akira and Katō Shūichi, eds., *Zeami, Zenchiku*, Nihon shisō taikei (Tokyo: Iwanami shoten, 1974), 24:38–39 (hereafter, referred to as *ZZ*), trans. in Thomas J. Rimer and Yamazaki Masakazu, *On the Art of the Nō Drama: The Major Treatises of Zeami* (Princeton: Princeton University Press, 1984), 32–33.

[15] See W.G. Aston, trans., *Nihongi* (Rutland, Vt.: Tuttle Books, 1972), book 2, 127. By the time of Emperor Kammu (r. 781-806), a branch of the Hata family was known for its musical performances. See Hirose, *Nō to Komparu*, 73.

[16] Imported from the continent during the Nara period, sangaku is considered the major prototype for what became sarugaku. See Hirose, *Nō to Komparu*, 78 ff.

[17] *ZZ*, 40. These items were the "three treasures" of the Komparu family and are mentioned by Zenchiku in his own writings. The *gigaku* mask attributed to Shōtoku Taishi is still in the family's collection. See Itō Masayoshi, *Komparu Zenchiku no kenkyū* (Kyoto: Akao shōbundō, 1970), 295–300.

[18] This diagram is a modified version of that in Itō, *Komparu Zenchiku no kenkyū*, 11. The recurring name Bishaō may echo Bishamonten (S. Vaiśravana), a Vedic god of good fortune said to be the underlying "Buddhist" essence (*honji*) of the deified Kōkatsu.

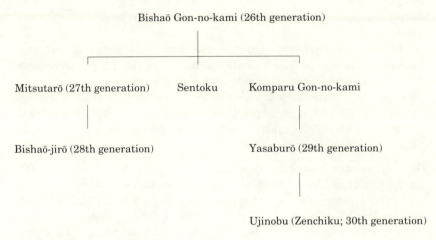

Bishaō Gon-no-kami (26th generation)

Mitsutarō (27th generation)   Sentoku   Komparu Gon-no-kami

Bishaō-jirō (28th generation)   Yasaburō (29th generation)

Ujinobu (Zenchiku; 30th generation)

FIG. 1-1. Komparu Lineage

Mitsutarō's son to the son of his brother, rather than a grandson. He speculates that Komparu Gon-no-kami—the first of the Emai-za to use the name Komparu—was a more popular performer than Bishaō-jirō and thus had sufficient leverage to install his own son Yasaburō as successor.[19] Presumably, the name Komparu was considered an important draw by all branches of the family.

Komparu Gon-no-kami is mentioned in the *Sarugaku dangi*.[20] By his time the Emai troupe had established a close relationship with Kōfuku-ji, the great Nara temple associated with the Fujiwara, and with its affiliated shrine Kasuga-taisha. Actors from the Emai troupe performed the most prestigious roles at the annual *takigi* (torchlight)[21] noh held at the Southern Great Gate of Kōfuku-ji and at the Wakamiya Festival at Kasuga, a tradition that continues to this day. Thus, the Komparu family dominated sarugaku in the Nara region, which maintained an aura of prestige as the site of the ancient capital. The ritual performances of *Okina* required of all sarugaku troupes were a particular point of pride in the Komparu fam-

---

[19] Dōmoto, *Zeami*, 200–201.

[20] "Concerning performances in the countryside: Komparu Gon-no-kami and Kongō Gon-no-kami never earned high success. The shogun did not attend their subscription performances in the capital. Komparu himself, in his subscription performances in Kyoto, was not a success, abandoned his series after two days, and retired to the countryside. Kongō, too, when performing in a noh competition at Nara, was asked to stop and leave after only two performances. Still, the fact that these two accomplished as much as they did in an age when the standards of sarugaku were so high (i.e., during Yoshimitsu's time) is quite significant." *ZZ*, 298; translation modified from Rimer and Yamazaki, *Art of Nō Drama*, 232–33.

[21] See note 41.

ily, an attitude that emerges with increasing clarity in Zenchiku's later writings.

Written many years before Zenchiku married into Zeami's family, the *Fūshi kaden* passages cited above demonstrate the Kanze troupe's recognition of the pedigree claimed by the Komparu troupe. In fact, Zeami often used the Hata surname in his signature. Dōmoto speculates that, despite the Kanze troupe's recent successes in the capital, it felt insecure.[22] The Komparu lineage within the sarugaku tradition was superior, and the *Fūshi kaden* was recorded, in part, to establish a parallel history within the Kanze family. The fourth section cites "a sacred work" as the source for this early history, and Dōmoto suggests that this was a genealogical text that originated in the Emai troupe. It was lent to Zeami, and permission was granted to use the Hata surname. In exchange, the Komparu family, in an unstable financial position since the passing of Zenchiku's grandfather Gon-no-kami, was afforded opportunities to perform in the capital, and to mingle with the rich and powerful of Zeami's acquaintance. Another hint of close ties is the "Moto" component of Zeami's personal name Motokiyo, perhaps adopted in emulation of the Komparu lineage, where it occurs frequently. Dōmoto even speculates that Zeami's wife may have been of the Komparu family.[23] In any case, the *Sarugaku dangi* suggests previous marriage between the two families,[24] and the Yamato troupes generally maintained cordial relations, despite the obvious professional rivalries for patronage.[25]

Zenchiku was born in 1405,[26] the son of Komparu Yasaburō. He makes no mention of his father, which suggests that Yasaburō died an early death. In any case, his father seems to have been an undistinguished performer who was largely responsible for the troupe's decline. Zenchiku's original name was Kanshi, later changed to Ujinobu. (Zenchiku is his Buddhist name, not used before age sixty-one). The date of his succession as head of the troupe is unclear. The postscript to Zeami's *Rikugi* contains the designation "head of the Komparu troupe" (Komparu-dayū), indicating that he succeeded no later than 1428, when he was in his early twenties.

Zenchiku's role in the history of sarugaku is closely linked to the for-

---

[22] Dōmoto, *Zeami*, 196–99.

[23] Ibid., 199.

[24] "In Yamato, the troupe at Takeda [the Emai], the Deai [forerunners of the Kanze troupe], and the Hōshō troupe are closely interrelated." *ZZ*, 302.

[25] Discussed in O'Neill, *Early Nō Drama*, 33–34.

[26] This date is determined from the inscription to Zenchiku's *Emai-za hōshiki*, which records his age as sixty-four. See Nose Asaji, *Nōgaku genryū kō* (Tokyo: Iwanami shoten, 1938), 469. This document is reproduced in Omote Akira and Itō Masayoshi, eds., *Komparu kodensho shūsei* (Tokyo: Wan'ya shoten, 1969), 310–11 (hereafter referred to as *KKSS*). Actually, the manuscript has no title; Omote and Itō call the work "Sarugaku engi."

tunes of the Kanze family. Zeami had three sons: Motoshige, Motomasa, and Motoyoshi. The last never established himself as a performer, eventually entering the priesthood. He is best known as the author of the aforementioned *Sarugaku dangi*, a kind of oral history and compendium of sarugaku lore as told by Zeami. Motomasa was trained to be Zeami's main successor and became head of the Kanze troupe in 1422. He is the author of the popular play *Sumidagawa*.

Motoshige, better known as Onnami, was born to Zeami's younger brother Shirō. He was adopted in 1398 or 1399 by the then childless Zeami, to insure an heir.[27] As Dōmoto notes, Zeami perhaps feared that Shirō would succeed him. For a time Onnami performed regularly with Zeami and Motomasa, but for unknown reasons he formed an independent Kanze group by the year 1429. Certainly one can imagine jealousy between Onnami and Motomasa, Zeami's natural son and preferred student. As Zeami lost the patronage he had enjoyed during Yoshimitsu's shogunate and his fortunes steadily declined, Onnami's popularity rose. He became a favorite of the new shogun Yoshinori, performing regularly before the most important audiences.

Zeami's greatest misfortune was yet to come: the sudden death of Motomasa in 1432. Onnami had been disowned, and yet because of his strong position he became the official "Kanze-tayū"; in fact, the current Kanze lineage is descended from him. Zeami was distraught and looked to Zenchiku as the best prospect to become his artistic heir. It appears that Zenchiku had already married Zeami's daughter before Motomasa's death, probably around 1427.[28] It is important to remember that Zenchiku was not adopted into the family in the conventional sense. Both Motomasa and Onnami were still alive, and Zenchiku remained head of his own troupe.

From an early age Zenchiku had a passion for waka.[29] This may have attracted him to Zeami, who, as a result of Yoshimitsu's attentions, had received a highly literate education, tutored by the aristocratic waka and *renga* poet Nijō Yoshimoto. Zenchiku received extensive personal instruction from Zeami, who composed two treatises, the *Rikugi* and *Shūgyoku tokka*, exclusively for his benefit. Significantly, the first of these is based on

[27] Although most Western accounts portray Onnami as merely Zeami's nephew, Dōmoto asserts with complete confidence that he was officially Zeami's eldest son, through adoption. His adult name Motoshige, containing the "Moto" found in the names of his adoptive father and brothers, is evidence of this. Also, in his childhood he was called "Saburō," a name received by both Kannami and Zeami when it was determined they were to succeed as head of the troupe. See Dōmoto, *Zeami*, 200–202.

[28] Itō, *Komparu Zenchiku no kenkyū*, 20.

[29] There is evidence of contact with the famous waka poet Shōtetsu (1381–1459). See ibid., 27–29.

the Six Principles of poetry mentioned earlier, and was perhaps written simply to appeal to Zenchiku; most scholars consider it out of character and one of Zeami's weakest efforts. On the other hand, the *Shūgyoku tokka* is one of Zeami's most difficult yet profound works, and it provided many of the key elements that resurface in Zenchiku's own rokurin ichiro treatises. There is also evidence that Motomasa was on very friendly terms with Zenchiku, showing him a work (probably the *Kakyō*) that contained proprietary Kanze secrets (see below). Similarly, before taking the tonsure Motoyoshi entrusted to Zenchiku copies of the *Sandō* and *Kakyō* he and Motomasa had received from their father.[30] Zeami's evaluation of Zenchiku's potential is evident in the following passage from the *Kyakuraika*, written the year after Motomasa's death:

> All the secrets of our art—from the legacy I received from my late father through what I have learned in old age—were transmitted to my son Motomasa, and I had only quietly to await the Great Matter at the end of my life. Just at that time Motomasa unexpectedly departed from the world, and our school's line was broken: our house is already in ruin.[31] My grandson is still but a young child. When I think of the lack of a successor for the art that my father and I leave behind, I feel the deep attachment of an old man; now this worry will be an impediment in the Great Matter ahead. If there were even a qualified outsider, I could at least teach him what I myself know, but there is no suitable performer to be found.
>
> Of course, the head of the Komparu troupe's fundamental style is correct, and he may be capable of preserving our tradition, but as of now he does not seem likely to become a great performer. Perhaps when he becomes older and his powers mature, he will become an uncommonly skilled actor with a distinctive style. However, as I do not expect to live that long, who will be able to transmit the seal of attainment to him? Still, Motomasa permitted Komparu to look at one of our most important secret treatises, no doubt thinking that other than he there was no one who could preserve our school's name for future generations.[32]

In fact, Zenchiku rose to a level of great accomplishment as a performer, although he never matched the popularity of Onnami. Under his leadership, the declining Emai-za was restored to a position of respect and

---

[30] See ibid., 21–22. Omote cites this incident as evidence of the importance of the *Kakyō*, which perhaps was given to Motomasa at the time of his offical recognition as Zeami's heir. *ZZ*, 556. Most likely this is the same *Kakyō* text lent earlier when Motomasa was still living. The Komparu manuscript of the *Kakyō*, dated Eikyō 9 (1437) and now in the possession of Hōzan-ji, is probably a copy made by Zenchiku himself from Motomasa's.

[31] Already Onnami had cut his ties with Zeami and was performing on his own as the "Kanze head."

[32] *ZZ*, 246. The manuscript mentioned is probably the *Kakyō* text mentioned in note 30.

financial stability. While Zeami was in exile on the island of Sado (1434–1437?), Zenchiku cared for his wife, herself perhaps of Komparu lineage.[33] During this period Zenchiku seems to have been deeply immersed in the study of Zeami's aesthetic theories. A letter from Zeami contains a detailed reply to a question about the proper performance of demon roles,[34] and the copy of the *Kakyō* written in Zenchiku's hand is dated Eikyō 9 (1437). Despite Zeami's initial misgivings, at his death in 1443 Zenchiku was his full-fledged artistic successor.

Zenchiku continued to perform at festivals in the Nara region and appeared in special performances before shoguns Yoshinori and Yoshimasa. In 1466, at the age of sixty-two, he surrendered his position as tayū to his elder son Sōin (given name Motouji), still performing occasionally as elder of the troupe. During this period he retired to the Tafuku-an, a retreat in the village of Takigi outside Nara. The putative site of the Tafuku-an is only a few hundred feet from the gate of the Shūon-an (popularly known as Ikkyū-ji), the country temple of the great Zen master Ikkyū Sōjun (1394–1481).

The relationship between Ikkyū and Zenchiku is unclear. Yoshida Tōgo, the editor of the first published collection of Zenchiku's writings, mistakenly attributed to Ikkyū an inscription at the end the first rokurin ichiro text,[35] actually written by one of his early companions, the poet Nankō Sōgen (or Shūgen, or Sōgan, 1387–1463). In fact, he was merely continuing a tradition within the Komparu School; such later performers as Komparu Anshō (d. 1621) also believed that Ikkyū had contributed to the rokurin ichiro manuscripts.[36] In this vein, several early scholars projected an Ikkyū influence on Zenchiku's writings.[37] As will be seen, while Zen elements do occasionally surface in the rokurin ichiro system, a result of the general cultural climate and also the explicit Zen terminology found in Zeami's writings,[38] its major Buddhist motifs are drawn from

---

[33] Suggested in Dōmoto, *Zeami*, 197.

[34] For the text of this letter, see *ZZ*, 318–19. Zeami's views on the portrayal of demons is discussed in chapter 3.

[35] For a discussion, see Itō, *Komparu Zenchiku no kenkyū*, 31-32.

[36] Anshō's remarks on Ikkyū's contribution are reproduced in Omote Akira and Oda Sachiko, eds., *Komparu Anshō densho* (Tokyo: Wan'ya shoten, 1978), 143.

[37] For example, see Haga Kōshirō, *Higashiyama bunka no kenkyū* (Kyoto: Shibunkakudō, 1981), 571–72. This misapprehension is common among non-Japanese commentators.

[38] Thomas Hare insists that despite Zeami's affiliation with the Sōtō temple Fugan-ji and his frequent use (and creative misuse) of Zen terminology, his spiritual commitment to Zen is doubtful. Thomas Blenman Hare, *Zeami's Style* (Stanford: Stanford University Press, 1986), 31. I agree that Zeami's writings reveal an artist rather than a religious aspirant; still, much of the Zen terminology demonstrates, at the very least, extensive contact with Zen clergy. Certainly Zenchiku's almost deliberate avoidance of Zen expressions, despite his obvious spiritual orientation, is in marked contrast to Zeami. This fact does not disprove an association with Ikkyū, however, since Zenchiku's major treatises predate this period.

Shigyoku's Kegon-based commentary. It is most likely that Ikkyū and Zenchiku did not become acquainted before the Tafuku-an period, when the major rokurin ichiro texts were already complete. On the other hand, since Nankō and Ikkyū were acquainted, it is not impossible that Zenchiku had met him earlier. In any case, Both Zenchiku and Ikkyū had fled to the countryside to avoid the disturbances of the Ōnin Wars. Ikkyū's official biography, the *Ikkyū Oshō nenpu* by his disciple Bokusai, records for the year Ōnin 2 [1468], "In the fall [Ikkyū] wrote a Dharma discourse for Zenchiku (the Komparu-dayū, now living in Takigi) of the Tafuku-an."[39] On the basis of this evidence, it seems likely that Zenchiku sought spiritual guidance from Ikkyū in the last years of his life.

Also of interest is the lively artistic community that gathered at the Shūon-an. Ikkyū was acquainted with the great renga poet Sōgi (1421–1502), and renga sessions at the Shūon-an are recorded in which his disciple Sōchō (1448–1532) participated.[40] Legends transmitted within the Komparu School suggest that Zenchiku performed noh for Ikkyū and his entourage, although there is no record of this.[41]

The date of Zenchiku's death cannot be determined precisely, but documentary evidence places it between 1468 and 1471.[42] It is clear from his writings—a journal of a pilgrimage with his wife to the Fushimi Inari Shrine,[43] and other fragments—that Zenchiku spent his last years engaged in a personal religious quest, and that he achieved a degree of spiritual peace.

Zenchiku is known as a skilled dramatist whose plays are still regularly performed; firm attributions include *Kamo*, *Bashō*, *Yōkihi*, *Ugetsu*, *Matsumushi*, *Oshio*, *Tamakazura*, and *Teika*.[44] Most of his works are based on literary classics from the courtly tradition and contain little dramatic action. The majority are third-category spirit plays; the *shite* tend to be abstracted composites of natural forces and poetic image, in contrast to

[39] *Zoku gunsho ruijū* 9, 2:763. Omote cautions, however, that after Zenchiku's death many fabrications crept into Komparu School accounts of his relationship with Ikkyū, which in turn may have influenced the Edo period manuscripts of Bokusai's biography. See *KKSS*, 62.

[40] See Donald Keene, "The Comic Tradition in Renga," in John Whitney Hall and Toyoda Takeshi, eds., *Japan in the Muromachi Age* (Berkeley: University of California Press, 1977), 272ff. Sōchō venerated Ikkyū both as a religious personality and as a poet.

[41] For a discussion of the various legends pertaining to Zenchiku and Ikkyū, see Itō, *Komparu Zenchiku no kenkyū*, 32ff. One of these falsely attributes the origin of the term *takigi nō* (torchlight noh) to the name of the village Takigi. Some suggest that *takigi* may denote the gathering of firewood for the Shunigatsu-e festival, rather than "torchlight" performances.

[42] See the extended discussion in Nose, *Nōgaku genryū kō*, 462–64.

[43] See appendix, no. 21.

[44] For a discussion of the Zenchiku attributions, see Itō, *Komparu Zenchiku no kenkyū*, 46–53. Hare discusses the style of Zenchiku's plays in *Zeami's Style*, 177–82.

Zeami's works, which are more vivid in characterization and varied in dramatic form. These plays consistently embody the neoclassical aesthetic ideal of yūgen, radiating a wistful sadness and nostalgia for the past brilliance and elegance of court culture. The art of poetry itself is a major theme, reflecting Zenchiku's stated view that waka is the essence of sarugaku.[45]

In recent years scholars have speculated that Zenchiku may have written additional plays often attributed to Zeami, including *Saigyō-zakura, Obasute,* and *Nonomiya.*[46] Surely the last, which depicts Prince Genji's visit to Lady Rokujō during her stay at the temporary "Shrine in the Fields" in Sagano, would be his finest effort, a work of extraordinary beauty and thematic complexity. The twentieth-century actor Kanze Hisao has written that Zenchiku's plays exhibit a circular form, whereby the shite returns to its original state without attaining final spiritual release, despite the efforts of the *waki*'s prayers.[47] Certainly this circularity suggests the Mahayana nonduality of delusion and enlightenment, and thus bears a strong resemblance to the rokurin ichiro sequence to be studied in the coming chapters.

THE MANUSCRIPTS

To conclude this chapter, I shall briefly summarize the manuscript history of the two works translated in chapter two. Due to the composite nature of the texts, a clear understanding of their evolution is important.

The *Rokurin ichiro no ki* (A record of six circles and one dewdrop; hereafter *Ki*) is the earliest and most important of the rokurin ichiro texts. It is a record composed by Zenchiku of the commentaries he had obtained from Shigyoku and Kaneyoshi. Therefore, when the subsequent rokurin ichiro works, all of which incorporate some of the concepts presented in the commentaries, are examined, it is possible to differentiate the contributions of these two scholars from Zenchiku's own ideas. It is a serious mistake, however, to assume that this manuscript contains a full expression of Zenchiku's initial conception of the rokurin ichiro. His brief remarks merely serve to identify each category, as a preface to Shigyoku's comments.

There are three extant manuscripts associated with the Komparu School that contain portions of the *Ki.* The most complete version is the so-called Hachiemon manuscript, which includes Zenchiku's own "personal re-

[45] This theme is expressed in several of Zenchiku's critical writings. See appendix, no. 2.

[46] For example, see Itō's remarks on the authorship of *Nonomiya* in his *kaidai* in Itō Masayoshi, ed., *Yōkyoku shū* (Tokyo: Shinchōsha, 1988), 3:450–53, and also Hare, *Zeami's Style,* 180–82. Dōmoto, in *Zeami,* argues for *Obasute* (724–26) and *Saigyō-zakura* (734–36).

[47] Discussed in Dōmoto, *Zeami,* 734–35, n. 110.

marks" (*shishi*), the commentaries of Shigyoku and Kaneyoshi, and an inscription by the poet and former Zen priest Nankō Sōgen.[48] This manuscript is part of a series of sixteen Zenchiku works, as well as some Zeami material, recorded in the early Edo period by Komparu Hachiemon Anki (1588–1661), the second son of Komparu Anshō (d. 1621), the sixth generation Komparu head after Zenchiku. Anshō had originally trained his eldest son Ujikatsu as his successor, but Ujikatsu died at the age of thirty-five, leaving a fifteen-year-old son, Shigekatsu. Because he considered his grandson too young to absorb the entirety of the teaching, Anshō took the unusual step of transmitting the orthodox Komparu teachings to Anki, who had already been adopted into the Hachiemon family of waki performers through marriage—a pattern that echoes the original transmission from Zeami to Zenchiku. In 1656 or 1657 he entrusted "secret" writings of Zenchiku and Zeami to Anki, who copied them in his own hand. Some of the resulting manuscripts have Anshō's seal and appended remarks. They were subsequently kept by the Hachiemon family and remain the largest single collection of Zenchiku manuscripts. There are, however, extant holograph versions of several of Zenchiku's works, as enumerated in the appendix.

The second manuscript, in the collection of Hōzan-ji in Ikoma, is the original inscription by Nankō in his own hand, dated 1455. It is one of several Zenchiku- (and also Zeami-) related manuscripts in possession of the temple, acquired sometime during the Meiji period.

The third manuscript, in the Yoshida Collection of the Tenri Library, was copied in the early Edo period. It contains only Shigyoku's commentary, interspersed with Zenchiku's "personal words" in the same fashion as the Hachiemon manuscript. However, it also includes a brief postscript (translated below) and date recorded by Shigyoku not found in the Hachiemon text. Both the Hachiemon and Yoshida manuscripts include the diagrams of each of the six circles and the sword—representative of the One Dewdrop—that are reproduced in my translation.

As noted, the Hachiemon manuscript is the most complete, and it has been utilized for the translation. There is one significant omission, however. At the end of Shigyoku's commentary, Zenchiku adds, "The next part is [Shigyoku's] postscript; however, I have eliminated the particulars. For his exact words, see the original." The Yoshida text records what is probably Shigyoku's postscript in full:

> Ujinobu, head of the Komparu troupe, is a great master among performers of successive generations, one whose surpassing excellence is without equal in the

---

[48] Little is known of Nankō's relations with Zenchiku, but he was a close acquaintance of Ikkyū in the mid-1430s. See James H. Sanford, *Zen-man Ikkyū* (Chico, Ca.: Scholars Press, 1980), 34, and Itō, *Komparu Zenchiku no kenkyū*, 31. Five of his poems are translated in David Pollack, *Zen Poems of the Five Mountains* (Decatur, Ga: Scholar's Press, 1985).

past or present. His accomplishments are extraordinary; he is the greatest performer under heaven. Above all, his supreme knowledge of both inner [Bud-
dhist] and outer works is seen in the profundity of the principles in this treatise.
Thus, I have recorded the particulars above with ceaseless wonder and great
deference.

> First Year of Bunnan (1444)
> Third Month, Eighteenth Day

At this time, Zenchiku would have been age forty, Shigyoku age sixty-
two.

In addition, this Yoshida manuscript concludes with an additional postscript that Itō Masayoshi believes was written by a later Komparu actor,
although it is signed "Ujinobu":

> This treatise is the most secret treasury among our great secrets, an extremely
> important and profound document. It must be kept in strictest confidence. It
> should not be transmitted to more than one son.

> Chōroku 3 [1459]
> Seventh Month, Twenty-eighth Day
> Ujinobu (seal affixed)

Itō observes that this final colophon, together with the omission of
Shigyoku's name and title (recorded twice in the Hachiemon manuscript)
and the lack of any divisions between the shishi and Shigyoku sections,
create the illusion that the entire text was written by Zenchiku.[49] This
might be a case of deliberate deception on the part of a partisan copyist.
Certainly the suspicious nature of the colophon supports this view. On the
other hand, the manuscript may be a copy of an earlier version of
Shigyoku's commentary and Zenchiku's shishi, which existed before the
Ki was assembled in its final form.

The omission of Shigyoku's postscript in the Hachiemon manuscript is
probably due to Zenchiku's modesty; in any case, it demonstrates that
Zenchiku himself edited Shigyoku's text in the process of assembling the
composite of the Ki. In the process, the date of Shigyoku's commentary
was also omitted.

Nankō's postscript is dated Autumn, First Year of Kōshō (1455); thus,
there is a gap of almost twelve years between the composition of these two
sections. The completed Ki text that we now have—the earliest extant
rokurin ichiro draft—was assembled by Zenchiku more than eleven years
after Shigyoku's commentary was composed, and even his own "personal
remarks" were in all likelihood recorded after both Shigyoku and Kaneyoshi had written their respective commentaries. It is not possible to

---

[49] Itō, Komparu Zenchiku no kenkyū, 112–13.

date the Kaneyoshi section. All that can be said is that it was completed by 1455.

The second work translated, the *Rokurin ichiro no ki chū* (Commentary to "A record of six circles and one dewdrop"; hereafter, *Kichū*), survives only in the Hachiemon manuscript, directly following the *Ki* text discussed above. It is dated the first month of Kōshō 2 (1456), only a few months after the completion of the *Ki*. This text is Zenchiku's first full explication of the rokurin ichiro theory in his own words, and he draws freely from the Buddhist and Neo-Confucian constructs devised by Shigyoku and Kaneyoshi. Most significant are Zenchiku's description of each circle in terms of the art of performance, material almost entirely lacking from the *Ki*, and his introduction of Shinto cosmology.

I have deliberately chosen to translate only these two texts, which record the formative stages of the rokurin ichiro system and highlight the contributions of the commentators. While the analysis in the succeeding chapters will frequently make reference to later texts in order to clarify certain themes, this study is not a comprehensive treatment of all of Zenchiku's theories, or even of all aspects of the rokurin ichiro texts. For example, Zenchiku's assigning of styles of poetry to the seven categories in some later drafts is not treated in detail. These characterizations seem somewhat arbitrary—an afterthought, when Zenchiku decided to combine his long-abiding interest in waka with his symbolic theory of performance—and in any case, due to their late date, they lie outside the central concern of this study: the dialogue among the three principals Zenchiku, Shigyoku, and Kaneyoshi.

Also, the reader should be aware that these texts were not widely studied and were essentially unknown outside the Komparu School. Thus, it is unlikely that later performance traditions were directly influenced by Zenchiku.[50] For this and other reasons, I emphasize that, although noh devotees may see many parallels with contemporary performance practice and aesthetics, this study is solely concerned with the rokurin ichiro system as a cultural monument of the fifteenth century.

---

[50] Dōmoto has remarked in public that the influence of Zenchiku's theories on the mainstream performance tradition was "absolutely zero." However, the early Edo period writings of Komparu Anshō, which draw from Zenchiku's theories and contain definitions and diagrams of the six circles, indicate continued interest within the secret tradition of the Komparu School. Furthermore, insofar as Zenchiku's aesthetics are derived from Zeami's views, they are not entirely irrelevant.

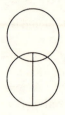

Chapter Two: Translations

A RECORD OF SIX CIRCLES AND ONE DEWDROP

Personal Remarks Concerning Six Circles and One Dewdrop

IN THE WAY of our family's profession of sarugaku, the body exhibits extreme beauty, and the voice produces [melodic] patterns.[1] In these [activities], the performer is not aware of specific arm movements, nor of where to place his feet;[2] is this not a wondrous function that is fundamentally without subjective control and objective awareness?[3] Thus, [the art] provisionally

[1] As discussed in chapter 1, the text is a composite of Zenchiku's brief definitions and commentaries written by Shigyoku and Ichijō Kaneyoshi. In the Hachiemon manuscript used for this translation, Zenchiku's descriptions are interspersed with Shigyoku's remarks for each of the seven categories (six circles and one dewdrop); Kaneyoshi's commentary is appended at the end, followed by Nankō Sōgen's postscript.

The text used is Omote Akira and Itō Masayoshi, eds., *Komparu kodensho shūsei* (*KKSS*; unless otherwise noted, "Omote" signifies the editorial presence therein).

[2] The diction of these opening remarks is borrowed from the opening of the Great Preface to the *Book of Songs*, the early classic of Chinese poetry. In Legge's translation, this passage reads: "Poetry is the product of earnest thought. Thought [cherished] in the mind becomes earnest; exhibited in words, it becomes poetry. The feelings move inwardly, and are embodied in words. When words are insufficient for them, recourse is had to sighs and exclamations. When sighs and exclamations are insufficient for them, unconsciously the hands begin to move and the feet to dance. The feelings go forth in sounds. When these sounds are artistically combined, we have what is called musical pieces." James Legge, *The Chinese Classics*, 4:34. This passage is quoted more fully in the preface of Zenchiku's *Kabu zuinō ki* (*KKSS*, 122).

[3] "Beyond subjective control and objective awareness" is a translation of *mushu mubutsu*. Zeami uses the term *mushu* (no-master) in the derogatory meaning of "lack of mastery" or "lack of one's own style." (See *Shikadō* passage, *ZZ*, 113–14.) Here, however, Zenchiku seems to emphasize the spontaneous and involuntary nature of intuitive artistic expression, as extolled in the Great Preface. The expression *mubutsu* appears in *Lao Tzu* (ch. 14), where it signifies "nothingness," that is, the lack of form or any objective characteristic that can be ascribed to the Tao. In this passage the term suggests the performer's lack of awareness of specific arm movements, and so forth.

Haga Kōshirō sees in this phrase a strong Zen flavor (Haga, *Higashiyama bunka*, 535–39), reinforced by the empty circle diagram that is reminiscent of the *ensō* frequently painted by Zen artists—a term used by Zenchiku in his

assumes the form of six circles and one dewdrop. The first [circle] is called the Circle of Longevity, the second the Circle of Height, the third the Circle of Abiding, the fourth the Circle of Forms, the fifth the Circle of Breaking, and the sixth the Circle of Emptiness; the One Dewdrop represents the most profound level.

FIG. 2-1. Circle of Longevity

The first [circle, the] Circle of Longevity [fig. 2-1] is the fundamental source of the yūgen of song and dance. It is the vessel[4] in which deep feelings develop upon viewing a performer's movement and listening to his singing. Due to its round, perfect nature and eternal life span, it is called the Circle of Longevity.

Section Written by [Shigyoku,] the Former Abbot of the Kaidan-in in the Southern Capital

Representing profound tenets in both the inner [Buddhist] writings and outer [non-Buddhist] works, these six circles are the ultimate in principle and truth.[5] In the case of the scriptures, they correspond to the heart of the esoteric teachings, the Six Great Elements[6] that embody the Dharma Nature. The heart of the exoteric teachings—[the doctrine of] all dharmas comprising Suchness-following-conditions[7] and the process of samsara and its extinction [into Nirvana][8]—is fully expressed by these six ranks.

Circle of Breaking definition. However, his assumption that Zenchiku was a disciple of Ikkyū at this time, due to the existence of the Nankō postscript (Nankō was an acquaintance of Ikkyū), is doubtful. See chapter 1.

[4] For Zeami's definition of "vessel" (*ki*), see chapter 3.

[5] The following was written by Shigyoku (1383–1463), a Buddhist priest of the Kegon Sect who served as abbot of the Kaidan-in at Tōdai-ji in Nara. For further biographical information, see chapter 4. Almost nothing is known about his relationship to Zenchiku. As noted above, Shigyoku's comments are interspersed with Zenchiku's descriptions of the seven stages and are identified as such in the translation.

[6] In esoteric Buddhism, the Six Great Elements (*rokudai*) are earth, water, fire, wind, space, and consciousness. This configuration differs from the more common exoteric systems of five (earth, water, fire, wind, and space) and four (earth, water, fire, and wind), which represent only matter.

[7] This is the doctrine of *shinnyo zuien* (C. *chen-ju sui-yüan*), first developed by the third

The first and last represent the original source of formless true Emptiness, and the middle four correspond to the four characteristic states of existence: birth, abiding, change, and extinction.[9]

First is the realm of emptiness devoid of characteristics, the wondrous essence of the one source of motion and stillness.[10] The passage in the *Avataṃsaka Sūtra*, "The Dharma Nature is fundamentally empty; it cannot be acquired, nor can it be seen,"[11] and the teaching in the *Mahāvairocana Sūtra*, "The letter A is primordial life; it is everywhere, in both sentient and nonsentient beings,"[12] both expound the eternal life of the Buddhist Law which is [represented by] this one rank.

FIG. 2-2. Circle of Height

[ZENCHIKU]

In the second [circle, the] Circle of Height [fig. 2-2], this [single] point

patriarch of the Hua-yen School, Fa-tsang (643–712). Briefly, it states that Suchness (*tathatā*), although itself an absolute, unchanging essence, undergoes transformation through contact with external causes and manifests as phenomena. See chapter 4.

[8] The first term, *ruten* (S. *pravṛtti*), denotes the traditional doctrine of samsara, the endless wheel of birth and death; the second, *genmetsu* (the manuscript provides the alternate reading *genmechi*; S. *nivṛtti*), expresses the process by which this cycle is broken, the illusory self disintegrates, and Nirvana is realized. See chapter 4.

[9] These are the four stages (*shisō*) that all existences undergo in a single "life cycle." See chapter 4.

[10] Shigyoku's probable source for this expression, *dōsei ichigen*, is a passage at the beginning of the *Hua-yen-ching shu*, a commentary on the *Avataṃsaka Sūtra* written by Ch'eng-kuan (738–820), the fourth Hua-yen patriarch. See chapter 4.

[11] This passage is found in chapter 14 of the eighty–chapter *Avataṃsaka Sūtra*, "Gāthā Atop Mount Sumeru." *T* 279.10.81c.

[12] Shigyoku has paraphrased and inverted the order of the verses in the sutra passage. The original text reads: "I [Dainichi nyorai] am of an equivalent mind, self-existing in all places, universally present in every seed, both sentient and insentient. The letter A is primordial life; the letter VA designates water; the letter RA designates fire; the letter HŪM designates anger; the letter KHA is identical to space; the point (M) is ultimate emptiness." *T* 848.18.38b–c.

Clearly, the significance of the letter A within the context of Mahāvairocana's mantra (OM A VA RA HŪM KHAM) is the issue here; the statement concerning sentient and insentient beings goes with the previous section. It is likely that Shigyoku's immediate source is not the sutra itself, but rather a quotation from this passage found in Kūkai's *Sokushin jōbutsu gi*, which is mispunctuated in this fashion. *Kōbō Daishi zenshū*, 1:509.

rises,[13] becoming spirit; breadth and height appear, and clear singing is born. This is the unsurpassed, highest fruition of feeling.

[SHIGYOKU]

Second is the stage of birth. That is to say, a single wave of transitory existence arises on the formless, tranquil sea of [Dharma] Nature. Master Tsao-po's[14] interpretation, "There is no wind on the Nature Sea, yet of itself a golden wave shimmers on its surface," expresses this concept.

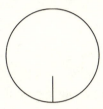

FIG. 2-3. Circle of Abiding

[ZENCHIKU]

In the third [circle, the] Circle of Abiding [fig. 2-3], the short line's position is the peaceful place where all roles take shape and vital performance is produced.

[SHIGYOKU]

Third is the rank of abiding. The myriad dharmas, comprising both material form and mind, flow in accord with conditions; the cycle of birth-and-death and [entrance into] Nirvana appears here, as the process of samsara and return to extinction continues without end. This is the enlightened rank of tranquil abiding, as dharmas exist freely in accordance with their natures. The passage in the *Lotus Sutra*, "Dharmas reside in the Dharma position; the forms of this world are eternally abiding,"[15] and

---

[13] The vertical line in figure 2-2 represents this rising point.

[14] Li T'ung-hsüan (635–730), a lay scholar best known for his extensive Hua-yen studies. Unfortunately, the quotation has not yet been identified. Itō Masayoshi notes that this image appears in a medieval work falsely attributed to Kūkai, the *Ryōgū gyōmon shinshaku* (*Kōbō Daishi zenshū*, 5:151). This passage is in turn paraphrased in the *Toyoashihara shinpū waki*, a medieval Shintō work written by Jihen (d. 1347?) that was an important influence on Zenchiku. See Itō, *Komparu Zenchiku no kenkyū*, 172–75; for the *Shinpū waki* passage, see *Zoku zoku gunsho ruijū*, 1:124. In fact this "golden wave" image also appears in Zenchiku's *Kabu zuinō ki*, as a metaphor for poetry that depicts "inherently tranquil things that temporarily become unsettled" (*KKSS*, 138–39) See chapters 4 and 6 for further discussion.

[15] From the "Skillfulness in Means" chapter. *T* 262.9.9b. The conventional interpretation of the first clause is "dharmas abide in their own dharma positions." In the Tendai School, however, the expression *hōi* is interpreted as Suchness; thus, all things abide eternally be-

Great Teacher Hsien-shou's[16] commentary, "Deluded views are exhausted, the mind clears and myriad images appear together," both expound this concept.

FIG. 2-4. Circle of Forms

[ZENCHIKU]

In the fourth circle, the Circle of Forms [fig. 2-4], the various forms of heaven and earth, all things in creation, are at peace.

[SHIGYOKU]

Fourth is the stage of change. Grasses, trees, and lands are all transformations of "consciousness-only":[17] the One Mind[18] transforms, and myriad forms are clearly visible. The passage in the *Avataṃsaka Sūtra*, "The essential nature of the Dharmadhātu makes no distinctions; the myriad images of all existence are none other than the Buddha's body. I do not recognize any dharmas as existing outside of *bodhi*, and therefore respect all dust [of the world],"[19] expresses this meaning.

cause they are supported by the underlying ground of the absolute. Bunnō Katō et al., trans., *The Threefold Lotus Sutra* (New York: Weatherhill, 1975), 70, n. 34. Since this is clearly Shigyoku's view, I have translated accordingly. See chapter 4.

[16] Fa-tsang (643–712), the third patriarch of the Hua-yen School and its major figure. The phrase quoted by Shigyoku is found in the *Wang-chin huan-yüan kuan*, although modern scholars now question the Fa-tsang attribution. For a translation and discussion of the original passage, see chapter 4.

[17] "Consciousness-only" (*yuishiki*) is the major Chinese branch of the Yogācāra School, one of the two major schools of Indian Mahayana thought. See chapter 4.

[18] "One Mind" (*isshin*) is the totality of existence, as treated in the *Ta-sheng ch'i-hsin lun* (The awakening of faith in the Mahayana); it is an important term in Shigyoku's Hua-yen/Kegon tradition. See chapter 4.

[19] The term *jin* (dust) may also be rendered "sense objects." According to Omote, this passage is not found in the sutra; perhaps it originates in one of the commentaries. However, a similar statement appears, cited in Chinese but unidentified, in *Sasamegoto*, the major treatise of the linked-verse poet Shinkei (1406–1474): "All forms of creation are the Dharmakāya, therefore I respect all dust [of the world]." Ichiji Tetsuo et al., eds., *Rengaron shū, nōgakuron shū, hairon shū* (Tokyo: Shōgakkan, 1973), 157. This suggests, at the very least, that Shinkei and Zenchiku were exposed to similar Buddhist concepts; most likely this was a popular dictum of the time. Shinkei is discussed in chapter 7.

FIG. 2-5. Circle of Breaking

[ZENCHIKU]

Fifth is the Circle of Breaking [fig. 2-5]. When the inexhaustibly varying shapes of the ten directions of heaven and earth are produced, they are originally born within this circle. However, since they temporarily break its round form,[20] I have named it the Circle of Breaking.

[SHIGYOKU]

Fifth is the stage of extinction, in which even worldly desires appear as *bodhi*, and even birth-and-death returns to Nirvana. The passage from the *Avataṃsaka Sūtra*, "The three worlds are just One Mind; outside of this Mind there are no separate dharmas; there is no distinction among Mind, buddhas, and sentient beings,"[21] and the interpretation of the Great Teacher of T'ien-t'ai,[22] "Whether one is reborn in hell or not rests completely upon the ultimate sage [the Buddha] himself; Vairocana's domain does not surpass a single thought of the ordinary man," both correspond to this stage. The passage from *The Awakening of Faith*, "Because one's wisdom is pure and clear, he breaks through the compound consciousness, puts an end to

[20] The term used here is *ensō*, the familiar empty circle painted by Zen artists to signify the empty yet complete, harmonious nature of Mind.

[21] According to Omote, this exact wording is not found in the sutra; he quotes two similar passages. However, a passage from the *Jigyō ryakki* of Genshin (942–1017), the well-known author of the popular Pure Land work *Ōjō yōshū* (The Essentials of salvation), opens with the identical words, followed by the sentence in the next quotation, which Shigyoku attributes to "Tendai Daishi" (see note 22). The *Jigyō ryakki* is a short work that contains brief summaries of various Mahayana doctrines, evidently intended to aid Genshin's personal practice. *Eshin sōzu zenshū*, 3:417.

[22] The title "Tendai Daishi" usually refers to Chih-i (538–597), the major figure of the T'ien-t'ai School. However, since the passage quoted is found in a treatise entitled *Chin-kang pei* (*T* 1932.46.781a) written by the sixth patriarch of the school, Chan-jan (711–782), Omote assumes the title refers to him. In my opinion, Shigyoku is in fact referring to Chih-i. Since the two previously unassociated passages combined here appear in the same configuration in Genshin's *Jigyō rakki* as noted above, it seems likely that this is Shigyoku's immediate source. Probably unaware of the second passage's origin in Chan-jan's work, he mistakenly attributed it to the more illustrious Chih-i.

the deluded mind of successive forms, and manifests the Dharmakāya,"[23] expresses this mind.

FIG. 2-6. Circle of Emptiness

[ZENCHIKU]

The sixth [circle, the] Circle of Emptiness [fig. 2-6], [is] the rank of no-master and no-form;[24] coming back to the beginning,[25] again one returns to the original Circle of Longevity.

[SHIGYOKU]

The sixth circle again returns to the first, formless One Principle. Empty, no traces remain; full, it dispenses with words. Having shed many times, there is nothing left to shed; having emptied over and over, nothing visible remains to be emptied.

[ZENCHIKU]

This One Dewdrop [fig. 2-7] does not fall into dualistic views of "emptiness" and "form"; it is free existence, unobstructed by a single speck of dust. Thus it takes the shape of the Sword of [Dharma] Nature.

[SHIGYOKU]

The final One Dewdrop is the ultimate, most profound stage, just as rain and dew, frost and snow all vanish, collecting into a single dewdrop.

[23] *T* 1666.32.576c, translation adapted from Yoshito S. Hakeda, trans., *The Awakening of Faith* (New York: Columbia University Press, 1967), 41. Shigyoku slightly alters the word order in the second line, but the meaning is not changed. According to Hakeda, "Compound consciousness" (*wagō no shiki*) refers to the *ālaya-vijñāna* (storehouse consciousness). See chapter 4 for further discussion.

[24] For "no-master," see note 3. However, here *mushu* is applied specifically to the Circle of Emptiness, and thus it denotes a lack of dualistic subject/object consciousness, rather than a lack of subjective control. "No-form" is the familiar Buddhist expression *mushiki* found in the *Heart Sutra* and elsewhere.

[25] The expression used here is *kōko kyakurai*, a Zen phrase that means "having experienced enlightenment, to return to the world [of phenomena]." An important term for both Zeami and Zenchiku, it is discussed in chapter 3.

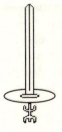

FIG. 2-7. One Dewdrop

In uniformly clearing away the above six gates[26] of form and no-form, it resembles a sword cutting through myriad obstructions. Therefore, it is called the Nature Sword. The teaching of the *Lankāvatāra Sūtra*, "Do not ponder anything at all, whether good or evil,"[27] and the passage in the *Consciousness-Only Treatise*, "The path of thinking vanishes, the way of words is cut off,"[28] both express this concept. This mysterious principle's firm and immovable qualities are called the sharp sword of Acalanātha;[29] this One Mind[30] is learned as the *prajñā* sword of Mañjuśrī's inner wisdom.[31] It is most profound and cannot be explained. It is just this one blade.

Thus, although the art of song and dance entertainment seems close at hand, it is distant; while seeming shallow, it is deep. Its fundamental source is the wisdom of the Buddha, and it first appeared long ago in the Age of the Gods, when the deities lit a bonfire and performed *kagura* at the door of the heavenly rock-cave [where Amaterasu was hiding].[32] The four Bodhisattvas of Wind Instruments, Stringed Instruments, Song, and

[26] That is, Zenchiku's "six circles."

[27] According to Omote, these exact words are not found in the sutra, but there are several similar passages. See *KKSS*, 584, n. 16.

[28] From the tenth *chuan* of the *Ch'eng wei-shih lun*, the central text of the Fa-hsiang School. *T* 1585.31.55b.

[29] This refers to the sword held in the right hand of Fudō-myōō (The Immoveable One), symbolizing the wisdom that cuts away all attachments. "Mantra King" is actually the original meaning of Myōō; the character *myō* is missing from the manuscript.

[30] For a possible connection between One Mind (*isshin*) and the dewdrop symbol within the Tōdai-ji tradition, see chapter 4.

[31] The sword of Mañjuśrī, the bodhisattva of wisdom, which cuts off the roots of ignorance.

[32] This famous myth from the *Nihon shoki* is recounted by Zeami in both his *Fūshi kaden* and *Shūgyoku tokka*. For an analysis of his interpretations, see chapter 3.

Dance[33] in the Pure Land of Tranquil Sustenance[34] are transformations of the Buddha Amitābha, and the four Bodhisattvas of Smile, Tress, Song, and Dance of the Diamond Realm Assembly[35] are emanations of Mahāvairocana, the Enlightened King. This [same principle] is [seen in] the bodhisattva Samantabhadra's inner realization,[36] the Dharma gate of child entertainers,[37] Kāśyapa's dignity,[38] and the prophecy of Prince

[33] "Bodhisattvas of Song and Dance" is a general term for the minor bodhisattvas who play music and dance as attendants of Amida; they are often depicted in paintings of Amida's Descent. The individual "Bodhisattva of Song" and "Bodhisattva of Dance," however, properly belong to the group of four Diamond Realm Mandala deities referred to in the next phrase of the text; in that context, only the Bodhisattva of Song is associated with Amida. Furthermore, the "Bodhisattva of Wind Instruments" and "Bodhisattva of String Instruments" do not exist as such, although the reference is probably to those who hold such musical instruments in the scenes of Amida's Descent. It appears that Shigyoku has simply created a Pure Land grouping parallel to the assembly from the esoteric pantheon.

[34] Another name for Amida's Western Paradise.

[35] These bodhisattvas are found in the central assembly of the Diamond Realm Mandala of esoteric Buddhism. Termed the *naishi kuyō*, "four offering bodhisattvas of the interior" (i.e., within the inner circle of the assembly), they represent offerings by Mahāvairocana to the four surrounding Buddhas: Akṣobhya in the east, Ratnasambhava in the south, Amitābha in the west, and Amoghasiddhi in the north, respectively. The Bodhisattva of Smile symbolizes the ecstasy that accompanies enlightenment; Tress represent the external flowering of all virtues, a manifestation of the presence of principle and wisdom; Song symbolizes the activity of preaching the Dharma; and Dance represents the playful spontaneity and freedom of the supernatural powers that accompany enlightenment. As a group, these four represent offerings of the subjective qualities of enlightenment, in contrast to the four "offering bodhisattvas of the exterior," who bear objective offerings to Mahāvairocana from the four Buddhas: incense, flowers, light, and perfume.

[36] Samantabhadra (J. Fugen) is often depicted in a Śākyamuni trinity, together with Mañjuśrī. Situated on Śākyamuni's right, he represents principle, meditation, and activity, while Mañjuśrī on the left symbolizes wisdom and knowledge. These two bodhisattvas are major figures in the Hua-yen School, appearing frequently in both the sutra and the major commentaries. Samantabhadra's significance in this passage is not clear; in esoteric Buddhism, he is said to represent the mind of enlightenment (*bodaishin*).

[37] The significance of this phrase is not clear; perhaps it alludes to celestial spirit-boys who perform music and dance.

[38] One of Śākyamuni's ten closest disciples, Kāśyapa became the leader of the sangha after the passing of his teacher. In this passage, the phrase "Kāśyapa's dignity" refers to a story recorded in the *Sutra Requested by the Kiṃnara King* (J. *Daijukinnaraō shomon kyō*). A heavenly musician, a "king of the Kiṃnara," played his lute and sang before a throng assembled to hear the Buddha preach. Upon hearing the performance, everyone present stood up and danced like small children, unable to contain themselves. Kāśyapa in particular was asked by a bodhisattva to explain his behavior (*T* 625.15.371a). This incident is alluded to in various Japanese literary works, where the emphasis is on Kāśyapa, who "forgot his dignity and arose [to dance]." For example, in the *Genji monogatari*: "'I have told you of my feelings about the world,'" said Kaoru. "'One result of them has been that I have not mastered a single art worthy of the name. But music—yes, I know how useless it is, and still I have a hard time giving it up. I do have a good precedent, after all. You will remember that music made the holy man Kāśyapa jump up and dance.'" From the "Shiigamoto" chapter, *NKBT* 17:384;

Shōtoku.[39] Dharma Teacher T'aehyŏn[40] of the Fa-hsiang School has said, "There is a single gate [to enlightenment] in all actions—the so-called acquisition of awareness. When awareness is acquired, all one's actions conform to the Dharma Nature,"[41] and Great Teacher Ch'ing-liang of the Hua-yen School[42] has recorded, "Raising and lowering the feet, all is the mind of Mañjuśrī; seeing, hearing, and understanding, all is the practice of Samantabhadra."[43] In the fifth year of Chōwa [1016], the Great Deity of Kasuga appeared before Major Prelate Rin'e,[44] the superintendent of Kōfuku Temple, proclaiming, "In striking a drum, blowing a flute, in song and dance, there is interest without limit; the sound of the drum is heard in the palace of Dharma Nature and Eternal Truth, and the swirling gestures of dance and voices of song are reflected in the mirror of the Four Wisdoms and Three Insights.[45] In fact, in their ability to establish connections [to the Way of the Buddha], these [performances] are far superior to preaching the Law. . . ."[46] Judging from this oracle, it seems that even the gods and buddhas are moved by this art; rulers and their ministers, nobility and commoners alike value it highly. Is there a reason for this? Truly, this is the essence of the notion that the very phenomena [of this world] are Truth. Does the direct cause of rebirth in the Pure Land exist outside of this?

---

translation modified from Edward G. Seidensticker, *The Tale of Genji* (New York: Alfred Knopf, 1975), 805.

[39] According to Omote, "Prince Shōtoku's prophecy" may refer to the *Sarugaku ennen no ki*, a document attributed to Shōtoku Taishi in the *Fūshi kaden* that has not survived. According to Zeami, the work cites precedents in India and China and argues that the performance of sarugaku will bring peace to the country and harmony to the hearts of the people. ZZ, 40. The pseudohistorical connection between Shōtoku Taishi and sarugaku was discussed in chapter 1.

[40] An important figure in Korean Buddhism. Active in the mid-eighth century, he is the author of commentaries on a wide range of sutras and texts, including *The Awakening of Faith*.

[41] From his commentary to the *Brahma's Net Sutra*. T 1815.40.690b.

[42] The fourth patriarch of the Hua-yen School, Ch'eng-kuan (737–838). "Ch'ing-liang" (clear and cool) is an epithet for Mount Wu-t'ai, the legendary home of Mañjuśrī and a major Buddhist center.

[43] The source for this quotation has not been identified. For the significance of Mañjuśrī and Samantabhadra, see note 36.

[44] Although the manuscript provides the reading Rinkai, Rin'e is standard. A member of the Nakatomi clan, the hereditary administrators of Kasuga Shrine, Rin'e (950–1025) became superintendent of Kōfuku-ji, the shrine's cognate Buddhist temple, in 1017.

[45] The Four Wisdoms are the Mirror-like Wisdom (*daienkyō chi*), the Wisdom of Equality (*byōdōshō chi*), the Wisdom of Observation (*myōkan zatchi*), and the Wisdom of Action (*jōsosa chi*). According to the teachings of the Yogācāra School, when enlightenment is realized, the four categories of consciousness—sensory consciousness, mental consciousness, ego consciousness, and *ālaya*-consciousness—are transformed into these four wisdoms, in reverse order. The Three Insights are the knowledge of former births, the knowledge of future destiny, and the knowledge of the origin of suffering and the path to its cessation.

[46] This incident is recorded in *Kasuga gongen kenki* 10 (*Gunsho ruijū*, 2:25–27; translated in Royall Tyler, *The Miracles of the Kasuga Deity* [New York: Columbia University Press, 1990]

[ZENCHIKU][47]

The next part is Shigyoku's postscript; however, I have omitted the particulars. His exact words are in the original text. Imprinted with the seal of the former Abbot of the Kaidan-in, the monk[48] Shigyoku.

The Following Section Is by Regent Ichijō [Kaneyoshi]

The origin of sarugaku has been treated fully in Shigyoku's commentary.[49] What more can be said? Yet there are three teachings[50] in the world, and like the three legs of a cauldron, one cannot be left out. For this reason, Master Fu[51] of the Liang dynasty wore a Taoist hat, Confucian shoes, and a

---

219–21), as well as other works. According to Omote, it is not clear what source Shigyoku used. *KKSS*, 585, n. 18. A more succinct account, in which the principal is Rin'e's teacher Shinki (930–1000), is presented in *Towazugatari*: "There was a high priest named Shinki, . . . resident monk of the Kita Cloister in Kōfuku Temple. Shinki felt that the sound of drums and bells hindered his meditation. Consequently he made a vow: 'If I ever become a head official of one of the six sects, the sound of drums and the clanging of bells will be prohibited.' When, shortly thereafter, his ambition was realized and he was put in charge of Kōfuku Temple, he immediately carried out his wish, and for a long while no music accompanied the worship at Kasuga. Lonely silence filled the crimson gates around the shrine, while the dancers grieved with ever-deepening sorrow. Yet they steadfastly trusted in the will of the gods. Shinki declared, 'No desires remain to me in this life. My only wish now is to devote myself wholly to the way.' Accordingly he entered religious seclusion, confidently offering to the gods the joy his religious understanding had brought him. The god of Kasuga Shrine appeared to him in a dream and declared: 'At the same time I foresook the Pure Realm and came to this defiled world of life and death determined to help ignorant man achieve enlightenment, you ordered the cessation of music and dance, making it more difficult than ever for men to achieve salvation. I resent your interference in my work. I will not accept your offering.' As a result of this dream, music was never again prohibited, no matter how troubled the times." *Nihon koten zensho*, 105:397. Translated by Karen Brazell, *The Confessions of Lady Nijō* (Stanford: Stanford University Press, 1976), 203–4.

[47] The following paragraph was probably written by Zenchiku when he copied Shigyoku's commentary. See chapter 1.

[48] Literally, "the monk who had visited China," a reference to Shigyoku's travels to the Ming court.

[49] The following commentary was written by the well-known scholar and court official Ichijō Kaneyoshi (or Kanera; 1402–1481). See chapter 5 for details of his life.

[50] The "unity of the three teachings" (*sankyō itchi*) is a major theme in Muromachi painting and thought. In its original form in China, the "three teachings" were of course Confucianism, Taoism, and Buddhism, and this was also the predominant grouping in Japan, especially in painting. Here, however, the three are the native Shinto teachings, Buddhism, and "the secular works of Confucius and Lao Tzu." See John M. Rosenfield, "The Unity of the Three Creeds: A Theme in Japanese Ink Painting of the Fifteenth Century," in John Whitney Hall and Toyoda Takeshi, eds., *Japan in the Muromachi Age* (Berkeley: University of California Press, 1977), 205–25, and Haga Kōshirō, *Chūsei zenrin no gakumon oyobi bungaku ni kansuru kenkyū* (Kyoto: Shibunkaku shuppan, 1981), 221–244.

[51] Fu-hsi (497–569). A lay Buddhist scholar, he is credited with the invention of the revolving sutra repository (*rinzō*). In the rarely performed noh play *Rinzō*, written by Nobumitsu, "Fu Daishi" himself appears as the guardian deity of the sutra repository of Kitano Shrine.

Buddhist robe. Po Chü-i[52] of the T'ang dynasty adorned his outward appearance with Confucianism, governed his mind with Buddhism, and nurtured a long life with Taoism. These examples both express the single flavor of the three teachings.

In his commentary [Shigyoku] discusses only the origins [of sarugaku] in the Age of the Gods and its relation to the Buddhist Law, omitting the principles recorded in Confucian and Taoist works. Thus I shall record some of what is on my mind, briefly explaining [these matters] from the Confucian point of view. In *Tso's Commentary* [*to the Spring and Autumn Annals*] it says, "In dance, one sets the rhythm of the eight instruments and moves with the eight winds."[53] In the *Classic of Filial Piety* it says, "There is nothing better than music to transform the habits of the people."[54] In the *Book of Rites* it says, "The basis of music lies in the Great Oneness."[55] Indeed, music nurtures the ears, color nurtures the eyes, and dance promotes circulation. The way of music and dance is truly great. When Confucius explained the great method for ruling the country, however, he proclaimed, "In music, one should perform the dance of Shun." Also, "Dispense with the songs of Cheng, for they are lewd."[56] Confucius made a distinction between the songs of Cheng and elegant music, but later Mencius proclaimed, "Today's music is like the music of antiq-

---

[52] The famous T'ang poet (772–846). It is fair to say that in his later years Po Chü-i considered Buddhism the most worthy of the three. Cf. the following lines from one of his poems, quoted by Omote and translated by Kenneth K. S. Ch'en: "Confucianism emphasizes ceremonies and regulations / Taoism nurtures the spirit and breath. / Emphasis on ceremonies gives rise to ostentatious display, / One nurtures the spirit to avoid ill omen. / They are not as good as practicing Ch'an meditation, / For in it there is profound meaning." Kenneth K. S. Ch'en, *The Chinese Transformation of Buddhism* (Princeton: Princeton University Press, 1973), 214.

[53] Kaneyoshi's quote differs slightly from the original, found in Legge, *The Chinese Classics*, 5:18.

[54] Omote has modified the Japanese reading of this quote to comply with the original. I have followed Omote in my translation. The meaning remains unchanged.

[55] These words are not found in the *Book of Rites*. A similar statement concerning rites (*li*), not music, is recorded in the *K'ung Tzu chia-yü*. See KKSS, 208, n. 10.

[56] These two statements are found in the *Analects*, 15:10: "Yen Yüan asked how the government of a country should be administered. The Master said, 'Follow the seasons of Hsia. Ride in the state carriage of Yin. Wear the ceremonial cap of Chou. Let the music be the Shao with its pantomimes. Banish the songs of Cheng, and keep from specious talkers. The songs of Cheng are licentious; specious talkers are dangerous.'" Legge, *The Chinese Classics*, 1:297–98. Legge translates Kaneyoshi's first motif as "the Shao with its pantomimes [dancers who kept time to the music]," but here Arthur Waley's view is more convincing: he calls it "the Secession Dance," because "this dance (at any rate according to later Confucian theory) mimed the peaceful accession of the legendary Emperor Shun." Arthur Waley, *The Analects of Confucius* (New York: Vintage Books, 1968), 101. Concerning the "songs of Cheng," Waley declares, "It was probably to the character of the music not to that of the words that Confucius objected (196n). . . . The tunes of Cheng and Wei are often referred to as 'new music' or the 'common music of the world'" (250).

uity."[57] For example, when music is shared with the people, even the songs of Cheng become elegant music; when the people are denied music, then even elegant music becomes the music of Cheng—this is his meaning. In addition, even Confucius said, "Music is properly called 'music.' Why is it not simply called 'bell and drum'?"[58] Benevolence is a virtue of the fundamental heart; when this virtue is acquired, voiced sounds return to its foundation. Master Hu Wu-feng[59] has said, "The principle of Heaven and human desire are the same in activity, differing [only] in feeling." His words have the same meaning as those of Dharma Master T'aehyŏn [quoted] in [Shigyoku's] commentary, "When awareness is acquired, all one's actions conform to the Dharma Nature."[60] Therefore, although it is said that today's sarugaku performances are nothing but the playful movements of actors, if there were no spectators in the stands and no one on the lawn to listen, then the means of presenting the art—every song, every play— would be lost. The moral benefits of sarugaku are the result of sharing music with the people. Is it necessary to mention that the previous quotations, such as "One sets the rhythm of the eight instruments and moves with the eight winds,"[61] of themselves express this principle?

The origin of the two characters [in the term sarugaku] is found in the first chapter of the "Age of the Gods" section in the *Chronicle of Japan*. When the great [sun] goddess Amaterasu was hiding in the heavenly rock-cave, the goddess Ama no Uzume took in hand a spear wreathed with Eulalia grass, donned a wig of *masaki* leaves and a sash of club-moss to tie up her sleeves, and performed a playful dance.[62] Because Uzume was a

---

[57] *Mencius*, book 1, part 2, chapter 1: "Another day, Mencius, having an interview with the king, said, 'Your Majesty, I have heard, told the officer Chwang, that you love music; was it so?' The king changed colour, and said, 'I am unable to love the music of the ancient sovereigns; I only love the music of the present age.'

"Mencius said, 'If your Majesty's love of music were very great, Ch'i would be near to a state of good government! The music of the present day is just like the music of antiquity, as regards effecting that.'" Legge, *The Chinese Classics*, 4:19.

[58] *Analects*, 17:11: "The Master said, ' "It is according to the rules of propriety," they say. "It is according to the rules of propriety," they say. Are gems and silk all that is meant by propriety? "It is music," they say. "It is music," they say. Are bells and drums all that is meant by music?'" Legge, *The Chinese Classics*, 1:324.

[59] Or Hu Hung (1100–1161), a Sung Confucian scholar of the Hunan School. His *Chih-yen* (2:1a) contains an almost identical passage: "The Principle of Heaven and human desires are the same in substance but differ in function. They are the same in operation but differ in feeling." Translated by Conrad Schirokauer, "Chu Hsi and Hu Hung," in Wing-tsit Chan, ed., *Chu Hsi and Neo-Confucianism* (Honolulu: University of Hawaii Press, 1986), 488. Although Hu cautioned against confounding human desire with the Principle of Heaven, Chu Hsi criticized him for implying that the two had a common basis.

[60] See note 41.

[61] See note 53.

[62] W. G. Aston translates this passage: "Moreover Ama no Uzume no Mikoto, ancestress of the Sarume no Kimi, took in her hand a spear wreathed with Eulalia grass, and standing

distant ancestor of the Lord of Sarume, such playful entertainments have come to be called sarugaku.[63] Also, in the latter "Age of the Gods" chapter of the same work, when her August Grandchild descended from Heaven, at the bidding of Amaterasu the god Sarudahiko cleared the way for him.[64] It is said that Sarudahiko's nose was seven hands long and his eyes were like eight-hand[65] mirrors. All the gods were intimidated by his countenance, and no one would stand up and face him; finally, Uzume confronted him, and at length Sarudahiko announced himself. The title "Lord of Sarume"[66] is derived from his name. According to tradition, the guise of the person who walks before the *mikoshi*, a function designated *ō no mai*[67] and found in various festivals, is based upon Sarudahiko's form.

The Creative, initiative, flourish, advantage, and perseverance[68] are the fundamentals of the way of the *Book of Change*, the ultimate principles of Confucianism. In the preface to Dhyāna Master Kuei-feng's[69] [*Abbreviated*

---

before the door of the Rock-cave of Heaven, skillfully performed a mimic dance. She took, moreover, the true Sakaki tree of the Heavenly Mount Kagu, and made of it a head-dress, she took club-moss and made of it braces [*tasuki*], she kindled fires, she placed a tub bottom upwards, and gave forth a divinely-inspired utterance." Aston, *Nihongi*, 44; *NKBT*, 67:112.

[63] In other words, the term sarugaku is formed by combining the character *saru* from Sarume no kimi's title with the character *gaku*, as found in the term *kyogaku* (playful entertainments). According to the *Nihon shoki*, Ama no Uzume was renamed "Sarume no kimi" as a result of the Sarudahiko incident alluded to by Kaneyoshi in the next section: "Saruta-hiko no Kami forthwith proceeded to the upper waters of the River Isuzu at Sanada in Ise. Ama no Uzume no Mikoto, in accordance with the request made by Saruta-hiko no Kami, attended upon him. Now the August Grandchild commanded Ame no Uzume no Mikoto, saying: 'Let the name of the Deity whom thou didst discover be made thy title.' Therefore he conferred on her the designation of Sarume no Kimi. So this was the origin of the male and female Lords of Sarume being both styled Kimi." Aston, *Nihongi*, 79; *NKBT*, 67:148–49.

A female member of the Sarume family traditionally occupied a hereditary position at court, entitled *sarume*; she performed kagura and various rituals at religious festivals.

[64] See *NKBT*, 67:148 (Aston, *Nihongi*, 77) for the full account.

[65] The exagerated dimensions have been retained in the translation for literary effect. The phrase *yata no kagami* here is unrelated to the sacred mirror of the Three Imperial Regalia.

[66] See note 63.

[67] The *Shaku Nihongi* states that the *ō no mai* is based on Sarudahiko's appearance; the large nose is explicitly mentioned. The red mask with the long nose often seen at shrine festivals, called *ō no hana*, is modeled on Sarudahiko.

[68] These five terms are translations of the most basic "text" of Ch'ien, the first hexagram of the *I ching*. The Wilhelm/Baynes translation renders this "The Creative works sublime success, furthering through perseverance." Richard Wilhelm and Cary F. Baynes, trans., *The I Ching or Book of Changes* (Princeton: Princeton University Press, 1969), 4. The origin and meaning of this terminology is discussed in chapter 5.

[69] The fifth patriarch of the Hua-yen School, Tsung-mi (780–841). He is best known for his synthesis of Hua-yen and Ch'an teachings. The work referred to compares the Four Qualities to the Four Attributes of Nirvana—permanence, bliss, selfhood, and purity: "Initiative, flourish, advantage, and perseverance are qualities of the Creative. They originate in the Primal Pneuma. Permanence, bliss, selfhood, and purity are qualities of the Buddha. Their basis is the One Mind. Concentrating upon the Primal Pneuma, one becomes gentle;

Notes on the] Perfect Enlightenment Sutra it says, "Initiative, flourish, advantage, and perseverance are qualities of the Creative. They originate in the Primal Pneuma."[70] Master Chou Lien-ch'i[71] says in his [*Explanation of the*] *Diagram of the Great Ultimate*, "The Ultimate of Nonbeing and the Great Ultimate!" Therefore if we apply these concepts to the Six Circles and One Dewdrop theory, the Circle of Longevity is the stage of the Creative. The four circles from the Circle of Height to the Circle of Breaking are the four qualities of initiative, flourish, advantage, and perseverance. These are the same as [Shigyoku's] four characteristic states of birth, abiding, change, and extinction.[72] The Circle of Emptiness is the stage of the Great Ultimate, and the One Dewdrop is the stage of the Ultimate of Nonbeing. I will explain the significance of these stages one by one below.

The first [circle, the] Circle of Longevity, is the so-called Circle of the Creative. The wheel of Heaven[73] revolves day and night without stopping for the interval of a single breath; the four seasons run their course, and various things are born. Is this not [due to] the power of the Creative? Thus, constant sincerity[74] is called the Creative. The Cre-

---

practicing the One Mind, one manifests the Way." *T* 1795.39.524a. It is unlikely, however, that Kaneyoshi's source is the original Tsung-mi text. This same citation appears in the *Ruijū jingi hongen*, compiled by Watarai Ieyuki (1256–1351), a major figure in the Ise Shinto movement. *Zokuzoku gunsho ruijū*, 1:10. For further discussion of this work, see chapter 6.

[70] A translation of *i-ch'i* (J. *ikki*). By itself, *ch'i* can mean breath, force, stuff, ether, pneuma, etc; here, *i-ch'i* refers to a kind of primal energy/matter that existed before heaven and earth were formed. When *ch'i* appears in its Neo-Confucian sense, as the complement of *li* (principle), I use Wing-tsit Chan's rendition, "material force."

[71] Chou Tun-i (1017–1073), the pioneer of Neo-Confucian thought. The work quoted here, the *T'ai-chi-t'u shuo*, is perhaps the single most important work in that tradition, establishing a cosmogony that influenced all of his successors. It begins: "The Ultimate of Non-being [*wu-chi*]and also the Great Ultimate [*t'ai-chi*]! The Great Ultimate through movement generates yang. When its activity reaches its limit, it becomes tranquil. Through tranquility the Great Ultimate generates yin. When tranquility reaches its limit, activity begins again. So movement and tranquility alternate and become the root of each other, giving rise to the distinction of yin and yang, and the two modes are thus established." Translated by Wing-tsit Chan, *A Source Book in Chinese Philosophy* (Princeton: Princeton University Press, 1963) (hereafter *SBCP*), 463.

Later in his commentary, Kaneyoshi assigns *t'ai-chi* and *wu-chi* to the Circle of Emptiness and the One Dewdrop, respectively. See chapter 5. It should be noted that Chou bases his cosmology upon these two "ultimates," the forces of yin and yang, and the five phases (*wu-hsing*), without discussing the Four Qualities introduced by Kaneyoshi.

[72] See note 9.

[73] See chapter 5.

[74] The immediate source for this expression is probably the *Doctrine of the Mean* (*Chung-yung*), chapters 25–26: "Sincerity means the completion of the self, and the Way is self-directing. Sincerity is the beginning and the end of all things. Without sincerity there would be nothing. Therefore the superior man values sincerity. Sincerity is not only the completion of one's own self, it is that by which all things are completed. The completion of the self means humanity. The completion of all things means wisdom. . . . Therefore absolute

ative is health, and health without end[75] is the heart of the Circle of Longevity.

The second [circle, the] Circle of Height, is the stage of initiative. In the *Book of Change* it says, "Great indeed is the initiating power of the Creative; all things owe their beginning to it."[76] In the [*Commentary to the*] *Words of the Text* it says, "Of all that is good, initiative is supreme."[77] The material force of the One Origin[78] is the beginning of the birth of all things. It is like [Shigyoku's] analogy of a golden wave [arising] on the Nature Sea. Among the four seasons it is spring;[79] among the five phases it is wood; among the five virtues, it is benevolence. In the *Book of History* it says, "People part company, birds and animals raise their young and mate."[80] This is the appearance of the quality of initiative in springtime.

The third [circle, the] Circle of Abiding, is the stage of flourish. In the [*Commentary to the*] *Words of the Text* it says, "Flourish is the coming together of all that is beautiful."[81] This indicates the stage at which all things and all virtues gather. Among the four seasons, it is summer.[82] Grasses and trees flourish, and birds and animals rarely become ill. After all, it is the season of peaceful living for all things. Among the five phases, it is fire; among the five virtues, it is propriety.

The fourth [circle, the] Circle of Forms, is the stage of advantage. This is not advantage in the sense of profit that accompanies fame; it is advantage in the sense of benefit for all things.[83] Among the four seasons, it is autumn.[84] In autumn, the five grains hang from their stalks, and grasses

---

sincerity is ceaseless. Being ceaseless, it is lasting. Being lasting, it is evident. Being evident, it is infinite." *SBCP*, 108–9.

[75] Cf. Ch'eng I's *I chuan*, chuan 1: "The Creative is Heaven. The heavens are Heaven's physical form; the Creative is its nature and feelings. The Creative is health; health without end is called the Creative."

[76] This is from the Judgment to Ch'ien. Translation modified from Wilhelm, *The I Ching*, 370.

[77] The *Wen-yen chuan*, the seventh of the Ten Wings traditionally attributed to Confucius, consists of four commentaries on the first two hexagrams only. Translation modified from Wilhelm, *The I Ching*, 376.

[78] Kaneyoshi's use of the term *ichigen* here is confusing. See chapter 5.

[79] Omote cites Chu Hsi's commentary to the first hexagram in his *Chou-i pen-i* (1:5) as a likely source for the correlates of the Four Qualities listed by Kaneyoshi. For discussion, see chapter 5.

[80] These phrases are quoted from the *Book of History*, part 1, chapter 2. Legge, *The Chinese Classic*, 3:18–21; see chapter 5.

[81] Translation modified from Wilhelm, *The I Ching*, 376.

[82] See note 79.

[83] Here Kaneyoshi distinguishes two common meanings of the character *ri*: "profit," as in *meiri* (fame and profit), and "to benefit [others]." His source is probably the *Wen-yen*, which reads "Because [the superior man] furthers all beings, he is able to bring them into harmony through justice." Trans. Wilhelm, *The I Ching*, 376.

[84] See note 79.

and trees bear fruit. Birds and animals prepare themselves for winter by growing additional fur.[85] Thus this is the stage of benefit for man and furtherance of all things. Among the five phases, it is metal; among the five virtues it is justice. Justice is suitability; everything assumes its own appropriate form.[86] Heaven is heavenly, earth is earthly. It is the stage in which birds and animals, grasses and trees all assume their own suitable forms.

The fifth [circle, the] Circle of Breaking, is the so-called stage of perseverance. In the [*Commentary to the*] *Words of the Text* it says, "Perseverance is the foundation of all actions."[87] It is the fundamental basis of all things. Among the four seasons it is winter,[88] when the leaves of grasses and trees turn color and fall, returning to their roots. Thus it is the cause of [the next stage of] initiative. In the *Book of History* it says, "[In winter] people gather together; birds and animals have soft, thick coats."[89] Among the five phases, it is water; among the five virtues, it is wisdom.[90] By nature water descends to the lowest point; it then ascends to heaven and again becomes rain and dew. This [circle] is an expression of the power of the foundation of perseverance, which governs the continuous cycle of all things. Again breaking its shape and returning to formlessness, it changes in the same manner that worldly desires become *bodhi*. Surely this is the wondrous function of the quality of wisdom.

The sixth [circle, the] Circle of Emptiness, corresponds to the stage of the Great Ultimate. The Great Ultimate is the supreme truth; the greatness of heaven and earth originates from the principle of this Great Ultimate. Thus it is said, "The Great Ultimate gives birth to the two essential forms [of yin and yang]."[91] Master K'ang-chieh[92] said, "The Tao is the Great Ultimate." Or again, "Mind is the Great Ultimate." Every speck of dust

[85] See note 80.

[86] Cf. Chu Hsi's remarks on "advantage" in the passage cited in note 79.

[87] Trans. Wilhelm, *The I Ching*, 376.

[88] See note 79.

[89] See note 80.

[90] See discussion of Chu Hsi's notion of "wisdom as hidden and stored" in chapter 5.

[91] From the *Ta chuan*, one of the Ten Wings to the *I ching*: "Therefore there is in the Changes the Great Ultimate. This generates the two primary forces. The two primary forces generate the four images. The four images generate the eight trigrams." Translation modified from Wilhelm, *The I Ching*, 318. This passage is the locus classicus for the expression *t'ai-chi* (Great Ultimate).

[92] The Sung Neo-Confucianist Shao Yung (1011–1077). The two remarks quoted by Kaneyoshi are found in reverse order in the "Kuan-wu wai-p'ien" section of his major work, the *Huang-chi ching-shih shu*. They are frequently cited by commentators, including Chu Hsi: "'Tao is the Great Ultimate. . . . Mind is the Great Ultimate. Tao is a term designating the natural principles of heaven and earth and all things. Mind is a term designating this principle when humans have obtained it and regard it as the ruler of their whole selves.' Chu Hsi commented: 'This is so, but the Great Ultimate just is one and does not form a pair with anything.'" Translation modified from Anne D. Birdwhistell, *Transition to Neo-Confucianism* (Stanford: Stanford University Press, 1989), 214.

and blade of grass possesses this principle: thus the commentary, "Everything possesses the Great Ultimate."[93] All dharmas return to the One Mind,[94] and so it is also said, "All things are at one with the Great Ultimate."[95] There are no dharmas outside the mind; there are no things outside the Great Ultimate. This also may be called the one principle of no-characteristic.

The One Dewdrop is the stage of the Ultimate of Nonbeing. In all the stages above, including the Great Ultimate, the dualism of principle and material force[96] is present. [In contrast,] the Ultimate of Nonbeing departs from the word-based distinction of being and emptiness; it does not lie within the realm of thought. The passage in the *Doctrine of the Mean*, "[The operations of Heaven] have neither sound nor smell,"[97] Tseng Tzu's "yes,"[98] and the spirit of Tseng Hsi's bathing in the River I[99] correspond to

[93] The source has not been identified.

[94] Cf. case 45 from the Zen koan collection *Blue Cliff Record* (C. *Pi-yen lu*): "The myriad things return to one. Where does the one return to?"

[95] Omote does not identify a direct source but notes that this sentence echoes the statement from the *T'ai-chi-t'u shuo*: "The five phases constitute one system of yin and yang, and yin and yang constitute one Great Ultimate." Translation modified from *SBCP*, 463.

[96] These two terms, *li* and *ch'i*, are a cornerstone of Chu Hsi's thought. For discussion see chapter 5.

[97] These words conclude the *Chung-yung*: "The *Book of Odes* says, 'I cherish your brilliant virtue, which makes no great display in sound or appearance.' [Ode 241]. Confucius said, 'In influencing people, the use of sound or appearance is of secondary importance.' The *Book of Odes* says, 'His virtue is as light as hair.' [Ode 260]. Still, a hair is comparable. 'The operations of Heaven have neither sound nor smell.' [Ode 235]." *SBCP*, 113.

Ode 235 is a long poem praising the virtues of King Wen. In Waley's translation the final stanza reads:

The charge [of Heaven] is not easy to keep.
Do not bring ruin on yourselves.
Send forth everywhere the light of your good fame;
Consider what Heaven did to the Yin (another name for the Shang).
High Heaven does its business
Without sound, without smell.
Make King Wen your example,
In whom all the peoples put their trust.

Arthur Waley, trans., *The Book of Songs* (New York: Grove Weidenfeld, 1987), 251.

[98] From the *Analects*, 4:15: "Confucius said, 'Ts'an [private name of Tseng Tzu], there is one thread (*i-kuan*) that runs through my doctrines.' Tseng Tzu said, 'Yes.' After Confucius had left, the disciples asked him, 'What did he mean?' Tseng Tzu replied, 'The Way of our master is none other than conscientiousness (*chung*) and altruism (*shu*).'" *SBCP*, 27.

[99] Reference to a famous incident in the *Analects* (11:25). When Confucius asked his disciples what they would prefer to do if given recognition in office, Tseng Hsi gave the most unorthodox response, which met with the master's approval: "'In the late spring, when the spring dress is ready, I would like to go with five or six grownups and six or seven young boys to bathe in the I River, enjoy the breeze on the Rain Dance Altar, and then return home singing.'" *SBCP*, 37–8.

this stage. Just as in Chuang Tzu's chapter "Discoursing on Swords," where the Son of Heaven's sword is discussed and contrasted to the sword of the feudal lord and so on,[100] the point of this one sword of the Ultimate of Nonbeing is all things of heaven and earth, and its swordguard is the primal force of the Great Ultimate. Cutting off material and human desires, it lays flat the evils in one's endowed temperament, and finally one is able to reach the peaceful place of no-action.

Kaneyoshi's postscript and seal are found here.

After the Diagrams of Six Circles and One Sword, the Following Was Recorded (by Nankō Sōgen) ←

Head of the Komparu troupe Ujinobu[101] stores in the family collection diagrams of six circles and one sword.[102] The explications of these are extremely numerous. The abbot of the Kaidan-in in Nara[103] delves into both the exoteric and esoteric with endless explanations that creak along with the sound of many carts, like a spinning-wheel in the mouth that won't stop. On the other hand, Lord Ichijō, regent at court,[104] searches widely in Confucian texts, matching up his cognates one by one. His discussions of the circles and sword are surpassingly beautiful and good. How could someone like myself add a single word to theirs? Nevertheless, [since Ujinobu is a master without equal,][105] I will attempt to say a few things.

When following the way of song and dance, the Buddhist patriarchs all would enter the *samādhi* of "backward practice," amusing themselves with wine and lascivious behavior. The Buddha and the Dharma completely reject this: letting his hands fly, Ho Shan beats the drum,[106] and Chin Niu

---

[100] In *Chuang Tzu*, chapt. 30, the sword of the Son of Heaven is described: "The valley of Yen and the Stone Wall are its point, Ch'i and Tai its blade, Chin and Wey its spine, Chou and Sung its swordguard, Han and Wei its hilt. . . . The five elements govern it, the demands of punishment and favor direct it. It is brought forth in accordance with the yin and yang, held in readiness in spring and summer, wielded in autumn and winter. . . . Above, it cleaves the drifting clouds; below, it severs the sinews of the earth." Translated by Burton Watson, *The Complete Works of Chuang Tzu* (New York: Columbia University Press, 1968), 342–43.

It is apparent from what follows that Kaneyoshi borrows only the general conception from Chuang Tzu; the description of his "sword" varies considerably.

[101] Zenchiku's personal name.

[102] The ex-Zen priest and poet (1387–1463). Nankō's original comments, in Chinese, survive; the Hachiemon manuscript reproduces them in native Japanese reading, with one omission (see note 105).

[103] Shigyoku.

[104] Kaneyoshi.

[105] This laudatory phrase is not reproduced in the Hachiemon manuscript, suggesting modesty on Zenchiku's part when he compiled the final *Ki*.

[106] A reference to case 44 of the *Pi-yen lu*. See chapter 7.

playfully dances.[107] Truly, the Buddha's eye does not glimpse the way of song and dance, the demon realm cannot fathom it.

However, if the tuft of hair on the Buddha's forehead is emanating spirituality, then song and dance are not alive. At such times, the "wondrous function" of the six circles and one sword is like eating the Ai family's [delicate] pears after cooking them[108]—what vitality is there? In the past, The Deity of Kasuga spoke through an oracle and praised [song and dance].[109] Indeed he was right. Therefore I will not remain silent and refuse to comment: choosing from the master's superlative song and dance pieces, I will write a *gāthā* in praise of him.

Indeed, the Lord and the Abbot are like Mount T'ai and the Great Bear [revered] in history, in appearance they are like [rare] *kirin* horn and phoenix down—my words are quite different from theirs. How can I avoid being called the dog's tail following the marten?[110]

The *gāthā* reads,

The pillowed glory of the traveler of Kantan,[111]
the barge of the Eguchi beauty,[112] alive with song and dance—
transmitted in the family, these are the true Buddhist Law;
the six circles and one sword are not mere elegance.

[Humbly recorded in the autumn of the first year of Kōshō [1455] by the fallen man of the fisherman's hut, Sōgen.][113]

---

[107] A reference to case 74 of the *Pi-yen lu*. See chapter 7.

[108] An allusion to the "Contempts and Insults" section of the *Shih-shuo hsin-yü*, a Chinese collection of tales, mostly from the Chin dynasty: "When Huan Hsüan saw someone who was not quick-witted, he would always say angrily, 'I suppose if you got some pears from the Ai family, you'd cook them before eating, wouldn't you?'" The commentary states that the Ai Chung family owned a pear tree whose fruit was so delicious that "it would dissolve in the mouth. . . . Stupid persons who did not discriminate among good flavors would cook them before eating." Translated by Richard B. Mather, *Shih-shuo Hsin-yü: A New Account of Tales of the World* (Minneapolis: University of Minnesota Press, 1976), 440.

Nankō himself seems to have been fond of firm, young pears. He wrote the following poem:

I head for the market with three sen to buy pears and stroll about,
chomping on the reddest, crunchier than plums;
this year, thank god, they're not "worth a thousand in gold"—
I can even afford one for the guardian deity Makora.

Gozan bungaku shinshū, 6:261, translated by Pollack, *Zen Poems of the Five Mountains*, 71.

[109] See notes 44 and 46.

[110] A proverb that denotes an inferior person following someone praiseworthy.

[111] A reference to the protagonist of the noh play *Kantan*, who slept on a magic pillow lent by a Taoist sorcerer during a stay at a traveler's inn. He dreamt of great glory, only to awaken.

[112] In the noh play *Eguchi*, the protagonist is a courtesan who, while performing on a pleasure barge, is revealed as a manifestation of the bodhisattva Samantabhadra.

[113] As noted in chapter 1, this colophon is not included in the Hachiemon manuscript. It

COMMENTARY TO "A RECORD OF SIX CIRCLES
AND ONE DEWDROP"

The six circles incorporate the teachings of the Gods, the Buddhist Law, and the Confucian Way—both the religious and the secular—to express the nature of the process by which heaven and earth divided.[114]

First of all, the Circle of Longevity, the form of heaven and earth before differentiation, is round like the egg of a bird.[115] This is the progenitor of the gods, and the primordial life of the Buddhist Law—the shape of the letter A [which represents] fundamental birthlessness;[116] or again, the rank of the Creative which is the heart of the way of the [*Book of*] *Change*, the [constant] movement of the wheel of Heaven night and day, without the interval of a single breath.[117] The round form of the Circle of Longevity is the mind that revolves without stopping for an instant. To take an example from the realm of song and dance, breathing joins together one's singing in a continuous, round form.[118] Using the voice, one must connect exhalation and inhalation without interruption. Truly speaking, without breath there can be no voice, but if the two are considered separate entities, the breath is a thread that connects the voiced words. When there are intervals between breaths, the performance has no life, but if this round form is not forgotten, one's singing has enduring life.[119] Since song and dance are one, this round form also represents the breath of dance. That is, the life of dance lies in not concentrating upon technique, but rather in smoothly connecting one's individual movements by utilizing this round form. [The Circle of Longevity] is the vessel that bears all things,[120] the root source of yūgen.

---

simply concludes with the remark, "This section has the seal of the fallen man of the fisherman's hut, Sōgen." Gyoan (fisherman's hut) was Nankō's literary sobriquet.

[114] The expression *tenchi kaibyaku* (the "opening" of heaven and earth, as they polarize from an amorphous state and come into being) refers to the Chinese-derived cosmogony in the opening passage of the *Nihon shoki*. See discussion in chapter 6.

[115] This image of the bird's egg is drawn from the *Nihon shoki* passage: "Of old, heaven and earth were not yet separated, and the yin and yang not yet divided. They formed a chaotic mass like an egg which was of obscurely defined limits and contained germs." *NKBT*, 67:76; translation modified from Aston, *Nihongi*, 1–2.

[116] The letter A is mentioned in Shigyoku's commentary; see note 12. It is Zenchiku, however, who here introduces the doctrine it symbolizes: *honpushō*, "fundamental birthlessness." For the significance of the letter A in medieval Shinto, see chapter 6.

[117] Cf. the *Ki* text, "The wheel of Heaven revolves day and night without stopping for the interval of a single breath." See chapter 5.

[118] The matter of proper breathing is more fully discussed in Zenchiku's *Go'on sangyoku shū*. See chapter 3.

[119] For a discussion of this concept, see chapter 3.

[120] For a further discussion of the "vessel," see chapter 3.

Next is the Circle of Height, where heaven and earth have already separated: the pure ascends and the impure descends. This is the form of primal force arising,[121] the progenitor of the gods. It is like that golden wave upon the Nature Sea,[122] or the stage of initiative—the supreme good—which is the inception of the birth of all things.[123] In spring, grasses and trees sprout. Or again, the words "By rising and falling to the tones *kyū* and *shō*, the voice brings forth melody. This is called 'music' "[124] [are represented by this circle]. The [deep] feeling produced by high, clear singing, pure and unsurpassed,[125] occurs here. In the case of dance, it is the birth of vital rhythm in which primal force arises for the first time, moving from *jo* to *ha*.[126] The sublime feeling produced by all roles and all pieces—indeed, by just one syllable or gesture—belongs to this rank.

Third is the Circle of Abiding, the form in which heaven is heaven and earth is earth, the place where all forms come to completion.[127] The myriad dharmas—both material and mental—flowing in accord with

[121] See notes 70 and 78.

[122] See note 14.

[123] See notes 76 and 77.

[124] These words are also recorded in the Komparu School manuscript of Zeami's *Kakyō*. The Zeami passage reads: "Through the upper and lower tones *kyū* and *shō*, the voice produces [pleasing] patterns; this is called 'music.' *Kyū* is yin; it corresponds to earth, *ryo*, and exhalation. *Shō* is yang: it corresponds to heaven, *ritsu*, and inhalation. When *ryo* and *ritsu* join together and the voice rises and falls, this is called 'melody.' These divide into five tones and twelve pitches—six *ryo* and six *ritsu*." *ZZ*, 84.

This section combines phrases from the Great Preface passage cited in note 2 and the commentary to that work by Cheng-hsüan (127–200).

[125] "High, clear singing" is discussed in Zenchiku's *Go-on sangyoku shū*: "*Ryo*, *ritsu*, and *chūkyoku*. *Ryo* is open, gentle singing and corresponds to the skin; *ritsu* is sharp, incisive appearance and pure, clear singing, corresponding to the flesh; *chūkyoku* is rapid singing that suddenly becomes delicate and shifts direction, corresponding to bone." *KKSS*, 171.

The concept of "deep feeling" alluded to here is related to a conception expressed in Zeami's *Goi*: " 'Feeling' is when the eyes and mind are surprised at an unexpected place. In the style of feeling, there are [three elements:] grasping the present mood of the audience, impressing their hearts, and catching their eye. When their disposition shifts [from a moment of delight], there is another, detached sensation of deep feeling. In the *Book of Songs* it says, 'Rectifying profit and loss, moving heaven and earth, impressing demons and gods. This is called "feeling." ' " *ZZ*, 170.

The above translation follows Omote (*ZZ*, 170n and 471–72, n. 91). The last sentence in the quotation is not found in the Great Preface to the *Book of Songs*. See chapter 3 for further discussion of this topic.

[126] That is, *jo* and *ha* within the rhythmic pattern of *jo-ha-kyū* (opening, development, and climax). Zenchiku's views on *jo-ha-kyū* are discussed in chapter 3.

[127] Cf. the following passage from Zeami's *Shūgyoku tokka*: "This fulfillment corresponds to *jo-ha-kyū*. The reason is that fulfillment is a matter of resolution. If there is no resolution, there can be no sense of completion. The moment when the performance is complete, the spectators experience an instant of deep fascination." *ZZ*, 190.

The topic of "completion" is discussed further in chapter 3.

conditions,[128] and [the process of entering] Nirvana after [leaving] the cycle of birth-and-death, are manifested here.[129] "Flourish is the coming together of all that is beautiful";[130] this is the stage where all things, all virtues gather. The appearance of summer trees and grasses growing luxuriantly is like the short vertical line in this circle. From here, styles [in the manner] of all things are performed; it is the wondrous place where all song and dance pieces are accomplished, imitating the various appearances of things. Having a place in which to reside, these forms leave and enter the mind, disappearing and appearing like thoughts. The mind that resides in this place, alternately standing and sitting, assumes a hidden form as the interval between movements.[131] Then, it again moves into the realm of performance, and the round form produces movements to the left and right; this is the living role in its manifest state. A single note, a single syllable resides in this position; however, if each does not come to completion, one does not know this circle. Since "dharmas reside in the Dharma position; the forms of this world are eternally abiding,"[132] this is where blossoms scattering and leaves falling before one's eyes embody eternal imperishability.[133] If one does not know this place, one does not know the fundamental seed—such [lack of understanding] is like a plucked flower.

These first three circles are the highest ranks, the profound essence of subtle feeling, the spirit of the Three Circles' purity.[134]

[128] See note 7.

[129] See note 8.

[130] See note 81.

[131] Cf. the following passage in Zenchiku's *Go-on sangyoku shū*: "Concerning interval and beat. All actions should be executed in the interval. If they are performed on the beat, they have little effect. The state when heaven and earth have not yet divided is the interval; the division is the beat. [The manifestation of] all things comprises arising from this interval. Also, one should realize that within the interval there is a beat, and within the beat there is an interval. In all performances, the interest lies in the fact that actions have a transient nature. This interest is particularly evident in these intervals. The details must be transmitted orally." *KKSS*, 184.

For the significance of the "division of heaven and earth" expression, see note 114 and the discussion in chapter 6.

[132] See note 15.

[133] The expression used here, *jōjū fumetsu*, more literally translated "eternally abiding and not disintegrating," echoes the *jū* of the Circle of Abiding. This conception is derived from the following passage in Zeami's *Shūgyoku tokka*: "A certain person asked, 'What is the heart of the impermanence of all things?' The reply was 'Flying petals and falling leaves.' He then asked, 'What is eternal imperishability?' Again the reply was 'Flying petals and falling leaves.' There is no fixed mental content in the direct experience of fascination. In many arts, those who engender fascination are called skillful, and those who can maintain this fascination for a long period are famed masters. Actors who have the ability to perform with interest in this way through their years of mature accomplishment [have managed consistently to create the transitory effect of *hana*, and so] are equivalent to the notion that 'flying petals and falling leaves embody eternal imperishability.'" *ZZ*, 186.

[134] "The Three Circles' purity" (*sanrin shōjō*) is a Buddhist expression. *Sanrin* refers to the

Fourth, in the Circle of Forms the myriad entities of all creation are diverse, evolving from the Three Functions of heaven, earth, and man in various ways. Even so, these various forms are extensions of the first three circles, having emerged from them. [This circle] is like the roundness of the world which encompasses mountains, rivers, and the great earth—all forms, both good and bad.[135] This is also the stage of advantage: furthering all things, benefiting man.[136] In autumn, the five grains, ripe, are bent over, and trees and grasses bear fruit. The mind that adjusts the [style of] song and dance in accordance with [the individual nature of] the object [portrayed] is called the Circle of Forms. Thus, although one distinguishes between the voices of the old and the young and colors each with an appropriate singing style, and even though these styles assume characteristics of the various objects portrayed, the mind that acts in accordance with the first three circles will generate performances of supreme yūgen. While these roles differ in appearance, they all lie within the round form[137] of the profound way of song and dance.

Fifth is the Circle of Breaking, in which everything is transformed into good or evil, breaking [the harmony of form]; even so, the round vessel—the bounds of heaven and earth—does not change. A country in disorder becomes peaceful again; what has been broken is always rebuilt. The world revolves in a recurring cycle of becoming, residing, dissolution, and emptiness.[138] This circle is the stage of extinction, in which birth-and-death itself is none other than Nirvana, and worldly desires are none other than bodhi. As the stage of perseverance,[139] it is the foundation of all actions, that which gives rise to initiative.[140] It is the basis of all things. Among the four seasons it is winter, when the leaves of grasses and trees turn color and fall, returning to their roots. Thus, although one breaks the circular form by acting as one pleases, the subtle essence of the first three circles is not abandoned. It has been said, "At seventy I could follow my heart's desire without transgressing moral principles."[141] Although one

---

alms-giver, the receiver of alms, and the alms given; when almsgiving is practiced without attachment, these three elements are equally pure. Within the present context, *sanrin* of course also refers to the first three circles of Zenchiku's system. For further discussion, see chapter 6.

[135] Cf. the following passage from Zeami's *Shūgyoku tokka*: "All forms in creation—good and bad, large and small, sentient and nonsentient—each and every one has its own *jo-ha-kyū*." *ZZ*, 191. See chapter 3.

[136] See note 83.

[137] See note 20.

[138] These are the "four ages" (*shikō*) that represent the progressive stages within a kalpa, one life cycle of the universe. Note that these terms are distinct from the "four characteristic states" (*shisō*) of existence (see note 9).

[139] See note 87.

[140] For further explication, see chapter 5.

[141] *Analects* 2:4. Chan's translation of this well-known passage reads: "Confucius said, 'At

displays rough, unrefined movements, the appearance of tranquility found in the higher ranks[142] is not lost. The power of an unorthodox solo vocal piece produces a feeling of profound beauty, and dancing an unusual, contrary style generates a fleeting, gentle flavor.

Sixth [is the] Circle of Emptiness: when the three great disasters[143] occur, the world is utterly destroyed and becomes empty. This is the form of return to the original beginning. The Great Ultimate is the supreme truth;[144] the vastness of heaven and earth originates from the principle of this Great Ultimate. After awakening, enlightenment is the same as the pre-enlightened state.[145] This is the return to the original Circle of Longevity after attaining [great mastery of the art], truly the rank of [withdrawing after] accomplishment and fame;[146] it is that which causes a single flower to remain on an old tree.[147] As all things wither and die, they faintly seem young; a single song, a single dance returns to the stage in which it first came to bud. That is to say, the original round form is restored.

The final One Dewdrop is the seminal master of heaven and earth, the spirit in the birth of all things. It is Acalanātha's sharp sword, representing this wondrous principle's firm and immovable nature, and Mañjuśrī's wisdom sword of inner illumination.[148] It has been said, "[In the stages] up through the Great Ultimate, the dualism of principle and material force is present. [In contrast,] the Ultimate of Nonbeing departs from the word-based distinction of being and emptiness; it does not lie within the realm of thought. The passage in the *Doctrine of the Mean*, '[The workings of Heaven] have neither sound nor smell,' Tseng Tzu's 'yes,' and the spirit of Tseng Hsi's bathing in the River I [all correspond to this stage]."[149] Although it displays no physical body, this is the spirit that oversees all compositions, the sword of the mind that cuts through all obstructions. Each song, each dance, each role—all possess this force. The sword trans-

---

fifteen my mind was set on learning. At thirty my character had been formed. At forty I had no more perplexities. At fifty I knew the Mandate of Heaven. At sixty I was at ease with whatever I heard. At seventy I could follow my heart's desire without transgressing moral principles.'" *SBCP*, 22.

[142] That is, the three highest of Zeami's "nine ranks," as defined in his *Kyūi*. The relationship between these stages and Zenchiku's categories is treated in chapter 3.

[143] The "three great disasters" are those caused by fire, water, and wind.

[144] For more on the Great Ultimate, see note 71 and chapter 5.

[145] This common Zen saying is quoted in Chinese in Zeami's *Shūgyoku tokka. ZZ*, 189.

[146] The expression *kō nari, na togetaru kurai* is derived from language in chapter 9 of *Lao Tzu*: "As soon as your work is accomplished and your fame achieved, you should withdraw—this is Heaven's Way."

[147] This image is found in the *Fūshi kaden* section on the performance of the old man role. *ZZ*, 22.

[148] See notes 29 and 31.

[149] This quotation is from the *Ki* text. For the references, see notes 97–99.

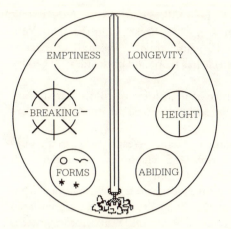

FIG. 2-8. The Eighth Mirror

forms, becoming the Great, Round, Mirror-like Wisdom[150] that has eight faces, all clear and luminous. However, as this treatise is entitled "Six Circles and One Dewdrop," one of these faces is not represented. [The eighth] possesses the qualities of each of these seven stages, but, in the spirit of the Nature Sword which returns to the One Mind and the "one thread,"[151] its shape manifests these multiple stages within a single mirror; thus it is not included in the sequential progression.[152]

Masukagami	A bright mirror—
ura o katachi no	know its inner essence by the forms
omote ni te	reflected on its surface,
omote o ura no	know the front as
hikari to mo shire	the light of the back.[153]

[150] See note 45 for the Four Wisdoms, of which the Mirror-like Wisdom is one.

[151] A reference to the *Analects* passage cited in note 98.

[152] In Zenchiku's *Nika ichirin*, the diagram depicted in figure 2-8 is supplied to illustrate this configuration. The large mirror that encompasses the symbols of the seven stages is the "eighth face."

[153] The *Rokurin ichiro dai'i* contains a variant for the second and third lines, "Ura o omote no / katachi ni te," which reinforces my interpretive translation. (*KKSS* 224). A more literal rendition of the original would be "Know the back by the front that has form."

This poem is difficult to interpret. On one level, it is an expression of the "eyes in front, mind in back" doctrine described in note 154; the actor should consider the "back," or detached view, as that which determines his appearance and provides the "light," or charisma, of a successful performance. I suspect that the poem's metaphysical meaning hinges upon a little-known quality of Chinese bronze mirrors. The reflecting front is polished smooth, while the reverse side exhibits a pattern or design cast in relief. When light is shined onto the front of the mirror, the reflected light projects a faint replica of the design on the back! This effect is due to slight irregularities on the mirror's face generated in the casting

[A synopsis of the essentials of each stage follows.]

First, the Circle of Longevity. In song, the breath is in the shape of a continuous round form. [Similarly,] a round form at the start of a dance connects beginning and end. This circle has front and back sides.[154] Orally transmitted.

Second, the Circle of Height. The excellent form of cold, clear singing arising. The feeling of superlative yūgen experienced during dance performances appears here.

Third, the Circle of Abiding. Song and dance—each piece, each syllable, each movement—are not in disarray.[155] Each comes to completion in its own position, the wondrous place of settling down.

Fourth, the Circle of Forms. Musical pieces and dance movements become like the objects portrayed; at this stage, things are differentiated appropriately, yet the first three circles of high rank[156] are not forgotten.

Fifth, the Circle of Breaking. Although the singing stands out[157] and unorthodox dance movements are performed, the tenets of [Zeami's] three highest ranks are preserved without effort. [Styles] that are said to "break" [the harmonious round form] lie within this circle.

Sixth, the Circle of Emptiness. Advancing further and further, song and dance wither—the appearance of a flower that remains on an old tree. [The

---

process. Thus, the poem expresses the mysterious interpenetration of the manifest and unmanifest aspects of reality, symbolized by the obverse and reverse sides of the mirror. It is included here as a bridge between the discussion of the missing "eighth face" and the following description of the Circle of Longevity, which is said to have both front and back sides.

[154] In the *Rokurin ichiro hichū* (*Kanshō bon*), Zenchiku records that "These front and back sides [of the Circle of Longevity] represent the practice of 'eyes in front, mind in back'" (*mokuzen shingo*; *KKSS*, 232). This is a reference to a concept discussed in Zeami's *Kakyō*: "In dance, there is the saying 'eyes in front, mind in back.' In other words, 'Look ahead with your eyes, and place your mind behind yourself.' . . . The performance of an actor as seen by the audience is a 'detached view' (*riken*), an objectification of his own form. That is, what the actor sees with his own eyes is a subjective view (*gaken*), different from the appearance he presents when seen from afar. Only when he looks at his own performance from afar (*riken no ken*) is his perception the same as that of the audience; at that moment, he achieves a complete view of his own form. . . . However, although he can see what is before his eyes, and to the left and right, . . . he is not aware of any weak points visible from the back. . . . Thus the actor must use the detached view to see himself from the perspective of the audience—to be aware of what his physical eyes cannot see—in order to present a graceful, harmonious form. Is this not placing the 'mind in back'?" *ZZ*, 88).

Zeami's "detached view" is discussed in Michiko Yusa, "*Riken no ken*: Zeami's Theory of Acting and Theatrical Appreciation," *Monumenta Nipponica* 42:3 (Autumn 1987): 331–45.

[155] See chapter 3.

[156] Zeami's upper three ranks. See note 142.

[157] The use of the word *takete* here implies Zeami's *rangyoku*, which means something like "sublime singing." Due to the adversative quality of the clause, however, I have translated the expression more literally. *Rangyoku* (and *ran'i*, the "rank of the sublime") and their relation to Zenchiku's Circle of Breaking are discussed in chapters 3 and 5.

art] becomes one of diminishing, and finally no style, as it returns to the original Circle of Longevity.

The One Dewdrop is the spirit that joins these six circles.

In general, one must understand these seven principles as they are manifested in each mental state, each song, each syllable, and each dance [as follows].

The appearance of characters upon entering the stage,[158] the round form where mind and matter are in harmony, and yūgen all comprise the Circle of Longevity. Then singing begins; the vitality of the sound rises high and cold, the style of distant whiteness.[159] This is the Circle of Height. To reside peacefully in this mind—namely, to come to completion—is to come to rest in the Circle of Abiding. These three levels are the highest, the ultimate in yūgen. Each movement of the sleeve, each individual style within each role, each step taken, and each note of a song—this is the stage where they all reside peacefully, embodying yūgen. Thus the five sections of dance[160] also come to rest here. If one learns the various roles within the Circle of Forms while abiding peacefully in the perfected three minds [of the previous circles], then one's art will belong to the upper ranks [of Zeami].[161] After that comes the Circle of Breaking, in which one descends to the lower ranks [of Zeami], deliberately performing any style at all. In unconventional portrayals—the movement of a child, or a savage person—the appearance breaks the [tenets of the] basic styles. However, one must not linger there and become tainted by the role; instead one should be like a nobleman performing in these lower ranks simply for amusement.[162] When these actions have been exhausted, one performs without style[163] or ornamenta-

[158] Although in Zeami demono means the "true form" of the shite role—in other words, the nochi-jite—here "demono no tei" seems to refer to the appearance of a character as he enters the stage, before speaking. See KKSS, 220, n. 1.

[159] The "style of distant whiteness" (tōjiroki tei) is a literal translation for a term that, in waka treatises, comes to signify "lofty," "impressive," and so forth. The images most prominently associated with this style are snow-covered peaks in the distance and a cold, clear moon in the dark autumn sky.

[160] The five dan of a dance: the opening (jo), one section; the development (ha), three sections; and the climax (kyū), one section.

[161] See chapter 3.

[162] See chapter 3.

[163] Zeami also uses the term mufū in the following passage from his Kakyō: "To completely master noh; to become a performer of extraordinary ability, then to enter the realm of ease, the rank of the sublime; to have not the slightest awareness of the movements one is performing; to exhibit the art of one who has attained the rank of no-mind and no-style (mushin mufū)—is this [level of performance] not close to the wondrous?" ZZ, 101.

At the beginning of this section (ZZ, 101) "the wondrous" (myō, taenaru) is defined as katachi naki sugata (appearance of no form).

tion,[164] while radiating fragrance and light. This stage is the Circle of Emptiness. The One Dewdrop is the spirit that preserves these [six] states of mind.

The above Six Circles and One Dewdrop are not just a compendium of the teachings I received from my teacher.[165] These principles, realized while I was in retreat at [the temple of] the Hatsuse Kannon, are an explication of Kannon's skillful means in benefiting the masses;[166] they are precepts to be observed by all sentient beings. Thus I have also named these [symbols] the Six Circles of Kannon.[167]

Kōshō 2 [1456], First Month, Lucky Day

Hata no Ujinobu[168]

[164] Zeami's *mumon*. Cf. this passage from his *Fūgyoku shū*: "There are differences in the perception of the art of ornamentation (*umon*) and the art of no-ornamentation (*mumon*). In the case of no-ornamentation, when there is considerable interest in the singing style yet the audience does not respond emotionally, this is the phenomenon of 'no-ornamention resulting from a lack of study.' However, there is also the situation where, although one's singing lacks ornamentation, the feeling it presents is sublime, and the experience is utterly captivating. This should be known as 'the style of no-ornamentation that surpasses the style of ornamentation.' It is the rank of a wondrous voice of the highest accomplishment." ZZ, 159–60.

[165] Zeami.

[166] The retreat mentioned here cannot be dated, but several passages in Zenchiku's writings attest to his deep faith in the Hase-dera Kannon. Evidence suggests that the temple was an important center of early Yamato sarugaku activity, and Zenchiku's predecessors in the Emai troupe performed there regularly. See Hirose, *Nō to Komparu*, 133–34, and Dōmoto, *Zeami*, 600, n. 16. The name Kanze, first used by Kannami, was probably derived from the "Kanzeon" of Hasedera. In addition, many of the legends surrounding the alleged founder of Yamato sarugaku, Hata no Kōkatsu, center in the Hatsuse area. See chapter 1.

[167] This appellation recalls the "Six Kannon," a grouping of six iconographical variants of the bodhisattva often aligned with the six paths of transmigration.

[168] Zenchiku. For the significance of the Hata surname, see chapter 1.

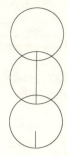

Chapter Three: Six Circles of Performance

WHATEVER the broader philosophical and cultural implications of the rokurin ichiro texts, one must never lose sight of their identity as artistic treatises. In recording these texts, Zenchiku's avowed intent was to record for posterity the essence of the art of sarugaku as transmitted from his teacher Zeami. For this reason, my goal in this chapter is to delineate the six circles as a dynamic repository of performance wisdom.

Nevertheless, when examining the various texts, it is at best difficult to isolate this performance stratum. There is no "pure" original record, untainted by the contributions of Shigyoku and Kaneyoshi. The *Ki* is the earliest extant manuscript, but already at this stage the commentaries comprise the great majority of the text. Indeed, the *Ki* appears to be primarily a record of these commentaries, with Zenchiku's brief definitions included merely to identify the seven categories. I strongly suspect that at least Shigyoku was shown a more detailed draft, or perhaps Zenchiku discussed the system with him in person.[1] Still, the *Ki* is a pivotal document because it isolates the material contributed by Shigyoku and Kaneyoshi, material that in later drafts is integrated into Zenchiku's text. When passages in such later works as the *Kichū* that are clearly derived from these commentaries are discounted, Zenchiku's own contributions begin to emerge. Of the material translated in chapter 2, the two summaries of performance principles found at the conclusion of the *Kichū* are the most direct and detailed. Yet one problem remains: it is difficult to determine whether any given conception in the *Kichū* (or later works) predates the *Ki* manuscript or was added later.

In my opinion, the most important clues to the original formulation of the rokurin ichiro system are the names of the seven stages themselves. These terms are consistent throughout the entire body of texts, and therefore they probably existed from the outset. Unfortunately, some of the designations are difficult to fathom on the basis of the *Ki* definitions alone.

[1] See chapter 1 for a description of the various manuscripts.

Applying the principles outlined above, however, it is possible to extract original Zenchiku material from later manuscripts that elucidate these terms. A careful comparison of these passages with the original *Ki* definitions will produce a comprehensible, although perhaps incomplete, view of the six circles.

Thus, this study begins by examining each of the six symbols individually with reference to its name, focusing on its practical significance for the performance of sarugaku. I will also occasionally expand slightly, referring to later applications of these concepts in order to clarify these provisional definitions.

THE CIRCLE OF LONGEVITY (*JURIN*)

The first stage is designated by the character *ju*, which has the felicitous meaning of "longevity," "long-lived," and so forth. Zenchiku's "personal remarks" (*shishi*) in the *Ki* describe the *jurin* as follows: "The Circle of Longevity is the fundamental source of the yūgen of song and dance. It is the vessel in which deep feelings arise upon viewing the performer's style and listening to his singing. Due to its round, perfect nature and eternal life span, it is called the Circle of Longevity."

The final sentence provides the rationale for the name. While the above can be read merely as an abstract description of the "source of yūgen," it is best understood with reference to material from the later *Kichū*: "To take an example from the realm of song and dance, breathing joins together one's singing in a continuous, round form. . . . When there are intervals between breaths, the performance has no life, but if this round form is not forgotten, one's singing has enduring life." The concept of longevity, then, is closely related to the notion of correct breathing in the art of singing. Smooth, harmonious breathing that continues in an unbroken cycle is the life-force of effective vocalization. As seen in the *Kichū*, Zenchiku also attaches cosmological significance to the principle of "uninterrupted breath";[2] however, the practical basis of the jurin conception is proper breathing in performance. The same principle extends to dance: "Since song and dance are one, this round form also represents the breath of dance. That is, the life of dance lies in not concentrating upon technique, but rather smoothly connecting one's individual movements by utilizing this round form."

A closely related concept is *inochi*, used above in the phrase "enduring life." While *ju* is a quality of the breathing process as experienced by the performer, a kind of storehouse of inexhaustible vitality, *inochi* —which

[2] This theme is first treated by Kaneyoshi in his commentary; see chapter 5.

usually denotes the life-force or life span of an individual—is used to express the longevity of the *effect* of the vocalization upon the audience. This principle is discussed in Zenchiku's *Go'on sangyoku shū*:

> Generally speaking, breath is the life of musical performance, and thus it is hardly necessary to mention it. Yet since there are so many dull performers of short[-lived] technique, unskilled in the way [of sarugaku], I shall write about this at length. After all, breath is the essence [of performance]. For example, it is like the thread that connects [a set of] jewels. In each section of a piece, one should sing the accented syllables during exhalation, and the final syllables where one comes to a stop at the point of inhalation. If the accented syllables come out at the point of inhalation, one will experience shortness of breath, and the life of the piece will be short. . . . Singing follows the progression *ryo–ritsu–ryo*,[3] but the process of first setting the pitch in one's mind and then beginning to sing from its fragrance is first of all a matter of breath. Setting the pitch is the breath of *ritsu*. Also, one concludes singing the final syllables with the breath. If one stops abruptly at the last syllable, the singing has no subtle fragrance, and its life is short (*inochi mijikashi*). The mind that concludes singing with the breath, and the return to the beginning to set the pitch, both are contained in the breath of *ritsu*. Thus it is like the shape of a round form, with no beginning or end. . . . The words are like jewels, the breath like a string.[4]

"Long life," then, implies a style of performance that is affecting yet subtle in expression, creating a lingering fragrance.

THE CIRCLE OF HEIGHT (*SHURIN*)

Concerning the *shurin* (or *ryūrin*), Zenchiku's "personal remarks" are: "In the second circle, the Circle of Height, this single point rises, becoming spirit; breadth and height appear, and clear singing is born. This is the unsurpassed, highest fruition of feeling."

Again, the name of the circle is derived from a concept found in Zeami's teachings on vocal technique. "Breadth" (*ō*) and "height" (*shu*) are discussed in Zeami's *Fūgyoku shū*:

> The singing voice has both breadth and height. In terms of *ryo* and *ritsu*, does not breadth correspond to *ryo*, and height to *ritsu*? The impulse to issue sound upon listening to the pitch is height; the stage of sounding the voice and actually singing is breadth. It is said, "Sing with breadth, conclude with height." Since the point where the pitch appears is height, however, the first words one sings

---

[3] For a discussion of the musical terms *ryo* and *ritsu*, see Eta Harich-Schneider, *A History of Japanese Music* (London: Oxford University Press, 1973), 134–38.

[4] *KKSS*, 177–78.

should be vertical. Therefore the flow of singing is from vertical to horizontal as one starts to sing, and again to vertical as one finishes. Breadth should be [thought of as] the handling of outgoing breath, height as the coloring of entering breath.[5]

Height, then, comprises the onset of the act of vocalization. It is the very first step, the mental impulse to begin singing at a precise pitch. This recalls the second stage in the principle of *itchō–niki–sansei* presented by Zeami in his *Kakyō*, which states that the performer should (1) listen to the pitch established by the accompanying musicians, (2) mentally set his own pitch and breath, and (3) only then begin to sing.[6] In contrast, the manifest vocalization takes place almost entirely in the horizontal dimension. The process is like a germinated seed sprouting straight upward, and then blooming outward on a horizontal plane. Zenchiku's shurin represents the initial germination, a distinct subjective state experienced in performance. The verticality of this stage emerges distinctly from the ground of the previous Circle of Longevity, which symbolizes continuous, circular breathing.

In a more objective sense, this circle also represents a style of high, clear singing, emerging from the tranquil vessel of the Circle of Longevity. Some commentators have speculated that "breadth" represents a strong, masculine voice, and "height" a more delicate, feminine style;[7] this may account for Zenchiku's characterization. In any case, in the later *Hichū* (*Bunshō bon*), Zenchiku modifies his definition to emphasize the "*cold, clear*" qualities associated with the "style of distant whiteness" of waka: "The Circle of Height is high, lofty in rank, rising with a chill (*hienobori*) in the style of distant whiteness: it is like the glow of cherry blossoms on a mountain peak in the mist, or the moon of an autumn night rising clearly from behind the clouds."[8] Here Zenchiku seems to have in mind the "chilling" effect described by Zeami in his *Kakyō*:

Noh that succeeds within the heart[9] occurs when, after performing many different types of pieces, an unsurpassed master is performing a piece that is not particularly distinguished in song, dance, acting, or plot: during a subdued, quiet passage, for no reason there is a point that is deeply moving. This is called a

[5] *ZZ*, 156.

[6] This doctrine is presented at the opening of the *Kakyō*. *ZZ*, 84. It is discussed further later in this chapter.

[7] *ZZ*, 443–44, n. 32.

[8] *KKSS*, 252.

[9] In the *Kakyō*, Zeami distinguishes noh that succeed through visual effect (*ken*), aural effect (*mon*), and an effect upon the heart (*shin*). In a slightly different sense, these three categories correspond to Zenchiku's first three circles; see the following discussion of this grouping.

chilling performance (*hietaru kyoku*). Even a relatively discerning audience does not understand this level; it is inconceivable that country audiences could appreciate it.[10]

For Zeami, the effect is attained at moments of no-ornamentation (*mumon*); again, the chill beauty is a phenomenon emerging from the plain ground of the tranquil Circle of Longevity. Furthermore, this conception depicts deep emotion arising in the hearts of the audience, a key aspect of the shurin to be examined later in this chapter.

THE CIRCLE OF ABIDING (*JŪRIN*)

The *Ki* text for the *jūrin* reads: "In the third circle, the Circle of Abiding, the short line's position is the peaceful place where all roles take shape and vital performance is produced." The significance of the jūrin in performance is not clear from this passage. The *Kichū* definition here is more helpful:

> From [the short vertical line in this circle], styles [in the manner] of all things are performed; it is the wondrous place where all song and dance pieces are accomplished, imitating the various appearances of things. Having a place in which to reside, these forms leave and enter the mind, disappearing and appearing like thoughts. The mind that resides in this place, alternately standing and then sitting, assumes a hidden form as the interval between dance movements.[11] Then, it again moves into the realm of performance, and the round form produces movements to the left and right; this is the living role in its manifest state. A single note, a single syllable resides in this position; however, if each does not come to completion, one does not know this circle.

Jū is an explicitly Buddhist term.[12] It appears in Zeami's writings in the compound *anju* (to reside peacefully), denoting the tranquil, assured mental state of an accomplished actor who is at ease performing various styles.[13] The emphasis in Zenchiku's jūrin is slightly different, however. In terms of performance, the jūrin is the mental state of ease that allows individual movements to arise smoothly, and then come to completion; the performer is constantly aware of the dynamic relationship between movement (manifest form) and interval (hidden form).

Perhaps the most closely related passage in Zeami's writings is a discussion of *jo-ha-kyū* and its relation to the concept of "fulfillment" (*jōju*).

[10] *ZZ*, 103.
[11] See chapter 2, note 131.
[12] See discussion of Shigyoku's jūrin commentary in chapter 4.
[13] For example, in the *Rikugi*. *ZZ*, 181.

Zenchiku's statement, "A single note, a single syllable resides in this stage; however, if each does not come to completion (*rakkyo*), they do not know this stage," echoes the following passage from Zeami's *Shūgyoku tokka*:

> The term *jōju* is a combination of words meaning "to become" and "completion." Therefore, in our art it too seems to mean something like "interesting." This *jōju* corresponds to *jo-ha-kyū*. This is because "to complete becoming" is equivalent to "coming to completion" (*rakkyo*). If there is no completion, then there will be no sense of "coming into being" in the minds of the audience. When the act of viewing reaches fulfillment, this is the moment of interest.[14]

The connection between *jo-ha-kyū* and this sense of fulfillment will be discussed at length in the second half of this chapter. It must be noted, however, that most of Zeami's remarks on "completion" are concerned with the subjective response of the audience. The explicit definitions of Zenchiku's jūrin, on the other hand, emphasize "completion" as a mental state of the performer: he experiences each individual motion (or sung phrase) arising freely, following its natural course, and then disappearing into the interval of hidden form.

THE CIRCLE OF FORMS (*ZŌRIN*)

The next three circles differ in scope. Zenchiku writes that the subjective qualities represented by the first three circles should be present in all performances;[15] in contrast, the final three represent concrete styles.

The *Ki* text for the first of these, the *zōrin*, reads, "In the fourth circle, the Circle of Forms, the various forms of heaven and earth, all things in creation, are at peace." Again, one must look to the *Kichū* for clarification:

> The mind that adjusts the style of song and dance in accordance with the individual nature of the object portrayed is called the Circle of Forms. Thus, although one distinguishes between the voices of the old and the young and colors each with an appropriate singing style, and even though these styles assume characteristics of the various objects portrayed, the mind that acts in accordance with the first three circles will generate performances of supreme yūgen. While these roles differ in appearance, they all lie within the round form of the profound way of song and dance.

The emphasis here is on the principle of differentiation. In performance, the actor must clearly delineate the unique characteristics of a given role:

---

[14] *ZZ*, 190.

[15] For example, in the *Hichū* (*Bunshō bon*): "In one role, one note, one flick of the sleeve, in one stomp of the foot, the minds of Longevity, Height, and Abiding are present." *KKSS*, 254.

for example, the differences among Zeami's Three Roles (*santai*: warrior, woman, and old man). In practical terms, the zōrin represents the art of *monomane*, the ability to portray an individual character convincingly. This mimetic style—originally the distinguishing characteristic of the Yamato sarugaku troupes,[16] in contrast to the more gentle, lyrical style of the Ōmi performers—must be mastered before the more advanced styles represented by the next two circles can be attempted. However, imitation without the inner grace of yūgen embodied in the first three circles is not permitted.

It should be noted that Zeami does not use the graph *zō* in this context. The term zōrin most likely derives from the expression *shinra banshō*, "the myriad forms of creation," which does appear in Zeami's *Shugyoku tokka*[17] and in the *Ki* text.[18]

THE CIRCLE OF BREAKING (*HARIN*)

Again, the *Ki* text ("When the inexhaustibly varying shapes of the ten directions of heaven and earth are produced, they are originally born within this circle. However, since they temporarily break its round form, I have named it the Circle of Breaking.") does not indicate the significance of this stage in performance. The *Kichū* records,

> Thus, although one breaks the circular form by acting as one pleases, the subtle essence of the first three circles is not abandoned. It has been said, "At seventy I could follow my heart's desire without transgressing moral principles." Although one displays rough, unrefined movements, the appearance of tranquility found in the higher ranks is not lost. The power of an unorthodox solo vocal piece produces a feeling of profound beauty, and dancing an unusual, contrary style generates a fleeting, gentle flavor.

The expression "rough, unrefined movements" recalls Zeami's views on the performance of demon roles. He distinguishes between two different types of portrayal: the "style of broken-down movement" (*saidōfū*) and the "style of forceful movement" (*rikidōfū*). Zeami approved of the former, describing it as follows: "The form is that of a demon, but the heart is human; thus when one performs without excessive force, one's movements are broken down finely. A role in the Style of Broken-Down Move-

---

[16] For insightful accounts of the importance of *monomane* in Yamato sarugaku, see Kitagawa Tadahiko, *Zeami* (Tokyo: Chūō kōron, 1972), 59 ff., and Toita Michizō, *Kannami to Zeami* (Tokyo: Iwanami shoten, 1969), 144 ff.

[17] *ZZ*, 191.

[18] *KKSS*, 201.

ment consists of an attitude of restraint and a lightness in the use of the body."[19] He says of the *rikidōfū*,

> Since this is the style of embodying strength in actions, it has no [admirable] quality. The heart is also that of a demon; thus in both respects it is a fearsome style that consequently is of little interest. However, if after having seen many different styles performed the audience views this style just once, in the manner of the *kyū* section [in a *jo–ha–kyū* sequence], it may provide a moment of pleasure, arousing their eyes and moving their hearts. It should not be performed frequently.[20]

In fact, the art of portraying demons had been a special feature of Yamato sarugaku. Gon-no-kami of the Kongō troupe and Mitsutarō of the Emai troupe were esteemed especially for their demon roles.[21] These performances were undoubtedly popular with both rural and urban audiences, and Zenchiku's interest is understandable. Thomas Hare describes Zeami's rejection of forceful demon roles as a reaction against Onnami's success with this style of performance, and as the result of his having embraced the yūgen style of Ōmi sarugaku.[22]

In his later years, Zeami restated his view of forceful demon roles. In reply to a letter (not extant) from Zenchiku, he wrote the following from Sado Island, where he was living in exile:

> I have read the part in your letter about the performance of demons. This is something unknown in our school. For example, beyond the Three Roles, we go as far as the Style of Broken-Down Movement; the Style of Forceful Movement, however, is something that other schools perform. Actually, my father did occasionally go so far as to express a demon-like power in his singing, and I too have learned this technique. I did this only after becoming a priest, however. Thus you should perform demon roles only in old age, employing the skill you have acquired in previous years by practicing your art over and over. Remember this well.[23]

This is precisely the situation that the *harin* represents: the accomplished, aging actor who has outgrown the passions of youth performs a forceful, inelegant demon role without displaying the vulgarity that a younger performer might reveal. As Zenchiku remarks, quoting the *Analects*, "At seventy I could follow my heart's desire without transgressing moral principles."[24]

[19] From the *Nikyoku santai ningyō zu*; *ZZ*, 128.

[20] *ZZ*, 129.

[21] Kitagawa, *Zeami*, 179. Mitsutarō's demon roles are mentioned in the *Sarugaku dangi* (*ZZ*, 266–67; trans. in Rimer and Yamazaki, *On the Art of the Nō Drama*, 181-2).

[22] Hare, *Zeami's Style*, 35.

[23] *ZZ*, 318–19.

[24] See *Kichū* translation in chapter 2. Also, see the discussion of Kaneyoshi's harin comments in chapter 5.

In the second half of his *Kichū* definition, Zenchiku broadens the scope of the harin. It represents not only the *rikidōfū*, but unorthodox styles in general. This recalls Zeami's category of *ran'i*, "the rank of the sublime." In the following passage from the *Shikadō*, Zeami uses the term to describe the effective performance of an accomplished actor who indulges in unorthodox or base techniques:

> The art of the rank of the sublime is a powerful vehicle that arises from the spiritual power of an artist who has already reached the highest levels. After many years of training from youth to old age, he learns all techniques, accumulating the good and rejecting the bad. Occasionally he mixes a bad technique—one he has despised and avoided in his years of training—with the good. You might ask why a master would perform in an incorrect fashion; but this is a special technique reserved for a master, proof of his skill. If he did not have only good techniques, he would not be a master. Thus, if his usually excellent technique loses its freshness and the audience seems overly accustomed to it, he occasionally mixes in faulty techniques; these have an appealing novelty due to his mastery. In this manner, incorrect technique seemingly becomes a virtue, as bad is transformed into good by the talents of the master. This creates a fascinating effect on stage.[25]

This phenomenon corresponds to another aspect of the harin. The perfection of external, conventional beauty, symbolized by the circle, is shattered, yet the internal mastery of the performer is manifest. The use of the term *ha* in this context is Zenchiku's innovation.

THE CIRCLE OF EMPTINESS (*KŪRIN*)

The *kūrin* is perhaps the most difficult of Zenchiku's six circles to describe in terms of performance. The *Ki* text reads, "The sixth circle, the Circle of Emptiness, is the rank of no-master and no-form; coming back to the beginning, again one returns to the original Circle of Longevity." The expression "no-master" (*mushu*) was noted in the previous chapter;[26] in contrast to Zeami, for whom it denotes a lack of mastery, Zenchiku uses the term to describe spontaneous, intuitive expression. *Mushiki*, the Buddhist term meaning no-form, recalls similar expressions found in the *Kichū*: no-style (*mufū*), no-ornamentation (*mumon*), and so on.[27] Perhaps the most notable aspect of the kūrin, then, is its lack of external characteristics: "one performs without style or ornamentation, and yet this rank gives off fragrance and light."[28]

[25] *ZZ*, 114.
[26] Chapter 2, note 3.
[27] See chapter 2, notes 163 and 164, for the use of these terms in Zeami's writings.
[28] From the *Kichū* translation in chapter 2.

However, the second component in the *kūrin* definition in the *Ki*, the expression *kyakurai*, has more specific implications for performance. Kyakurai is a Zen term that signifies the act of returning to the secular world upon attaining enlightenment and consequently realizing that Nirvana and samsara are one. It is used by Zeami in the *Kyūi* to describe the intentional indulgence in "base" roles by a master actor,[29] as outlined in the preceding discussion of the harin. In the *Kyakuraika*, however, Zeami alludes to another kyakurai style:

> The art of the Style of Return is a secret tradition of the highest, most wondrous style. It is said, "One desires to return, but this style of enlightened return cannot be attained in a hurry." As this is a secret style that can only be transmitted orally, I taught it only to Motomasa. He has died young, however, and as it now appears that in the future no one will even know the name of this style, I am recording it here. [A] most profound, most secret [matter].[30]

The next section of the treatise provides no further details or concrete examples.

Konishi Jin'ichi presents the following argument, by which the second meaning of Zeami's kyakurai can be deduced from Zenchiku's writings.[31] In his *Go'on sangyoku shū*, Zenchiku defines the five basic styles of composition and performance (*go'on*) originally devised by Zeami: congratulatory, yūgen, love, sorrow, and the sublime (*rangyoku*). He divides *rangyoku* into two categories. The first is the "demon-quelling style" (*rakki-tei*),[32] in this context equivalent to Zeami's *ran'i*. The second is the "style of the young voice" (*jakusei-tei*), defined as follows:

> The art of the sublime represents a stage attained after many years of success and the acquisition of fame; an actor of such rank is advanced in years. For him the voice of an old person is natural, and consequently there is no need to perform with it. To learn a young voice in old age—this is the sublime art of return (*kōko kyakurai no rangyoku*). There is an ancient poem that reads:
> (said to show the tottering walk of a child:)

Uguisu yo	O nightingale,
nado sa wa naku zo	why do you cry?
chi ya hoshiki	Do you want milk?
konabe ya hoshiki	Do you want food?
haha ya koishiki	Do you miss your mother?[33]

---

[29] ZZ, 176. For an excellent discussion of *kyakurai* as a Zen term, see Konishi Jin'ichi, *Nōgakuron kenkyū* (Tokyo: Hanawa shobō, 1961), 216.

[30] ZZ, 247.

[31] Konishi, *Nōgakuron kenkyū*, 231 ff.

[32] This is one of Fujiwara Teika's Ten Styles (*jittei*) of waka. See appendix, no. 13, for an example poem.

[33] KKSS, 169. This poem also appears in the *Saigyō Shōnin danshō*; there it is recorded,

The "tottering walk" refers to the choppy rhythm of the poem. This quality, combined with the naive viewpoint, produces a charming effect. The poem is also quoted in Zenchiku's *Kabu zuinō ki* to express the poetic essence of the play *Yoshino Saigyō* (not extant): "The appearance [of the shite] is that of an old man, but his heart is young. It is like the tottering walk of a child." (The poem follows.)[34] Zenchiku presents the play as an example of the *myōka fū* (the style of the wondrous flower), the highest of Zeami's Nine Ranks.

Konishi concludes that the "style of the young voice" is the *kyakurai fū* alluded to by Zeami. The accomplished, aged actor returns to the young, untutored style of the child actor, expressing a most profound beauty through the performance of naive, child-like dance and singing styles. On balance, Konishi's argument is persuasive. And without question this is the art that Zenchiku has assigned to his own kūrin: "This is the return to the original Circle of Longevity after attaining [great mastery of the art], truly the rank of [withdrawing after] accomplishment and fame; it is that which causes a single flower to remain on an old tree. As all things wither and die, they faintly seem young; a single song, a single dance return to the stage in which they first came to bud."[35]

ONE DEWDROP (*ICHIRO*)

In the early rokurin ichiro texts, the *ichiro* does not represent any particular aspect of performance; as Zenchiku notes in the *Kichū*, "It is the spirit that joins together the six circles." The symbolism of the ichiro will be examined in later chapters.

The topics treated above represent core meanings of the six circles, derived from the names of each. While these meanings are not necessarily the most important, they are clearly related to an early stage of the rokurin ichiro system—the stage at which these names were determined—and each has been linked to an aspect of performance. The teachings discussed might appear disordered to the reader not intimately familiar with Zeami's writings; however, they would be easily assimilated by Zenchiku's intended audience. In general, he displays a preference for themes that appear in Zeami's later treatises. I suspect this is due to the increasingly theoretical and transcendental aspects of these works, and to Zenchiku's personal contact with Zeami dating from this period.

"Written by Tsurayuki's daughter at age nine. Shunrai read this poem and wept." *Nihon kagaku taikei*, 2:296.

   [34] *KKSS*, 124; also in *Go'on sangyoku shū*, *KKSS*, 168.

   [35] For this passage, see chapter 2; for the flower image, see chapter 2, note 147.

In the remainder of this chapter I would like to address the significance of the six circles from a different perspective. It is relatively easy to interpret the practical "meaning" of each of the six circles; but considered as a group, a new set of problems emerges. Why has Zenchiku chosen to group together these aspects of Zeami over other teachings that are equally important? And what are the implications of the six-stage structure he has devised to present them?

To answer these questions, I will focus on a group of concepts within Zeami's writings that are discussed, and implicitly correlated, in the rokurin ichiro system. These will then be compared to Zenchiku's own representation of these concepts. My goal is not simply to compare the views of the two men on these topics. Rather, it is to unearth certain relational patterns that direct the flow of nōgakuron discourse. As will be seen, Zenchiku's categorizations are a powerful tool in such an undertaking.

THE CENTRIFUGAL AND THE CENTRIPETAL

For the purposes of this discussion, it will be useful to introduce two basic principles: the centrifugal and the centripetal.[36] The centrifugal tendency is movement from the center of a symbolic circle to its periphery; here, centrifugality is defined as a progression or evolution from an origin or essence. There is always a sense of the true essence as a source, followed by trace-manifestations, which are less pure or less fundamental. It is tempting to call this an emanationist model, but emanation is only one of many possible centrifugal paradigms. The contrasting model, the centripetal, describes movement toward the center: this may represent either a kind of "return" to an original or prior state, or the striving for a transcendental essence or peak experience. Again, there are many different types of centripetal models, and the distinctions are important. Here I shall simply note that the centripetal mode usually occurs within an epistemological, or experiential, context. That is, an individual is engaged in a process of knowing, the goal of which is to experience directly a "higher" or more central locus than conventional reality. In contrast, the centrifugal mode is customarily utilized in an ontological context, where a theory is put forth to describe various planes of being. Most commonly the discussion is on the nature of an Absolute and the process by which subsequent relative planes of being are generated or manifested.

These principles are relevant to the rokurin ichiro system for several reasons. First of all, the six circles represent not simply six static categories;

---

[36] The single mention of these terms in Itō, *Komparu Zenchiku no kenkyū*, 214, inspired the following discussion.

they are stages in a progression. This sequential structure is utilized to represent several different parallel processes. Furthermore, the concepts of centrifugality and centripetality indicate the directionality of the processes that will be examined, and so further help to categorize them. The flexibility of this terminology offers an advantage over more specific concepts such as emanation or noesis, enabling one to discern associated patterns and implicit relationships not immediately apparent from a more fixed perspective.

THE CENTRIFUGAL: THE PROCESS OF GENERATION

In the context of nōgakuron, the centrifugal most commonly appears as a process by which a particular performance technique or effect is generated. In a general sense, it represents a sequence in which the unmanifest becomes manifest. A prominent example of this is the principle of *itchō–niki–sansei*, or "first pitch–second breath–third voice," alluded to earlier in this chapter:

> Pitch is preserved by the breath. Listening to the pitch of the accompanying flute, the performer aligns himself with his breathing, closes his eyes, draws in his breath, and then issues sound. If he follows this pattern, his initial tone will be emerge at the proper pitch. However, if he only concentrates on pitch and attempts to sing without regulating the breath, he will not invariably be able to begin singing at the proper pitch. Since the pitch is first commingled with the breath and then sound is generated, the proper sequence is defined as "first pitch, second breath, third voice."[37]

This may appear to be a trivial example of centrifugality. It illustrates, however, a three-stage process of generation, a structure that is formally represented by Zenchiku's first three circles, as shall be seen. The unmanifest stage here is a mental state in which the performer gauges the musical pitch; in the second stage the breath is prepared, and finally the physical sound is generated. In this centrifugal sequence, the mental realm is treated as the source for the subsequent physical manifestation.

BUSHŌ IKON: SONG BECOMES DANCE

Of greater interest is the following theme of "song as the basis for dance (*bushō ikon*)," presented in Zeami's *Kakyō*. It treats the origins of the arts of song and dance in both historical and metaphysical terms:

> Dance cannot effectively project emotion unless it emerges from what has been sung. A wondrous power is generated at the point of transition, as the

[37] *ZZ,* 84.

fragrance from the final line of a vocal passage extends into the opening of the dance. Similarly, the point at which a dance concludes should blend in with the musical emotion [of what follows].

Indeed, it is said that song and dance originate from the *tathāgatagarbha*. First the breath emerges from the five organs; it then differentiates into the five colors and becomes the five tones and six modes.[38] . . . When the voice arises from the five organs, it moves into the five parts of the body and becomes the basis of dance.[39]

This passage is a prime example of centrifugality, wherein the component parts of music itself are said to have arisen from a transcendental source, the matrix of the tathāgatagarbha. The tathāgatagarbha is the womb or embryo of Buddha Nature that exists within each person.[40] It represents a pure, undefiled element that, if nurtured, will eventually develop into the enlightened mind. The five organs and five colors mentioned here are associated with the native Chinese theory of the five phases (C. *wu-hsing*, J. *gogyō*), a notion that originally has no connection whatever with the Buddhist tathāgatagarbha doctrine.[41] The character *zō* in the expression *nyoraizō* forms a weak verbal link to the five organs (*gozō*), which are representative of the five phases. Through this chain of symbolic and linguistic association—common modes of medieval argumentation— music (and subsequently dance, as the five parts of the body begin to move) is said to derive from the seed of the Absolute. Thus the *ordered* structure that is the basis of music and dance is a direct outgrowth of the Buddha Nature. And by ordering one's vocal sounds, an individual can partake of an order inherently more pure than conventional speech. This configuration is diagrammed in figure 3-1. The representation expresses both the *sequentiality* of the three stages and the *expansion* of the seed-like essence of tathāgatagarbha into fully mature sound.

The conclusion of this passage introduces another mode of generation, bestowal through divine intermediary:

The temporal modes (*toki no chōshi*) are divided into the four seasons, and also into the twelve times of day. The latter correspond to the [musical modes of] *sō*, *ō*, *ikkotsu*, *hyō*, and *ban*. Also, there is the theory that the temporal modes derive from a time when heavenly beings danced and sang, and the reverberation of their rhythms was transmitted to our [earthly] realm. Surely it is unlikely that the temporal divisions in Heaven are irregular, so both theories seem to be in

[38] See Rimer and Yamazaki, *On the Art of the Nō Drama*, 77–78n, for a discussion of these musical terms.

[39] *ZZ*, 86–87.

[40] The tathātagatagarbha doctrine is discussed in greater detail in chapter 4.

[41] This same association is found in the musical theory of *shōmyō*, the liturgical chant of Japanese Buddhism. See Konishi, *Nōgakuron kenkyū*, 251, and *ZZ*, 442–43.

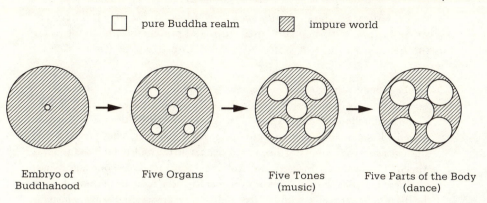

☐ pure Buddha realm   ▨ impure world

Embryo of
Buddhahood

Five Organs

Five Tones
(music)

Five Parts of the Body
(dance)

FIG. 3-1. Song Becomes Dance

accord. Along the same lines, it is said that the secret tradition in this country of
the dances of Suruga dates from the time when a celestial maiden descended
from Heaven and bestowed [upon the human realm] this form of music and
dance.[42]

In the cases noted here, musical modes are transmitted, as is, from the
divine to the human realm; it is this *shift* to a less numinous sphere that
constitutes a centrifugal progression. This contrasts with the *growth* of the
central, pure seed within the material sphere in the previous example. It is
also important to note that the very order of the seasons, and by extension
all temporal process on earth, is a gift from Heaven. This function of
divinity to establish order amid the chaos of the material world will reappear in the next section.

The themes discussed to this point illustrate the flexibility of the centrifugal paradigm. It can be applied to the microcosm of the process of vocalization, and the macrocosm of cosmic order. Furthermore, it can represent
both an atemporal metaphysical relationship between the absolute and
relative spheres and also a chronological sequence of historical genesis.
The modalities introduced here are evident in a complex synthesis in the
next example: Zeami's interpretation of the famous rock-cave myth from
the *Nihon shoki*.

THE GODDESS EMERGES: THE MYTHOLOGY
OF AUDIENCE RESPONSE

Undoubtedly the most widely known myth associated with the Japanese
performing arts is the story of the sun goddess Amaterasu's seclusion

[42] *ZZ*, 87.

behind the door of the heavenly rock-cave (*ama no iwa(ya)to*). There are several allusions to this episode in Zeami, and predictably, he identifies it as the historical origin of sarugaku. For example, in the *Fūshi kaden* he writes,

> The beginnings of sarugaku in the age of the gods, it is said, occurred when Amaterasu, the sun goddess, concealed herself in the heavenly rock cave, and the whole earth fell under endless darkness. All the myriad deities gathered at the heavenly Kagu mountain, in order to find a way to calm her. They played sacred music (*kagura*) to accompany their comic dances. In the midst of this the goddess Ama no Uzume came forward, and, holding a sprig of *sakaki* wood and a *shide*, she raised her voice and, in front of a fire that had been lighted, she pounded out the rhythm of her dance with her feet and became possessed by divine inspiration as she sang and danced. The sun goddess, hearing the voice of Ama no Uzume from within, opened the rock door slightly. The land became light, and the faces of the gods shone white. It is said that such entertainments marked the beginning of sarugaku.[43]

The rock-cave myth—originally, of course, inspired by the natural phenomenon of a solar eclipse—is utilized by Zeami on several levels. In the above passage, it serves to legitimize sarugaku as an art of ancient and divine origin. Appropriately, Zeami goes on to cite "origins of our art" in India, during the time of the historical Buddha. This dual focus on Japan and India reflects one of the major cultural themes of Zeami's age: the emergence of Buddhist-Shinto syncretism and the debate on the preeminence of either the Japanese gods or the buddhas of India.

As portrayed above, this incident can be seen as a parable of dramatic performance and audience response. The sun goddess functions as an audience: she hears the music performed by Ama no Uzume, and, intrigued, she opens the door. Then "the land became bright and the faces of the gods shone white." In this sense, the opening of the door is a metaphor for emotional response experienced by the goddess. Conversely, the assembled deities can be seen as representative of the performer's function. They sing and dance with great energy and ingenuity, hoping to coax the goddess from her seclusion, like a performer trying to arouse the interest of the audience. The sense of anticipation and excitement is heightened by an awareness of the goddess's luminous presence behind the closed cave door, beyond the limits of perception. When the performance succeeds, the effulgence of the goddess's response bathes the scene in a wondrous rush of blinding light. The assembly's initial surprise and amazement gives way to rejoicing, as the world is restored to its normal condition.

Such a reading is certainly plausible, in accord with the widely pro-

---

[43] *ZZ*, 38; translation modified from Rimer and Yamazaki, *On the Art of the Nō Drama* 31.

moted view that the music and dance performed by the assembled deities was the origin of kagura. In particular, it supports the divinity of aesthetic response in a fashion reminiscent of the anecdote concerning the Deity of Kasuga alluded to in the Shigyoku commentary.[44] However, Zeami's extended discussion of this incident in the later *Shūgyoku tokka* takes a different position. Rather than analyzing the individual roles of the sun goddess and the performers, he considers the phenomenon as it might be experienced by an observer at the scene. The audience here is, if anyone, the onlooking deities, assembled outside the cave, who respond to the phenomenon of the goddess's emergence. The incident is used to introduce a set of three principles—*myō*, *hana*, and *omoshiro*. The key passage reads as follows:

Question: How did the expression *omoshiro* come into being? The term *hana* is a metaphor; but what of the exclamation "Fascinating!", uttered without realizing it? This is not a metaphor—what is its origin?

Answer: This is a matter that should be investigated after the phenomenon of hana has been fully understood. The three elements mentioned earlier—*omoshiroki*, *hana*, and *mezurashiki*[45]—are all different names for one entity. It goes under the names of the Wondrous, the Flower, or Fascination,[46] but these are actually one phenomenon that has three aspects: high, middle, and low. Myō is the extinction of the workings of the mind that cuts off the use of words. To actually experience this state of myō is hana; when it is grasped as an object of awareness,[47] it is omoshiro.

The expression *omoshiroki* dates from the time when the (sun) goddess opened the door of the rock-cave, responding with delight to the playful performance of kagura at the heavenly Mount Kagu. The faces of the assembled deities all became brightly visible; thus the expression omoshiro (face-

---

[44] See chapter 2, note 46.

[45] Here only, Zeami substitutes *mezurashiki* for *myō*.

[46] I have utilized Rimer and Yamazaki's translation for *omoshiro*, "Fascination."

[47] The expression used here, *itten tsuketaru toki* (the moment when one point is added), is difficult. Konishi interprets it as a metaphor borrowed from ink painting: a single stroke drawn on a blank sheet thus represents the initial appearance of form. See Konishi, *Nōgakuron*, 228 and 299, n. 191. The most comprehensive discussion is found in Kuroda Masao, *Zeami nōgakuron no kenkyū* (Tokyo: Ōbaisha, 1979), 502–18.

Some scholars have posited a possible influence of the Five Ranks (*goi*) of Sōtō Zen upon the three categories of *myō*, *hana*, and *omoshiro*. The stage of *myō* corresponds to "[enlightenment] achieved between [universality and particularity] combined (*kenchūtō*)," represented by a black circle; *hana* corresponds to "[enlightenment] arriving from [universality and particularity] combined (*kenchūshi*)," represented by a blank (or white) circle; and *omoshiro* corresponds to "[enlightenment] emerging from universality (*shōchūrai*)," symbolized by a black dot within a white circle. Zeami's association with the Sōtō Sect in his later years lends some credence to this theory. See Kōsai Tsutomu, *Zeami shinkō* (Tokyo: Wan'ya shoten, 1962), 24–26, and *ZZ*, 477, n. 102.

white) came into being.[48] The instant the door opened should not be termed omoshiro; rather, omoshiro is the name for the moment when a conscious awareness of the event was established. What indeed can one call the moment before this objectivity arises?

Considered from the standpoint of our art, the mental instant when a performance is perceived as "fascinating" is the sensation of no-mind. . . . When the goddess shut the rock-door, the entire world and its lands were plunged into constant darkness; was the feeling not simply one of joy at the instant when, without warning, [the world] became bright? This is the moment when a subtle smile crosses the face without thinking.[49] The state when the rock-door is closed and everything is blackness, when all speech has been cut off, is myō; hana is the stage at which this turns to brightness; and omoshiro is the stage of objective awareness.[50]

Myō, hana, and omoshiro are most easily understood as terms that describe the psychology of audience response. Myō is a state of mystery and speechless expectation:[51] the audience is stunned by the sudden darkness, as their conventional perception and mental functioning are suspended. At the same time, they sense the numinous presence of the goddess just beyond their perceptual field. The subsequent stage of hana is the feeling of surprise and wonder experienced at the instant when the rock-cave has opened and the direct presence of the sun goddess is first encountered. It is a spontaneous response, which occurs before the conscious mind realizes what has happened. Omoshiro is the final stage, when the mind understands that "the door has opened" and is able to associate this fact with the sublime emotion just experienced at the stage of hana. In this

[48] This explication of the expression *omoshiroshi* appears in other works, including the ninth-century Shinto history recorded by Imbe no Hironari, *Kogo shūi*. (*Gunsho ruijū*, 25:3–4; trans. in Genchi Katō and Hikoshirō Hoshino, *Kogoshūi: Gleanings from Ancient Stories* [London: Curzon Press, 1972], 26). Surprisingly, this eytomology is supported by some modern scholars. In the *Iwanami kogo jiten*, Ōno Susumu et al. state that omoshiroshi originally denotes a state in which "the eyes open wide upon seeing a bright object"; this meaning extends to the delight experienced at music and dance performances. The *Kokugo daijiten* lists this and several other possible etymologies.

[49] This is a reference to the famous "wordless transmission" from Śākyamuni to Kāśyapa. During the course of a sermon on Vulture Peak, Śākyamuni held up a flower; no one understood his meaning except Kāśyapa, who smiled. The Buddha then announced that the True Dharma Eye had been transmitted.

[50] *ZZ*, 188.

[51] In two other works, Zeami alludes to a passage from an unidentifiable source, which he calls the "Tendai myōshaku": "[Myō is the place where] the way of words is cut off, and the activities of the mind are extinguished." See *Yūgaku shūdō fūken* (*ZZ*, 166) and *Goi* (*ZZ*, 170). The phrase "Tendai myōshaku" may refer to "interpretations of the term myō within the Tendai tradition," rather than representing the title of a work.

progression, the spontaneous subjective delight gives way to fascination.

This psychological interpretation does not, however, exhaust the meanings of the three categories. In the original myth as recounted in the *Nihon shoki*, the sun goddess is portrayed as an individual subject to human-like emotions; she is first upset, then curious as her fellow *kami* entice her from seclusion. But in Zeami's age, the sun goddess has become a more august deity; the Ise Shrine has assumed national importance, and the Dual Shinto movement has elevated the sun goddess to a transcendental position, explicitly the equivalent of the cosmic Sun Buddha, Mahāvairocana.[52] As a result, it becomes increasingly difficult to portray her emergence from the cave as the result of mere curiosity. She is no longer the audience, but rather a transcendental presence that manifests when the performance is of the highest possible quality. In this sense, the aesthetic experience is implicitly elevated to the level of the transcendental. The arousal of deep aesthetic response is equivalent to a revelation of the ontological source of being, represented by the sun goddess. Zeami reinforces this sense of the transcendental with his reference to the wordless transmission of Mind from Śākyamuni to Kāśyapa celebrated in Zen circles, neatly linked by the association of hana with the flower raised by the Buddha.[53]

As a symbol of the Absolute, the sun goddess is the source of these psychological effects. Hidden, she provides the anticipation; furthermore, it is this very hidden quality that creates the potentiality for hana to appear. Through the cave metaphor, myō becomes a state of commingled yin and yang, a stage of gestation that highlights the pristine nature of the hana response to follow. And finally, at the stage of omoshiro, the illuminating function of the goddess provides the ability to discern the delight, to see bright faces absorbed in fascination.

One caveat is in order, however. In a Buddhist context, myō is teleological, a final step in the path to enlightenment. In the same sense, these three categories delineate *one* phenomenon of "no-mind," which has three components: suspension of cognition, profound emotion, and awareness of what has happened. Strictly speaking, there is no gap, no sense of anticipation; the opening of the cave *symbolizes* the emotional response to its closing, as darkness and brilliance are experienced simultaneously. For Zeami, this state can occur suddenly during an exceptional performance.

The centrifugal nature of myō, hana, and omoshiro should be evident. The three are not separate effects, but successive stages in a single moment of aesthetic experience. These may be represented as in figure 3-2.

---

[52] This is one of many pairings of Buddhist and native Shintō deities found in medieval Buddhist-Shinto amalgamation; Amaterasu is also sometimes paired with the Eleven-Headed Kannon.

[53] See note 49.

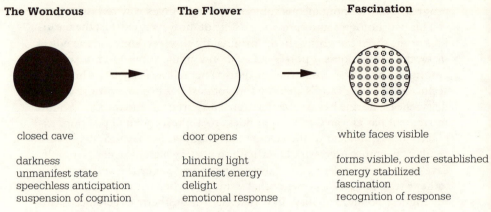

The Wondrous   **The Flower**   **Fascination**

closed cave   door opens   white faces visible

darkness   blinding light   forms visible, order established
unmanifest state   manifest energy   energy stabilized
speechless anticipation   delight   fascination
suspension of cognition   emotional response   recognition of response

FIG. 3-2. The Wondrous–The Flower–Fascination

THE RHYTHM OF CONSCIOUSNESS: *JO–HA–KYŪ*

This psychological orientation underlies one of Zeami's best known aesthetic principles—*jo–ha–kyū*. Originally terms used in *gagaku, jo, ha,* and *kyū* are most widely understood as principles of tempo, applied to a program of plays, sections of a play, and even individual lines of vocalization. Jo represents a slow, stately opening; ha the development or quickening of pace; and kyū the climax, the resolution that is always performed at a rapid tempo. This principle is considered important because it produces in the audience a sense of "fulfillment" (*jōju*): "When a day's program of sarugaku is successfully completed and one receives uniform praise from the spectators, this is due to the fulfillment of the jo–ha–kyū of the day. This is an auspicious completion. Similarly, there is fulfillment whereby the audience responds deeply in unison before one's eyes."[54] Certainly, in this sense the jo–ha–kyū structure is not unique to Japanese music or drama. Similar patterns can be observed in the arts of most cultures. In particular, this sense of emotional fulfillment, generated by some type of resolution, is a common phenomenon.

Zeami, however, views jo–ha–kyū as more than simply a structural guideline for the tempo of a performance or composition. In the *Shūgyoku tokka,* he discusses *jo–ha–kyū* as a structural feature of audience perception, using one of the terms just discussed, omoshiroki: "Fascination (omoshiroki) occurs through a process of jo–ha–kyū within the viewing experience of the audience; the style of the action is the jo–ha–kyū of the performer. There is jo–ha–kyū even within a single sound that causes the audience to gasp in admiration."[55] Here one sees that the very process of

[54] ZZ, 191.
[55] Ibid.

experiencing "fascination" (omoshiro) contains a jo–ha–kyū–like progression and thus has its own sense of fulfillment. Since both this passage and the previous rock-cave passage appear in the *Shūgyoku tokka*, it is not unreasonable to describe the relationship among myō, hana, and omoshiro as analogous to a jo–ha–kyū progression.

Given this, the statement that a single note (and a single gesture in dance) has its own jo–ha–kyū has two implications. First, the forms of the natural world tend to follow this rhythm, and so a successful performance should mimic them. This is jo–ha–kyū as external, objective structure, as represented in Zeami's famous pronouncement that "All forms of creation— good and bad, large and small, sentient and insentient—each and every one possesses its own jo–ha–kyū. Even within the chirping of birds, the cries of insects, each call has its own allotted pattern, which is jo–ha– kyū."[56] More profound, however, is the implication that the final completion takes place not as an external climax, but as a psychological event within the minds of the audience. In a general sense, the internal process of spontaneous attraction (or repulsion) and subsequent recognition of the object which generated that emotional response enables one to organize amorphous sensory data and perceive it mentally as a discrete event.[57] In aesthetic experience there is a close counterpart: the psychological process of anticipation–delight–fascination that defines a discrete object of consciousness as a distinct, and successful, *waza*. That is, the very delight and subsequent recognition of a single note experienced by the audience is what gives it structure. And the deliberate imitation of this internal structure through the external rhythm of jo–ha–kyū—slow opening, increasing tempo, climax—is successful precisely because it mimics the rhythms of consciousness.

Thus, jo–ha–kyū is centrifugal in two respects: it represents both the natural progression of birth, development, and rapid extinction exhibited by natural forms, and also the psychological process by which cognition arises. This second aspect is closely related to the myō–hana–omoshiro sequence previously discussed. In general, *rakkyo* can be seen as this objective process of formation, while *jōju* is the subjective fulfillment experienced by the audience, their sense of delight.

Another relevant perspective is that of yin–yang theory, so often utilized by Zeami in his writings. The conventional view is simply that yang and yin represent complementary principles such as light and darkness, male and female, active and passive, and so on. In his writings on Chinese medicine, however, Manfred Porkert gives more comprehensive and in-

---

[56] Ibid.

[57] This psychological mechanism is reminiscent of the Buddhist doctrine of the five skandhas: form (*shiki*), sensation (*ju*), conception (*sō*), volition (*gyō*), and consciousness (*shiki*). In particular, hana and omoshiro closely resemble the second and third stages.

sightful definitions of yin and yang as alternating poles of natural process. He defines yang as the stage of initiating action, the active component that is determining in function but of itself undetermined; yin is its "constructive" counterpart, comprising "more definite or permanent states, including completion, confirmation, repose, stasis, consolidation, concentration, concreteness, and solidity (as well as contraction and extinction), and in general the state of being determinate or determined (as opposed to both [the] determinant and undetermined [character of yang])."[58] Thus Zeami's "completion" (rakkyo) can be seen as the stage of yin, following the activation of yang: in the previous rock-cave analogy, the yang force of blinding light stabilizes, as the faces of the assembled deities are fully delineated and visible. In this sense as well, the principle of jo–ha–kyū within noh echoes both the natural world and our perception of it. Of course, from a traditional Buddhist perspective, these two realms are not only complementary but identical.

The themes from Zeami's writings discussed here share this quality of centrifugality. But what is the significance of these diverse themes for Zenchiku? To answer this, one must look at the centrifugal sequence as it appears in the rokurin ichiro system: the grouping of the first three circles.

JŌSANRIN: THREE CIRCLES OF YŪGEN

The first three circles of the rokurin ichiro system—the Circle of Longevity, the Circle of Height, and the Circle of Abiding—are often treated as a group by Zenchiku; he refers to them as the jōsanrin. For example, in the Kichū they are described as "the highest ranks, the dark essence of subtle feeling." The language here (yūjō no gentei)[59] strongly suggests that this essence is none other than yūgen. The statement in the Hichū (Kanshō bon), "He who does not know these three circles does not enter the realm of yūgen,"[60] confirms this view.

But what is the nature of this conception of yūgen? And how is it represented by the first three circles? To state it succinctly, yūgen for Zenchiku is not a particular style of performance, the graceful beauty most frequently denoted by the term in Zeami's writings, it is a *mental* attitude cultivated by the performer.[61] In another passage from the Hichū (Bunshō bon) Zenchiku remarks, "In short, among the highest levels, the three

[58] Manfred Porkert, *Chinese Medicine* (New York: William Morrow, 1988), 69.

[59] ZZ, 337.

[60] ZZ, 386.

[61] For more on the differing views of yūgen held by Zeami and Zenchiku, see Arthur H. Thornhill, "*Yūgen* after Zeami," forthcoming.

circles are actions of the mind (*kokoro no waza*), the rest are the behavior of the body (*mi no furumai*)."[62] And so, while these three circles symbolize certain performance techniques, as discussed in the first part of this chapter, in a general sense they represent psychological states that must be cultivated by the performer. When achieved, these are the essential components of yūgen.

The clearest explication of these mental attitudes is found near the end of the *Kichū*. In addition to the circularity of breath and dance discussed earlier, the Circle of Longevity represents "the appearance of characters upon entering the stage, the round form where mind and matter are in harmony."[63] In the *Hichū* (*Bunshō bon*) Zenchiku explains that the actor should begin by concentrating upon embodying the appearance (*sugata*) of the role, "becoming the thing itself," rather than focusing on specific movements to be performed. As a result, his mind will assume the inner form of the role, and conversely his mental state will manifest forcefully on stage, thus producing the "yūgen of the nonduality of mind and matter."[64]

In contrast to the visual effect of the Circle of Longevity, the Circle of Height represents an aural phenomenon, as "cold, clear singing" arises from the tranquil, focused background. This is compared to the distant whiteness of clouds in the sky, and the appearance of the cold, clear moon. For the performer, the requisite attitude is the focusing of vocal energy and emotion into this initial onset of form; at this moment the audience experiences the "feeling of superlative yūgen," which arises within the "vessel" of the Circle of Longevity. The emphasis on the arising of emotional response within a type of enclosure—the vessel— betrays the unmistakable influence of Zeami's categories of myō and hana. Indeed, Itō Masayoshi identifies the myō–hana–omoshiro terminology—which appears in the *Shūgyoku tokka*, a work written expressly for Zenchiku—as the strongest influence upon the *content* of the first three circles.[65]

The last of this group of three circles, the Circle of Abiding, is a stage of mental ease, as defined earlier. The *Kichū* elaborates that this is the locus where "song and dance—each piece, each syllable, each movement— are not in disarray. They come to completion in this position, the wondrous place of settling down." This clearly echoes Zeami's concept of *rakkyo*. Thus this circle represents the performer's ability to differentiate clearly and individual notes and movements, and also larger structural components.

In later works, Zenchiku makes the contrasting visual, aural, and men-

[62] *KKSS*, 250.
[63] *KKSS*, 220.
[64] *KKSS*, 250–51.
[65] See Itō, *Komparu Zenchiku no kenkyū*, 112 ff.

tal qualities of the first three circles explicit by assigning to them a tripartite yūgen of body, speech, and mind.[66] The underlying Buddhist typology of body, speech, and mind karma is suggested by the three circles, which spin like the wheel of samsara; yet, when the performer is detached and pure in mind, the circles become "pure" (shōjō)[67] and his performance naturally radiates the fragrance of yūgen. Still later, this conception is aligned with the Three Mysteries (sanmitsu: mudra, mantra, and meditation) of esoteric Buddhism.[68] The ritual practice of the Three Mysteries is considered the direct expression of the Buddha's body, speech, and mind, and so it is a fitting model for a performer who aims for a transcendental effect in his art.

The term "vessel" (ki), often used by Zenchiku in connection with the Circle of Longevity, merits further comment. Zeami borrowed the expression "vessel" from the Analects, where it indicates the function of man as a vessel of the Confucian teachings.[69] He writes in his Yūgaku shūdōfū ken:

> Now, to consider the significance of "vessel" in our art—first of all, the few accomplished actors who use the Two Skills (song and dance) and the Three Roles (old man, woman, and warrior) as the basis for performance of all pieces exhibit the function of the vessel. This is the power to acquire mastery in one body of many styles, spanning a wide range of appearances in various basic forms. The visual and aural [beauty] of the two skills and the three roles extends its emotion to all [styles], resulting in nonincreasing, nondiminishing effect and merit—this is the vessel function.
>
> In terms of being and nonbeing, being is appearance, nonbeing its vessel. That in which being manifests is nonbeing. For example, water crystal is a pure substance, an empty form with no color or feature, yet heat and water are both produced from it. Under what conditions can such diverse things as fire and water be produced from a formless, empty substance? A certain poem reads

Sakuragi wa	If you smash a cherry tree
kudakite mireba	to look inside,
hana mo nashi	there are no blossoms.
hana koso haru no	Flowers only bloom
sora ni sakikere	in the spring sky.

It is the emotive power of the performer's entire being, the root of his heart, that produces the seeds that flower in the form of entertainments. Truly, just as the

[66] For example, in the Hichū (Kanshō bon). KKSS, 236.
[67] The "purity of the three circles" is discussed in chapter 6.
[68] See Shidō yōshō, KKSS, 274.
[69] As indicated by the comment attributed to K'ung An-kuo (c. 130–90 B.C.) in Zeami's text, ZZ, 166.

empty substance of water crystal produces water and fire and the colorless nature of the cherry tree bears flowers and fruit, the accomplished performer who exhibits the subtle shadings of different pieces through his expressive style, drawing from the inner resources of his heart, is indeed a vessel.[70]

Thus "vessel" represents the fundamental Two Skills and Three Roles, and also a ground of nonbeing, a kind of mental and/or metaphysical emptiness that must be cultivated. Once the performer has developed this tranquil, empty state, expressed emotion arises clearly and forcefully from it, like the flowers of the cherry tree blooming in the spring sky. In terms of an actor's career, this vessel is a deep inner tranquility that develops as his mastery of the art matures; it is apparent in the kind of commanding intensity that results from his simply standing immobile on the stage, a specific effect represented by the Circle of Longevity. In turn, this vessel functions as the matrix within which the deep emotional response of the audience—symbolized by the Circle of Height—takes shape.

To describe the transition from the Circle of Longevity to the Circle of Height, Zenchiku frequently uses the terminology of pattern (*mon* or *aya*): "The tones *kyū* and *shō* rise and fall, and the voice forms patterns. This is called music." The monotone neutrality of the first circle transforms into differentiated, relational form and sequential pattern, and the performance is under way.

The parallels to the centrifugal themes of Zeami discussed above should be apparent. They correlate as follows:

CIRCLE OF LONGEVITY	CIRCLE OF HEIGHT	CIRCLE OF ABIDING
first, pitch	second, breath	third, voice
jo	ha	kyū
The Wondrous	The Flower	Fascination
(before yin and yang)	yang	yin
body	speech	mind
vessel	spirit arising	
uniform ground	differentiated pattern	

THE CENTRIPETAL

As noted earlier, the centripetal describes movement toward a center; this often takes the form of "return" to an original or prior state, or the striving

[70] *ZZ*, 166–67. The poem is probably derived from the Zen tradition; see *ZZ* 472–73, n. 94.

for a transcendental essence. It is my contention that the progression of the second group of three circles in Zenchiku's system—the Circle of Forms, the Circle of Breaking, and the Circle of Emptiness—represents a centripetal process.

This aspect of the second group of three circles is best understood from the perspective of *gei'i*, or absolute ranks of artistic achievement. As discussed in the previous section, these three circles—Forms, Breaking, and Emptiness—symbolize Zeami's categories of the Three Roles, the Rank of the Sublime, and the Flower of Return. Briefly, these represent a progression from the basic styles learned by a beginning student on through to the most difficult and highest achievements of the master actor at the end of his career. The centripetal aspect of this process is symbolized by the final goal of the Circle of Emptiness, which in turn is identical to the first Circle of Longevity. In this sense, arrival at the sixth circle represents a return to the first circle, the original "center" of the centrifugal paradigm.

To grasp fully the nature of the process represented by these final three circles, the pedagogical dimension of Zeami's writings must be investigated.

SHŪDŌ: LEARNING THE WAY

A primary focus in Zeami's earliest treatises is the training of the actor (*shūdō*). He discusses in great detail the appropriate path of study, and the psychology of the learning process. For example, in the *Fūshi kaden*, training is presented that is appropriate for an actor at age seven, at twelve, and so on through ages twenty-five, thirty-five, forty-five, and over fifty. At each stage, different skills should be learned. First the basic skills of song and dance are mastered; at a later age, the essentials of role-playing (*monomane*) are studied. It is important to note that the prescribed sequence does not simply represent a progression from basic to more difficult or advanced techniques. Equally important is the suitability of learning a given skill at the appropriate age. For example, certain vocal and dance techniques cannot be mastered until the young boy has reached physical maturity. Zeami is also very aware of the charm of the untutored movements of a child actor: "Since a [boy of twelve] still has the appearance of a child, whatever he does has a graceful effect (yūgen). It is also an age when his voice is appealing."[71] Nevertheless, this particular variety of charm will vanish as he gets older: "However, this flower (hana) is not the true flower; it is only temporary. During this period of training, everything has a sense of ease, but this does not mean that this will be the case throughout his

71 ZZ, 15.

career. At this age, the boy should sense the flower through his ease, while also paying close attention to technique."[72] In other words, because a boy of twelve is able to please the audience without extraordinary effort, he should use the opportunity to develop basic skills that reinforce the successful effect. This taste of having produced a charming effect, and the requisite skill, will not vanish after the natural beauty of this youthful stage has disappeared.

Here we see an essential feature of Zeami's writings. The ultimate criterion for the success of an actor's art is the appearance of hana, that affecting quality that pleases the audience. Hana will appear at different times in a performer's career for various reasons; it is his responsibility constantly to grow and adapt in order to take advantage of this process. His career as an artist can be charted by the appearance of various forms of hana at different stages. To generate the appropriate effects at each stage, a strict training regimen should be followed. The highest achievement of the performer is not simply to acquire the ability to generate the most profound effect; it is the ability to adapt to his circumstances and produce the *appropriate* effect.

The experience of shūdō, then, is a centripetal process. The performer aspires to develop ever higher levels of ability, adapting skillfully to the natural course of the aging process. Thus, while one might expect certain physical skills to deteriorate with age—dancing ability, for example—the master performer can adjust his technique to reach ever higher levels of accomplishment. The preferred sequence of development is most succinctly stated in the *Kyūi*. This famous work presents a system of nine levels of the performing art. Zeami divides these into three groups as follows:[73]

UPPER RANKS

1. The Wondrous Flower (*myōka fū*)
2. The Flower of Profundity (*chōshinka fū*)
3. The Flower of Tranquility (*kanka fū*)

MIDDLE RANKS

4. The True Flower (*shōka fū*)
5. Versatility and Precision (*kōshō fū*)
6. Early Beauty (*senmon fū*)

LOWER RANKS

7. Strength and Delicacy (*gōsai fū*)
8. Strength and Coarseness (*gōso fū*)
9. Coarseness and Dullness (*soen fū*)

[72] *ZZ*, 16.
[73] *ZZ*, 174–75.

It must be emphasized, however, that Zeami's initial ranking of these levels does not represent the proper pedagogical order. A student does not begin at the bottom and work his way to the top. According to the text, it is best to begin by studying the middle three levels, then the upper three. Thus the proper course is to progress from number 6 through to number 1, finally attaining the Wondrous Flower, "that level beyond words, where the actor's inward design and outward appearance are wondrously indivisible."[74] Clearly, the learning of these six levels is a centripetal process that results in a transcendent effect on stage when the highest level is attained.

But the master actor need not stop here. In the *Kyūi*, Zeami notes that he may proceed to indulge in the three lower styles simply "to amuse himself." He brings a special ability to the performance of these base roles that transforms them into highly expressive vehicles. Nevertheless, in this text, such performances are not touted as further evolution of his art. Zeami's point is that one who begins his study with the coarse movements of the three lowest styles will not develop properly.

In other works, however, unorthodox styles are accorded much greater importance. Most notable is the *ran'i*, or "rank of the sublime," described earlier in this chapter. A related concept, *rangyoku*, is discussed in Zeami's *Go'ongyoku jōjō*. As mentioned earlier, it is the last of five varieties of vocal style or composition: congratulatory, yūgen, love, sorrow, and "the sublime" (*rangyoku*). *Rangyoku* is represented by the following poem:

Itsu shika to	Before we know it,
kamu sabinikeru	the cryptomeria has grown,
Kaguyama no	straight as a spear,
musugi ga moto ni	to divine stature on Mount Kagu—
koke no musu made ni	a layer of moss lies at its root.[75]

In this fivefold scheme, then, the introduction of unorthodox technique is the art that develops last and is arguably the highest. The character *ran* is also read *taketaru* and thus indicates maturity and great stature. The grandeur of the towering *sugi* within the sacred compound is more impressive than the beauties of the cherry or red maple.[76] It is not its external beauty that impresses, but rather its stature. In this way, the very presence and command of the mature actor dominates; rather than concentrating on the conventional techniques he has mastered, he uses his stature to expand his

<hr />

[74] *ZZ*, 176.

[75] The text is from Zeami's *Go'ongyoku jōjō*, *ZZ*, 200; the poem is a variant of *Man'yōshū* 259.

[76] In the Zeami text, the yūgen style is equated with the *sakura*, and the love style with the *momiji*.

sphere of influence, to transform the superficially uninteresting or coarse into the profoundly affecting. In his later writings Zeami introduces an even more advanced stage, the *kyakuraika* or Flower of Return, which was detailed earlier. The word kyakurai is used in the *Kyūi* to describe a casual descent into the lower levels. However, the kyakurai style—that is, the "style of the young voice," represented by Zenchiku's Circle of Emptiness—is an even more advanced stage than the ran'i. It is not even alluded to in the *Kyūi* text.

In sum, the learning process begins from the fourth level of the nine; it then progresses through increasingly difficult stages to the Wondrous Flower, the highest style of performance. From there, the master actor may progress to ran'i, the rank of sublimity, where superficially crude elements are incorporated to heighten the effect. Finally, the Flower of Return may be performed in old age. While this is externally less spectacular than the three upper ranks, it is a uniquely affecting style that can only be performed by a master at the conclusion of his career.

This learning process is centripetal. The actor develops ever higher levels of accomplishment, as his art moves from conventional charm and physical beauty to a realm in which subtle effects transcend external appearance. This is symbolically equivalent to a return to the formless Absolute, a quintessential feature of the centripetal. In contrast, the original order of the nine ranks, which represents their absolute ontological value in descending order, is centrifugal. These two aspects of the nine ranks, with Zenchiku's final stage added, can be represented as follows:

CENTRIFUGAL (ONTOLOGICAL)	CENTRIPETAL (EPISTEMOLOGICAL)
1. Wondrous Flower	6. Early Beauty
2. Flower of Profundity	5. Versatility and Precision
3. Flower of Tranquility	4. True Flower
4. True Flower	3. Flower of Tranquility
5. Versatility and Precision	2. Flower of Profundity
6. Early Beauty	1. Wondrous Flower
7. Strength and Delicacy	Rank of the Sublime (Descent to 7–9)
8. Strength and Coarseness	Flower of Return
9. Coarseness and Dullness	

The alert reader might question the lack of symmetry here. How can ranks 7–9 represent a higher, more "central" position than the Wondrous Flower within the centripetal model? This can be explained by figure 3-3. Once the stage of the Wondrous Flower is attained, the performer enters a new realm of nine levels. Here, the relationship between external form and

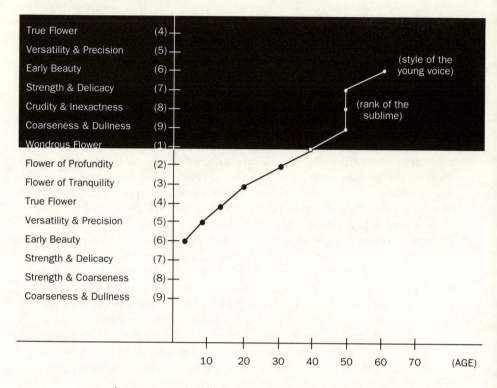

		(style of the young voice)
True Flower	(4)	
Versatility & Precision	(5)	
Early Beauty	(6)	
Strength & Delicacy	(7)	
Crudity & Inexactness	(8)	(rank of the sublime)
Coarseness & Dullness	(9)	
Wondrous Flower	(1)	
Flower of Profundity	(2)	
Flower of Tranquility	(3)	
True Flower	(4)	
Versatility & Precision	(5)	
Early Beauty	(6)	
Strength & Delicacy	(7)	
Strength & Coarseness	(8)	
Coarseness & Dullness	(9)	

10 20 30 40 50 60 70 (AGE)

NOTE: the ages represented here are only approximations, based on material from the *Kyūi and Fūshi kaden* texts

FIG. 3-3. Zeami's Nine Ranks

inner spirituality is reversed, and so even the first rank in this second "octave" is higher than the ninth rank of the first. The actor moves through the lowest ranks (7, 8, 9), which represent the *ran'i*, and finally attains the Flower of Return. Here, the external style is the same as that which he performed as a child (level 6),[77] but his consummate mastery and advanced age transform the performance into one of surpassing beauty. Zenchiku's final two circles accurately portray these final stages of achievement with a clarity lacking in Zeami's original nine-rank system.

[77] There is no firm proof that the "style of the young voice" is equivalent to level 6; however, this is where the young boy begins his training, and his childish voice and movement are what lend charm to his performance.

ESSENTIAL FLOWER AND FUNCTIONAL FLOWER

There is one more aspect of Zeami's Nine Ranks relevant to this discussion: the distinction between Essential Flower (*shōka*) and Functional Flower (*yōka*).[78] This topic appears in the *Shūgyoku tokka*:

> I have devised my own categories [to distinguish the suitability of a style to an audience], the Essential Flower and the Functional Flower. The Essential Flower represents the three highest flower [ranks]; it is the cherry blossom. This level is suited to the sensibility of upper class audiences. The highest of the middle three ranks is named the True Flower, and it too is the cherry, but the flower of this rank is not limited to the cherry blossom. It encompasses many varieties: the cherry, the plum, the peach, the pear, and so on. The sight of red and white plum blossoms creates a particularly elegant effect. Michizane himself enjoyed this sight.[79]
>
> In our art, the principal aim is to generate a moving effect that all types of audiences can appreciate. Within this context, the experience of "fascination" explained previously is the proof of a sophisticated audience. However, there are differences in the manner of appreciation. For example, the charming effect of a young boy's performance is like the first bloom of a single-layered cherry—its fresh appearance is the Functional Flower. Those who respond with delight only to this [kind of art] exhibit the level of appreciation of the middle and lower classes. The refined viewer also finds such a performance charming and enjoys it accordingly, but he does not consider it the true Essential Flower. An ancient or famous tree, the blossoms at Yoshino, Shiga, Kiyomizu, or Arashiyama— these correspond to [the art of] performers of established reputation in our profession.[80]

Here, the beauty represented by the three highest ranks is compared to the cherry blossom; this supreme beauty may also appear in performances of the lower ranks, but the knowledgeable viewer can distinguish between the essence of this highest flower in its true form (shōka) and its temporary appearance in a lesser context (yōka). It is important here to remember that

[78] The categories of *shō* and *yō* (or *yū*) closely resemble the *t'i/yung* (substance/function) pairing widely used in Chinese Buddhism and Neo-Confucianism. In a Buddhist context, *shō* (C. *hsing*) is often an approximate equivalent for *t'i*, although it usually appears by itself, as in the expression *Busshō*, "Buddha Nature." "Nature Flower" is a more literal rendition of *shōka*, but such an English expression is easily misinterpreted. "Essence" is a common English equivalent for *t'i* in Buddhist contexts.

[79] Sugawara Michizane (845–903), the famous scholar and calligrapher whose spirit is worshipped at Kitano Shrine, renowned for its plum blossoms. In the text, Michizane is referred to simply as Tenjin. The expression *yōkan*, taken here as "enjoyment" or "appreciation," may also mean "celebrated [in his poetry]."

[80] *ZZ*, 187.

Zeami's ranks are properly described as *ifū* (rank-styles). That is, each stage represents both an evaluation of an actor's ability (his rank) and a style of performance associated with that rank. Since the distinction between shōka and yōka differentiates performances, and not necessarily performers, it is clear that here Zeami is describing a formal relationship among specific styles represented by the Nine Ranks. This formal relationship is independent of the proper learning sequence.

Thus one finds at least three different functional relations among the nine levels: the simple ranking according to absolute value, from highest to lowest (1, 2, 3 . . . 9); the representation of the proper learning sequence (6, 5, 4, top 3, lower 3); and finally, the categories of shōka and yōka (first 3 as shōka, the fourth as yōka).

The shōka/yōka categorization is important for our purposes because it is the closet counterpart to the distinction between the two groups of three circles in the rokurin ichiro system. Zenchiku uses this terminology at the conclusion of his *Nika ichirin*:

> The innermost repository of this Way is not simply the longevity of one lifetime.[81] The Essential Flower that in height spans the three ages[82] and in breadth extends in the ten directions [is] the first three circles. The Functional Flower [is] the two circles of Forms and Breaking. The two ranks of Emptiness and One Dewdrop are the spirit of the sun and moon, the enlightened ranks of the perfection of Buddhahood.[83]

This scheme utilizes Zeami's *shō/yō* (or *yū*) distinction to illustrate the difference between the first three circles, which represent the mental foundation of yūgen as discussed above, and the actual performance styles of the fourth and fifth circles. The categories of Essential Flower and Functional Flower are presented as ontological terms to express this distinction. Zenchiku then groups the final Circle of Emptiness with the One Dewdrop, choosing to emphasize its transcendental, rather than manifest, aspect.[84]

Zenchiku diverges from Zeami's conception of shōka and yōka in one important respect. Despite the philosophical overtones of these terms, it is important to remember that Zeami introduces them to distinguish two related styles of performance: in particular, two different types of hana. As such, they represent an ad hoc solution to a problem raised in a work written several years after the *Kyūi*. They should not be considered an

---

[81] This is an oblique reference to the Circle of Longevity.
[82] Past, present, and future.
[83] *KKSS*, 223.
[84] I suspect this is due to the influence of Kaneyoshi's *Ki* commentary. Kaneyoshi groups the last two stages (kūrin and ichiro) together as representative of the Great Ultimate and Ultimate of Nonbeing. See chapter 5.

essential feature of the Nine Ranks as originally conceived. Nevertheless, Zenchiku seizes upon these terms, transforming hana—originally a metaphor for a pleasing or beautiful effect—into a symbol for the ontological essence that underlies *all* successful performances, including those of unorthodox appearance. This can be seen most clearly in Zenchiku's inclusion of the Circle of Breaking in his Functional Flower grouping. Zeami only applied yōka to his own fourth rank, which corresponds to Zenchiku's Circle of Forms (see below). Zenchiku's expansion of the scope of yōka serves to illustrate that the purity of his first three circles—now symbolized by the Essential Flower—underlies even the superficially imperfect art of the Circle of Breaking.

Zenchiku's own interpretation of the Nine Ranks is recorded in his *Yūgen sanrin.* Although the shōka-yōka terminology does not appear here, the scheme presented exhibits a similar conception:

> In terms of the learning path represented by the six circles and one dewdrop, I consider the first three circles to be the foundation of yūgen. Even when spanning across all styles to perform heterodox roles or demons, if one's art is endowed with the yūgen of the first three circles, the Three Causes of Buddha Nature are attained. The performance radiates virtue and perfection, illuminating the realm in accordance with the enlightened path of benefiting all sentient beings.
>
> In this connection, levels [of performance] are [also] grouped together in Zeami's nine varieties of essence and rank. To add my own thoughts, the three styles of his highest ranks correspond to the first three of my six circles. The middle, miscellaneous qualities [correspond] to the Circle of Forms. The lower varieties are the Circle of Breaking. The Circle of Emptiness and the One Dewdrop are the highest levels of superior fruition, the Nature-ranks (shōi) of unobstructed, self-existing *samādhi* and liberation.[85]

Thus, the two systems correlate as follows:

ZEAMI	ZENCHIKU
Wondrous Flower	Circle of Longevity
Flower of Profundity	Circle of Height
Flower of Tranquility	Circle of Abiding
middle three ranks	Circle of Forms
lower three ranks	Circle of Breaking
("Nature-ranks")[86]	Circle of Emptiness, One Dewdrop

Through the structure of his six circles, Zenchiku represents Zeami's middle and lower ranks as an *emanation* of the upper three. This is the

[85] *KKSS*, 264–65.

[86] See note 84 for the pairing of the kūrin and ichiro. The use of the expression shōi here is not related to shōka; it is merely introduced to set off these two final categories.

shō-yō structure, projected onto the original nine ranks. In the process, the lower three ranks are equated with the Circle of Breaking, and thus to ran'i—an aspect of the these categories only implied in the *Kyūi*.

The correlation of the first three circles with Zeami's three highest ranks is quite suggestive. In one sense, the two *groups* of three are equivalent, simply because they represent the higher level of accomplishment that follows the cultivation of *monomane*. At the same time, the *individual* categories can be equated. Each of Zeami's definitions contains an allusion to a Zen koan that employs imagery based on a light–dark dialectic, imagery that resonates with the evolving definitions of Zenchiku's first three circles. For example, the Wondrous Flower is described, "In Silla, the sun shines at midnight."[87] This image of brilliant light amidst darkness suggests the unity of opposites—mind and matter, the constant circulation of inhalation and exhalation—found in the Circle of Longevity. Above all, it recalls the stage of myō, whereby the sun goddess is secluded within the rock-cave, and the whole world is in darkness. Similarly, the Flower of Profundity is described, "Amidst a thousand white peaks, why is just one not covered?"[88] Here, the light and darkness have differentiated, just as sound and feeling emerge in the Circle of Height; this recalls the flash of light emitted as the rock-cave opens. And finally, the Flower of Stillness is represented by "Snow piled up in a silver bowl."[89] Now, individually bright objects are in harmony, like the smoothly integrated dance movements of the Circle of Abiding, and the individuated, illuminated white faces of the deities assembled outside the cave. In general, the dialectic of light and darkness is central to yūgen as an aesthetic ideal,[90] and thus these images are befitting analogues for Zenchiku's first three circles, which represent the yūgen of body, speech, and mind.

The topics discussed in this chapter touch upon many structural similarities in the typologies presented in the writings of Zeami and Zenchiku. The reader may feel a certain dissatisfaction, however. The centrifugal–centripetal paradigm has been applied to account for the contrasting processes represented by the two groups of three circles. Furthermore, these two groups have been provisionally linked through the Essential Flower–Functional Flower relationship. However, the latter model cannot accom-

---

[87] This image appears in many Zen collections; for example, it is used at the conclusion of Musō Soseki's *Muchū mondō*. From the perspective of inland China, in the middle of the night the sun is already shining in the Korean Kingdom of Silla. For additional analysis and information on possible sources, see Mark J. Nearman, "Zeami's *Kyūi*: A Pedagogical Guide for Teachers of Acting," *Monumenta Nipponica* 33:3 (Autumn, 1978), 319–25. For an extended discussion of Zeami's use of Zen terminology, see Kōsai, *Zeami shinkō*, 20–39.

[88] This phrase also appears in several collections, including the recorded sayings of Hsü-t'ang (1185–1269). *Zoku zōkyō*, 121:341b.

[89] This image is found in case 13 of the *Pi-yen lu*.

[90] As discussed in Thornhill, "*Yūgen* after Zeami."

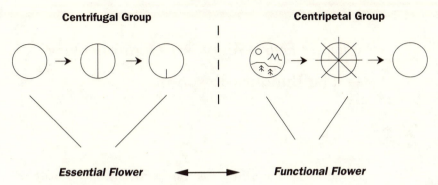

FIG. 3-4. Six Circles of Performance

modate the sequential aspect of the individual stages: the first three circles—at least as symbols of the Essential Flower and as three varieties of yūgen—are static, and thus the two models do not easily combine to account for the six circle structure in toto. In particular, the transition between the third and fourth circles is an abrupt shift in ontological status that interferes with the continuity of the self-regenerating six-stage cycle. Figure 3-4 illustrates this transition. To solve this problem, the Shigyoku and Kaneyoshi commentaries must be considered.

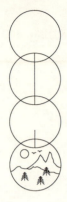

Chapter Four: Shigyoku's Commentary —The Buddhist Response

IN THE LAST CHAPTER, the rokurin ichiro system was analyzed from the perspective of performance theory. Inevitably, in such a context the principles set forth in the treatises of Zeami form the basis of all discussion. Zeami defines the criteria for successful performance, and as his artistic heir Zenchiku transmits these teachings essentially intact. From the standpoint of content, Zenchiku's writings at times seem little more than a restatement of Zeami's positions.

It is the formal structure of the rokurin ichiro system, however, that is its most notable feature and its greatest strength. Zenchiku's treatises represent a significant attempt to systematize a body of teachings that appear in many different works written over a span of almost three decades, works that themselves often lack internal consistency or discernible structure. While the rokurin ichiro system is not comprehensive, it does provide an easily learned framework of seven categories that future generations of performers might utilize to assimilate a selected core of Zeami's teachings. Inevitably, certain themes emerge as dominant, certain relationships are clarified or even created, as a result of Zenchiku's restructuring. Nevertheless, the general practical content of the rokurin ichiro system is a faithful transmission of Zeami's teachings.

The explication of the individual circles in the previous chapter does not, however, adequately represent their intrinsic aesthetic worth and conceptual power. Even after their "meaning" has been explained, the poetry of the terminology and the expressiveness of the diagrams lingers in the mind. Elusive relational patterns, only dimly suggested by the symbolic structure, haunt the reader. This fascination is what drove Shigyoku and Kaneyoshi to write their thoughtful commentaries. In fact, they exhibit almost no interest in the particulars of performance or artistic theory; their contributions are two personal responses to the allure of these symbols.

SHIGYOKU AND THE KEGON TRADITION

Shigyoku was a prominent cleric of his age, a respected teacher of the Kegon Sect headquartered at Tōdai-ji in Nara. The Nara sects experienced a revival in the Kamakura period, responding to the challenge of the new Pure Land teachings of Hōnen and his followers. In the Kegon tradition, the most notable figures are Gyōnen (1240–1321), the author of the still widely studied *Hasshū kōyō*, a compendium of the basic teachings of the "eight sects" of Japanese Buddhism, and Kōben (popularly known as Myōe Shōnin, 1173–1232), renowned for his waka, his diary of dreams (*Yume no ki*), and his outspoken criticism of Hōnen.

Born in 1383, Shigyoku studied both Kegon doctrine and the monastic regulations (J. *ritsu*, S. *vinaya*) at the Kaidan-in, one of the major subtemples of Tōdai-ji.[1] In 1417 he traveled to China, and the following year he was invited to lecture on the *Avataṃsaka Sūtra* at the Ming court, presumably because there were no native priests who could match his knowledge of the Hua-yen tradition, long defunct in China. Shigyoku was bestowed the title National Teacher P'u-i by the Ming emperor. Upon his return to Japan five years later, he lectured at the Great Vairocana Hall at Tōdai-ji and received the same title (Fu'ichi Kokushi) from the Japanese Emperor Shōkō. Shigyoku actually appears in the lineages of both the Ritsu and Kegon sects. While serving as abbot of the Kaidan-in, he lectured at various temples, including Kōzan-ji, the Kegon temple in Toganoo best known as the home of Kōben. Shigyoku's major extant work is the *Gokyōshō kenmon*,[2] an extended commentary on Fa-tsang's *Wu-chiao chang*, a seminal treatise of Chinese Hua-yen thought. He died at Kōzan-ji in 1463 at age eighty-one.

Although often ignored in accounts of medieval Buddhism, the Kegon tradition played a significant role in the culture of Zenchiku's age. Such Kegon doctrines as the inseparability of the absolute and phenomenal realms (*riji muge*) and the interpenetration of all phenomena (*jiji muge*) are widely studied in Zen koan practice, and indeed the histories of these two schools in China are closely connected. Shigyoku himself served as a spiritual adviser to the shogun Ashikaga Yoshinori, bestowing on him the lay precepts in 1429.[3] Of particular interest is a formal portrait of Shigyoku in the possession of Tōdai-ji that bears the inscription of the famous artist

---

[1] As its name (Ordination Hall) suggests, the Kaidan-in was a center of *vinaya* learning. The details of Shigyoku's life are drawn from his biography in the *Honchō kōsō den*, Dai Nihon Bukkyō zensho, 102: 264–65, and from Takamine Ryōshū, *Kegon shisō shi*, 2d ed. (Kyoto: Hyakkaen, 1963), 443–44.

[2] This work is discussed later in this chapter.

[3] Haga, *Higashiyama bunka no kenkyū*, 692–93.

Shūbun.[4] Shūbun was also a close acquaintance of Yoshinori, and Haga Kōshirō speculates that Shigyoku's Kegon world view may have had a significant impact on Shūbun's monochrome ink paintings, which are among the greatest achievements of medieval "Zen culture."[5]

The circumstances surrounding the writing of Shigyoku's commentary are not known. Presumably, Zenchiku showed him a rokurin ichiro text, now lost, and Shigyoku responded with the remarks contained in the *Rokurin ichiro no ki*. As discussed in chapter 1, Shigyoku's commentary was probably completed in 1444, when he was age sixty-two and Zenchiku was age forty. Judging from the evolution of these texts, I suspect that the two men had little further contact. The early rokurin ichiro works repeat large sections of his commentary verbatim, and the additional Buddhist material that appears in the later drafts is largely based on doctrines associated with the Tendai Sect.

SHIGYOKU'S COMMENTARY

Shigyoku's commentary is brief but expressive. Virtually every sentence presents a carefully measured analogy or cognate to Zenchiku's system, culled from Shigyoku's vast knowledge of Buddhist texts. His introduction states that, while the rokurin ichiro system contains both Buddhist (inner) and non-Buddhist (outer) elements, it can be analyzed successfully from the Buddhist perspective, both esoteric and exoteric. In fact, the subsequent references to esoteric doctrine are few and largely decorative.[6] This opening statement provides rhetorical symmetry, as the inner/outer categories balance with the esoteric/exoteric pair. The exoteric analogies introduced here are the key to the Shigyoku commentary. They are summarized in two sentences:

> The heart of the exoteric teachings—the doctrine of all dharmas comprising Suchness-following-conditions (*shinnyo zuien*) and the process of samsara and its extinction (*ruten genmetsu*)—is fully expressed by these six ranks. The first and last represent the original source of formless true Emptiness, and the middle

---

[4] See discussion in ibid., 687 ff. The Shūbun attribution is not universally accepted, however.

[5] Ibid., 694 ff.

[6] Only two explicitly esoteric terms are used: the Six Great Elements (*rokudai*) in the introduction, and the letter A (*A-ji*) which is used to describe the Circle of Longevity. See chapter 2, notes 6, 12, and 116. The Six Elements are in no sense analogous to Zenchiku's six circles; they are mentioned simply because the number six appears in each expression. However, Tōdai-ji's close ties with the Shingon Sect may have prompted Shigyoku to mention these esoteric motifs. In general, the underlying unity of exoteric (*ken*) and esoteric (*mitsu*) doctrine is a common theme in Japanese Buddhism.

four correspond to the four characteristic states of existence (*shisō*): birth, abiding, change, and extinction.

To appreciate the broad implications of these two sentences I shall examine three of its components in considerable detail: *ruten genmetsu*, *shinnyo zuien*, and *shisō*.

RUTEN GENMETSU: SAMSARA AND ITS EXTINCTION

The expression *ruten genmetsu* is comprised of two terms. The first is *ruten* (S. *pravṛtti*), functionally equivalent to samsara, the wheel of birth and death. Here we encounter the basic teachings of early Buddhism. Due to ignorance, the individual mistakenly believes that he possesses a discrete self (*ātman*) or ego. Through the twelvefold chain of causation, this ignorance generates desire, greed, and so on, in an endless cycle. Sensory perceptions of the external world are organized through the workings of the five skandhas—form, sensation, conception, volition, and consciousness—in a manner that reinforces the illusion of self. Thus, although there is actually no substantial entity that can transmigrate, this aggregate of mental energies revolves endlessly on the wheel of birth and death. This is ruten.

The second component of the expression, *genmetsu* (or *genmechi*; S. *nivṛtti*) represents the prescribed escape from the cycle of samsara. By eradicating erroneous views through the balanced practice of the Middle Way, the illusory nature of the self is directly experienced. When an individual's karma has been fully purified, he will no longer be subject to the chain of causation; after physical death he will not be reborn in any of the Six Paths of transmigration. This is the extinction of the illusory self, an annihilation into Nirvana—a state that can be described only as a cessation of what was before. This is the process represented by genmetsu.

In the analysis of Shigyoku's commentary it will be convenient to diagram a series of relationships between the absolute and relative planes, or aspects, of existence. While imprecise, the concepts of "absolute" and "relative" must remain flexible to support a broad range of configurations and nuances that will arise. The first diagram is given in figure 4-1. On the upper samsaric plane, an individual is represented by a single small circle or wheel, which revolves endlessly. He is the sum of his experiences of the objective world; the intersecting lines represent these sensory objects/experiences. Once his ignorance is eradicated, this discrete existence, delineated by the web of cause and effect, vanishes. In the above symbolic representation, the individual consciousness drops through the openings in the web of the samsaric plane, falling gently like vaporized specks of dust. Upon reaching the plane of Nirvana, it is no more.

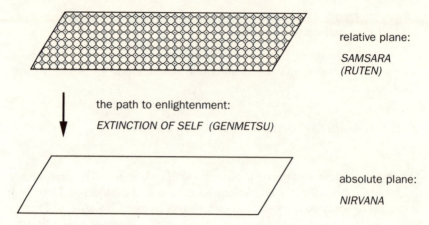

relative plane:

*SAMSARA
(RUTEN)*

the path to enlightenment:

EXTINCTION OF SELF (GENMETSU)

absolute plane:

NIRVANA

FIG. 4-1. Samsara and Its Extinction

Many objections could be raised to this method of diagramming. The web of samsara is without beginning or end, and so it should have no boundaries. Furthermore, in early Buddhism, Nirvana has no characteristics at all; the inference that it is a metaphysical plane of being[7] is anathema to those who refuse to entertain such ontological conceptions. The diagram is best viewed as the provisional symbolic representation of a psychological state and a nonstate.

SHINNYO ZUIEN AND THE PERFUMING OF SUCHNESS

The expression *shinnyo zuien* represents a much later stage in the history of Buddhist thought.[8] It first appears in an influential commentary to *The Awakening of Faith in the Mahayana* written by Fa-tsang (643–712), the third patriarch and most important figure of the Hua-yen School. Because of its importance, I will present a brief outline of various doctrinal developments that lie behind the conception this expression represents.

It is generally held that the appearance of the Prajñāpāramitā (perfection of wisdom) sutras marks the beginning of Mahayana Buddhism.[9] In re-

[7] This caution can be applied to all uses of the word "plane" in this chapter, since it implies a kind of ontological substantiality that Buddhism formally denies. It is a convenience, however, when describing certain aspects of Chinese Buddhist discourse, which often contains notions that are, practically speaking, ontologies.

[8] The following discussion of shinnyo zuien is inspired by chapter 3 of Whalen Wai-lun Lai's study, "*The Awakening of Faith in the Mahayana*: A Study of the Unfolding of Sinitic Mahayana Motifs" (Ph.D. dissertation, Harvard University, 1975).

[9] The history of early Mahayana Buddhism is not yet fully understood. For the problems involved, see Andrew Rawlinson, "The Position of the Astasāhasrikā Prajñāpāramitā in the

sponse to this body of scriptures, the Mādhyamika School arose in the second century, and the doctrine of Emptiness (śūnyatā) derived from the Prajñāpāramitā literature became the basis for many significant new trends in Buddhist thought. It proclaims that all things, all entities, are mutually conditioned and arise only due to dependent causes. Not only the self, but physical objects, even teachings such as the Four Noble Truths and the five skandhas, are declared to be empty of any permanent, discrete identity or self-nature (svabhāva).

Perhaps the most impressive achievement of the Mādhyamika School is the famous "eightfold negation" of its founder Nāgārjuna. In the words of Edward Conze,

> [Nāgārjuna and his school] developed the method of *prasanga*, an argumentation which demolishes all possible alternatives and which aims at the *reductio ad absurdum* of all beliefs. By drawing out the implications of any view, the Mādhyamika shows its self-contradictory character. . . . The famous motto of Nāgārjuna's chief work is the verse:
>
> "Not by itself nor by another, nor by both, nor without any cause
> Do positive existents ever arise in any way whatsoever."
>
> Each of the four theses is accepted hypothetically, and then rejected as self-contradictory, with the result that "Non-production" emerges triumphant.[10]

One of the most famous dictums to emerge from this form of argumentation is the statement that there is ultimately no distinction between samsara and Nirvana. In this way, the essential identity of the absolute and relative aspects of existence is proclaimed. It must be emphasized, however, that such dualistic pairs as form and emptiness and samsara and Nirvana are treated as dialectical pairs in the context of logical argument: they are identical in the sense that one cannot exist or even be discussed without reference to the other.

The Chinese, however, never really embraced this form of discourse. The Chinese language is weak in abstract expression, and precise logical argument is difficult to sustain. In particular, it does not gracefully support the either/or, neither/nor syntax necessary to express the subtlety of dialectical negation in its original form. Furthermore, the at least overtly negative tone of the doctrine of Emptiness did not appeal to the native sensibility.

Certain seeds were planted within Indian Buddhism, however, perhaps by non-Buddhist traditions, which exhibit a shift toward a more affirma-

Development of Early Mahayana," in Lewis Lancaster, ed., *Prajñāpāramitā and Related Systems* (Berkeley: Berkeley Buddhist Studies Series, 1977), 3–34.

[10] Edward Conze, *Buddhist Thought in India* (Ann Arbor: University of Michigan Press, 1967), 241.

tive mode of expression.[11] Most notable of these is the *tathāgatagarbha* (embryo, or womb, of the Tathāgata) theory, which expresses the potential for enlightenment that exists within all human beings.[12] It utilizes the image of an embryo, an embryo of the enlightened mind—or alternatively, a womb in which it develops—that may be nurtured within the impure, deluded consciousness until it matures and final liberation is experienced. Strictly speaking, the tathāgatagarbha is said to represent only the potentiality, or incipient cause, of Buddhahood, in order to avoid connotations of a substantial essence that might resemble a permanent self. Nevertheless, for the first time a pure, undefiled element is said to exist within the very plane of samsara.

The Chinese were very receptive to this biogenetic model for the process of enlightenment. The metaphysical models of Taoism, as well as the cosmogonic schemes adopted by Confucianists, are strongly biogenetic, based either on the model of human reproduction (the Tao, yin–yang), or the temporal order of the seasons (the *I ching*). For example, the yin–yang paradigm supports the concept of two entities—in the case above, delusion and enlightenment—each implicit in the other, each growing from the other, the two functionally interacting in a harmonious fashion. Thus the yang-like seed of the tathāgatagarbha germinates in the yin field of dark delusion and gradually grows to dominance.

As the tathāgatagarbha doctrine and the similar concept of Buddha Nature (which first appears in the *Parinirvāṇa Sūtra*) were absorbed into the mainstream of Chinese Buddhism, this biogenetic modality began to influence earlier forms of Mahayana thought. In particular, yin–yang dualism was adapted and utilized to *simulate* the Mādhyamika dialectic described above. Actually, yin–yang dualism represents a pseudo-organic process of harmonious mutual influence, based on a temporal model of bipolar, alternating cycles.[13] This is quite different from the atemporal, logical categories of dialectical negation. Nevertheless, this yin–yang

[11] In the nomenclature of contemporary Buddhology, the negative or paradoxical language used by Nāgārjuna and others to convey a sense of something by exhaustively expressing what it is not is termed "apophatic discourse"; the use of positive descriptions of a concept's qualities is termed "kataphatic discourse." See Robert E. Buswell, Jr., trans., *The Collected Works of Chinul* (Honolulu: University of Hawaii Press, 1983), 259, n. 50, for a fuller discussion.

[12] The most influential Indian text that treats the tathāgatagarbha doctrine at length is the *Śrīmālā-sūtra*; for a translation and extensive commentary, see Alex and Hideko Wayman, *The Lion's Roar of Queen Śrīmālā* (New York: Columbia University Press, 1974). This scripture is said to have influenced *The Awakening of Faith*, which also presents a version of the tathāgatagarbha doctrine.

[13] For an extended discussion of bipolarity in Chinese thought and literature, see Andrew H. Plaks, *Archetype and Allegory in the Dream of the Red Chamber* (Princeton: Princeton University Press, 1976), 44 ff.

modality came to influence all forms of discourse concerning the nature of the absolute and the relative.

A pivotal text in this regard is *The Awakening of Faith in the Mahayana* (C. *Ta-sheng ch'i-hsin lun*). Reputedly the translation of an Indian work attributed to a certain Aśvaghoṣa, about whom almost nothing is known,[14] *The Awakening of Faith* is considered the single most important work in the establishment of the "original enlightenment" (C. *pen-hsüeh*, J. *hongaku*) doctrine, which is central to almost all subsequent developments in East Asian Buddhist thought. The lack of an extant Sanskrit version, as well as a wealth of internal evidence, has led modern scholars to question its Indian origins, and in fact its modes of argument and categorization are suspiciously Chinese in character.

The work is based on a conception of the all-inclusive totality of existence, the One Mind (*i-hsin*), which in turn has two aspects, functionally equivalent to the absolute and the relative. The absolute is represented by the term *chen-ju* (J. *shinnyo*)[15] a not particularly literal rendition of *tathatā*, or Suchness. In most Indian texts, *tathatā* is virtually synonymous with Emptiness, as Suchness is omnipresent being itself, empty of any characteristic whatever.[16] The relative aspect of One Mind is samsara, rendered in Chinese as *sheng-mieh* (birth-and-extinction).

In *The Awakening of Faith*, the relationship between Suchness and ignorance is analyzed in several ways. On the one hand, they are proclaimed to be nondual in traditional Indian fashion:

> It should be understood that the essential nature of Suchness is neither with marks nor without marks; neither not with marks nor not without marks, nor is it both with and without marks simultaneously. . . .
>
> In short, since all unenlightened men discriminate with their deluded minds from moment to moment, they are alienated [from Suchness]; hence the definition "empty"; but once they are free from their deluded minds, they will find that there is nothing to be negated.[17]

---

[14] See Hakeda, *The Awakening of Faith*, 5–8, for a discussion of the problems surrounding the authorship of the text.

[15] In the current discussion, Japanese pronunciations are utilized when the term has actually been used by Shigyoku; this usage will continue even if the term is subsequently discussed in a Chinese context.

[16] This brief and somewhat simplified definition of Suchness is its most prominent meaning in *The Awakening of Faith*. Near the end of the text, however, Suchness is also described in kataphatic terms: "It is endowed with the light of great wisdom, [the qualities of] illuminating the entire universe, of true cognition and mind pure in its self-nature; of eternity, bliss, self and purity" (*T* 1666.32.579a; trans. Hakeda, *The Awakening of Faith*, 65). See note 43 for more on these last four qualities.

[17] *T* 1666.32.576a–b, trans. Hakeda, *The Awakening of Faith*, 34–35.

Yet in many other places, Suchness and ignorance are treated as two quasi-ontological entities that interact functionally. For example, the following sections speak of the way in which Suchness and ignorance "perfume" (*hsün-hsi*) each other:

> Clothes in the world have no scent in themselves, but if man permeates them with perfumes, then they come to have a scent. It is just the same with the case we are speaking of. The pure state of Suchness certainly has no defilement, but if it is permeated by ignorance, then the marks of defilement appear on it. The defiled state of ignorance is indeed devoid of any purifying force, but if it is permeated by Suchness, then it will come to have a purifying influence.

> How does the permeation [of ignorance] give rise to the defiled state and continue uninterrupted? It may be said that, on the ground of Suchness [i.e., the original enlightenment], ignorance [i.e., nonenlightenment] appears. Ignorance, the primary cause of the defiled state, permeates into Suchness. Because of this permeation a deluded mind results.[18]

Conversely,

> How does the permeation [of Suchness] give rise to the pure state and continue uninterrupted? It may be said that there is the principle of Suchness, and it can permeate into ignorance. Through the force of this permeation, [Suchness] causes the deluded mind to loathe the suffering and to aspire for nirvana. Because this mind, though still deluded, is [now] possessed with loathing and aspiration, it permeates into Suchness [in that it induces Suchness to manifest itself].[19]

Such passages generated great controversy among later commentators. Many considered heretical the notion that Suchness could exist in an impure form. Also revolutionary is the implication that the phenomenal world is actually a kind of modulation, or delimited form, of Suchness. In this sense the text affirms the inherent purity of the phenomenal realm.

The term under discussion here, shinnyo zuien (C. *chen-ju sui-yüan*), appears in Fa-tsang's comments on this "perfuming" passage:

> Suchness has two aspects: the Unchanging (C. *pu-pien*, J. *fuhen*) and that which goes along with [changing] condition (C. *sui-yüan*, J. *zuien*). Ignorance also has two aspects: that which is nonsubstantive, empty, and that which [nevertheless] actively functions and completes affairs [of the world]. Analyzed in terms of the "true" and the "false," the first [of the two above pairs] combine

---

[18] *T* 1666.32.578a, trans. Hakeda, *The Awakening of Faith*, 56.
[19] *T* 1666.32.578b, trans. Hakeda, *The Awakening of Faith*, 58.

to produce the Gate [aspect] of Suchness, while [the other two] the Gate of life and death (samsara).[20]

This statement that Suchness both is changeless and transforms in response to conditioned reality was widely commented on by Fa-tsang's descendants in the Hua-yen lineage. Shigyoku himself treats the contrasting categories *fuhen* and *zuien* in his own *Gokyōshō kenmon*.[21] Once again following Zenchiku's precedent, one might "provisionally" represent the configuration of fuhen and zuien as in figure 4-2.

In this diagram, both the absolute and relative planes are round, representing perfection and purity. The bottom circle is Suchness in its changeless aspect; the upper circle represents Suchness as it exists within the phenomenal realm, having "followed conditions." It must be emphasized here that the bottom circle does not represent an antecedent ontological source; the upper circle is in no sense generated by the lower. Rather, the two circles represent two aspects of Suchness that exist simultaneously. As the diagram indicates, there are actually two nondual pairs here. First, the two aspects fuhen and zuien are nondual in the logical, Indian sense. In addition, the zuien category itself contains two elements: Suchness and the realm of conditions. These are related through a functional process, indicated by the verb *zui*—"to follow"—and are nondual in the Chinese sense of harmonious interaction.

The above summary of the doctrinal background of shinnyo zuien is included here to indicate the rich modalities of Mahayana discourse that Shigyoku had at his disposal. While a layman such as Zenchiku could not be expected to be sensitive to every nuance, Shigyoku's scholastic accomplishments insured that he himself was keenly aware of the full significance of the terminology he employed. In particular, I have tried to demonstrate how the empty circle might at once represent the austere Emptiness of classic Mādhyamika thought—an absolutely pure state or category beyond all conceptualization—and yet at the same time represent the ground from which phenomenal existents arise. The modalities discussed here reappear in Shigyoku's comments on the first three circles, each of which treats the absolute and the relative in a distinct configuration.

[20] *T* 1846.44.255c, trans. in Lai, *The Awakening of Faith*, 207. From here, Fa-tsang develops his scheme to incorporate pairs of dialectical poles: each subcategory itself contains two aspects, one of self-affirmation and one of self-denial, ultimately resulting in eight subdivisions.

[21] The *Gokyōshō kenmon*, ostensibly a commentary on Fa-tsang's *Wu-chiao chang*, is Shigyoku's major extant work. Based on his lectures, it was actually recorded in ten *kan* by his disciple Gen'on. It contains remarks on a wide variety of doctrinal issues treated in the Kegon scholarship of the period. All citations are from an Edo period woodblock edition in the collection of Ryūkoku University. For discussions of fuhen and zuien, see *kan* 3.

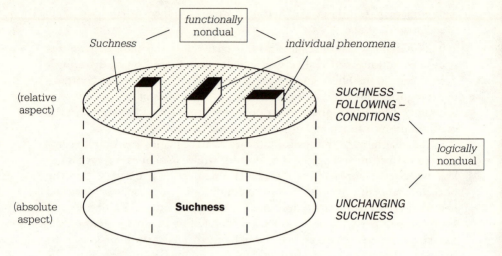

FIG. 4-2. Suchness-Following-Conditions

Through the juxtaposition of the terms shinnyo zuien and ruten genmetsu, Shigyoku accomplished much. Each expression represents an entire epoch of Buddhist thought—shinnyo zuien the Mahayana, ruten genmetsu the pre-Mahayana. Furthermore, in a general sense the contrasting
words *banpō* (myriad dharmas) and *shijū* (process) used in the text emphasize that both ontological speculation and the experiential process of enlightenment are represented within this one system. As will be seen, this
provides an excellent framework on which to fashion Shigyoku's comments on Zenchiku's six circles. The first three circles will represent the
ontological relation of Emptiness or Suchness to the phenomenal realm;
the second three will depict a psychological process by which the phenomenal world comes into existence and show how the suffering that accompanies it can be extinguished.

SHISŌ: THE FOUR CHARACTERISTIC STATES OF EXISTENCE

The second half of Shigyoku's comprehensive overview states: "The first
and last ranks represent the original source of formless true Emptiness, and
the middle four ranks correspond to the four characteristic states of
existence—birth (*shō*), abiding (*jū*), change (*i*), and extinction (*metsu*)." To
understand the significance of this statement, one must first examine the
origins of the Four Characteristic States of Existence (hereafter the Four
Characteristics).

These terms were first used by the theorists of the early Buddhist schools to designate four stages in a human lifetime: (1) birth and the years through adolescence (S. *jāti*); (2) the stage of early adulthood, when one's external appearance does not change noticeably (S. *sthiti*); (3) the stage from middle age onward, as signs of aging steadily increase (S. *anyathātva*); (4) old age and death (S. *nirodha*). As has been seen, the teachings of early Buddhism proclaim the insubstantiality of the self and the impermanence of human life. As the scope of analysis in Mahayana Buddhism was broadened to include all phenomena, the Four Characteristics were applied to the "life-cycle" of individual dharmas. In this sense, they represent the process of birth, development, decay, and death that each phenomenal existent undergoes, be it a human being, a plant, an idea, a gust of wind, or a speck of dust. The Four Characteristics are represented in figure 4-3.

Shigyoku's rationale for this implementation of the Four Characteristics is clear. The first and last circles share a common symbolic representation, the empty circle, and Zenchiku himself emphasizes their essential unity in his own remarks. Furthermore, the names of the middle circles resemble those of the Four Characteristics: *jū* is identical to the third circle, and *shō* for the Circle of Height and *metsu* for the Circle of Breaking are closely related semantically. Thus Zenchiku's first and last circles represent the "formless true Emptiness," and the Four Characteristics are aligned with the middle four. In this configuration, the middle four circles come to symbolize the life cycle of a phenomenal entity that arises from, and returns to, the ground of Emptiness.

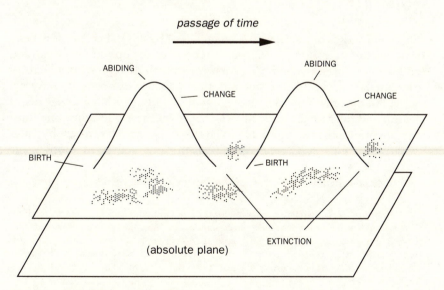

FIG. 4-3. Four Characteristic States

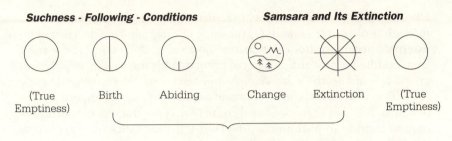

The Four Characteristics

Fig. 4-4. Shigyoku's Six Circles

The stage is now set for consideration of Shigyoku's remarks on the individual circles. Figure 4-4 summarizes the structural correspondences that have been discussed to this point. Note that the application of the Four Characteristics terminology results in a 1-4-1 division of the six circles, providing the smooth transition from the third to fourth circles lacking in the paradigms discussed in chapter 3. The rationale for apportioning the two groups of three circles into the shinnyo zuien and ruten genmetsu categories will become clearer in the following discussion.

THE CIRCLE OF LONGEVITY: ONE SOURCE OF MOTION AND STILLNESS

Shigyoku writes of the Circle of Longevity, "First is the rank of formless, tranquil Emptiness, the wondrous essence[22] of the one source of motion and stillness." Clearly, for Shigyoku the first circle represents a locus of absolute being, the Suchness or Emptiness discussed above. But how is it related to the phenomenal realm? How does it fit in with our categories of logical and functional nondualism? To answer these questions, one must investigate another powerful Hua-yen paradigm introduced here by Shigyoku: *dōsei ichigen* (C. *tung-ching i-yüan*), "one source of motion and stillness."

The first-known appearance of the expression is in the *Hua-yen-ching shu*,

---

[22] "Essence" is the standard translation for *t'i* (J. *tai*) in Buddhist contexts. This rendition is not entirely satisfactory, however, since—unlike the Chinese word—it implies a distillation or reduction process. The original sense of *t'i* is closer to "substance"; that is, an entity whose activities are characterized as "function" (*yung*; J. *yō*). Nevertheless, "substance" is considered unacceptable because it suggests the ontological substantiality that Buddhism explicitly rejects.

a commentary on the *Avataṃsaka Sūtra* written by Ch'eng-kuan (737–838), the fourth Hua-yen patriarch:

> Going and returning without limit,
> motion and stillness have One Source:
> Comprising all wonders with ease,
> going beyond word and thought,
> it is simply the Dharmadhātu.[23]

Commenting on these lines, Ch'eng-kuan writes in a later work, "Now, what is called 'becoming confused in the Dharmadhātu' and 'being reborn in the six transmigratory states' is going, it is movement. 'Awakening to the Dharmadhātu' and 'returning to the One Mind' is coming, it is stillness. All are functions of the Dharmadhātu. When confused, delusion is born; awakening is when delusion vanishes."[24]

Here one sees the processes of delusion and enlightenment represented as motion and stillness (*ching* is actually a verb here, meaning to become tranquil), respectively. As bipolar opposites, *tung* and *ching* are perhaps the most widely discussed yin–yang components in the metaphysics of the Sung Neo-Confucian philosophers, and there is ample evidence that the Hua-yen conception under discussion here was an important influence.[25] In the current context, motion is the arising of delusion on the previously tranquil, lucid surface of One Mind. Its inertia gradually slows as the stillness pole begins to assert itself, and eventually movement ceases. This process of coming to rest is the abatement of confusion, culminating in enlightenment.

The underlying metaphor in Ch'eng-kuan's commentary is the famous water and waves analogy of *The Awakening of Faith*.[26] The mind is likened to an ocean; when the wind of ignorance blows, phenomena (waves) arise.

---

[23] T 1735.35.503a.

[24] T 1736.36.2a.

[25] Imai Usaburō discusses the origins of the *dōsei ichigen* doctrine at length in his *Sōdai ekigaku no kenkyū* (Tokyo: Meiji shoin, 1958), 437–43. He demonstrates how this Hua-yen teaching was undoubtedly an influence upon the use of the terms *tung* and *ching* in the writings of Chu Hsi and other Neo-Confucianists.

[26] The passage from *The Awakening of Faith* reads, "[The nonduality of ignorance and enlightenment] is like the relationship that exists between the water of the ocean [i.e., enlightenment] and its waves [i.e., modes of mind] stirred by the wind [i.e. ignorance]. Water and wind are inseparable; but water is not mobile by nature, and if the wind stops the movement ceases. But the wet nature remains undestroyed. Likewise, man's Mind, pure in its own nature, is stirred by the wind of ignorance. Both Mind and ignorance have no particular forms of their own and they are inseparable. Yet Mind is not mobile by nature, and if ignorance ceases, then the continuity [of deluded activities] ceases. But the essential nature of wisdom [i.e., the essence of Mind, like the wet nature of the water] remains undestroyed." T 1666.32.578a, trans. Hakeda, *The Awakening of Faith*, 55–56.

Thus the phenomenal world, although a product of ignorance, is in essence no different from Mind, since it is composed of water. When the waves subside, conventional phenomena are exhausted, but the true essence of the mind—its originally enlightened nature, represented by water—remains undestroyed. Thus, as in Ch'eng-kuan's poem, the motion (of the waves) represents delusion, and their calming represents enlightenment. This metaphor of water and waves is commonly discussed as the relationship between *t'i* (substance. or essence) and *yung* (function). First used by the Neo-Taoist philosopher Wang Pi (226–229), this terminology was widely adopted by Chinese Buddhists. In his comments above, Ch'eng-kuan states that *tung* and *ching* "are functions of the Dharmadhātu," the totality of existence. [27]

The *t'i–yung* paradigm as it functions in *The Awakening of Faith*, [28] however, does not approach the subtlety of the dōsei ichigen configuration. In the former, *t'i* is merely an inert substance that moves when acted upon by external forces—the winds of ignorance. Therefore, this function—and thus the phenomenal realm represented by the waves—cannot be said to be truly intrinsic to the nature of Mind itself. In Ch'eng-kuan's poem, however, the process of motion/delusion and stillness/enlightenment is an entirely natural function of the Dharmadhātu, one that continues endlessly by itself. In this sense, the ocean is not simply an inherently inert body of matter (water); it is a dynamic repository that contains all of existence in potential form.

Through the use of the single expression dōsei ichigen, Shigyoku presents the Circle of Longevity as a symbol of infinite life, a kind of antecedent state that comprises the totality of existence. Indeed, the character *ju* is often used in Buddhist contexts to represent not merely longevity on a human scale, but the infinite life of the cosmic Buddha. [29] Shigyoku thus

[27] The notion of the Dharmadhātu (C. *fa-chieh*, J. *hokkai*) is succinctly defined by Minoru Kiyota as "the embodiment of Buddhist truth in the form of the realm of sentient beings or the universe." (Minoru Kiyota, *Shingon Buddhism: Theory and Practice* [Tokyo: Buddhist Books International, 1978], 163). For the Hua-yen doctrine of Four Views of the Dharmadhātu, see note 51. In the context of the current discussion, it is sufficient to emphasize that, while the Dharmadhātu comprises both the relative (exhibiting characteristics) and absolute (formless) aspects of existence, it reveals the true aspect of things in their totality, in distinction to any partial or deluded views. Therefore the category of the Dharmadhātu can be assigned to the absolute plane, in the sense that it represents truth. This is consistent with the dōsei ichigen paradigm, where *dō* and *sei* represent the arising and subsequent subsiding of delusion, on the ground of truth (*ichigen*). Furthermore, in many Mahayana contexts, the Dharmadhātu is functionally equivalent to Suchness.

[28] Actually, the *t'i/yung* terminology does not appear in the original water/waves passage itself; it is applied by later commentators. These expressions are used elsewhere in the text, however, as is the tripartite categorization *t'i*, *yung*, and *hsiang* (characteristics).

[29] For example, in the title of chapter 16 of the *Lotus Sutra*: "Nyorai juryō bon," "The Eternal Life of the Tathāgata."

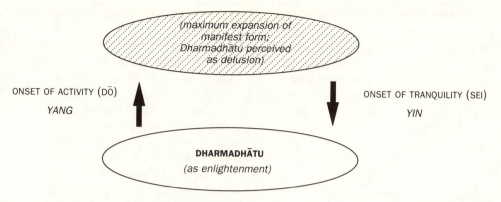

FIG. 4-5. One Source of Motion and Stillness

mentions here the "infinite life of the Buddhist Law," and the "Life of the letter A."

The dōsei ichigen paradigm is represented in figure 4-5. This diagram represents both the dō and sei functions. The relative plane represented by the upper circle expands and contracts accordingly; however, the emphasis is upon the mental states of delusion and enlightenment.

It is interesting to note that there are three implicit nondual relationships here. First, ichigen and dōsei are nondual in their roles as essence and function. In addition, the pair of dō and sei are nondual both because they are harmoniously interacting yin–yang functions, and because they share the same source. This biogenetic imagery—which also appears in such expressions as *pen* (root) and *mo* (trace), for example—is a powerful Chinese innovation. It introduces a new antecedent ontological plane, and it implies both the underlying unity of all resultant phenomena and the act of generation itself. In this sense, the diagram of dōsei ichigen attributes a dynamic and creative function to the empty circle (here the equivalent of the Circle of Longevity). This contrasts with the earlier shinnyo zuien/fuhen model, in which the empty circle represents the static (fuhen) aspect of Suchness. Furthermore, even the zuien aspect represents only a *dynamic* Suchness; it does not support the conception of a *creative* Suchness.

In a general sense, dōsei ichigen provides a model for the cyclical arising from, and subsequent return to, the "formless tranquil" state represented by the first and sixth circles. It is not meant, however, to be a detailed structural prototype for all six. For example, while the Circle of Height might conceivably represent the onset of delusion, the enlightenment process represented by the Circle of Breaking can hardly be characterized as "stillness." The emphasis here is on ichigen, the One Source that is a generative matrix for the middle four circles.

THE CIRCLE OF HEIGHT: THE LOCUS OF NATURE ORIGINATION

Shigyoku's remarks on the Circle of Height are brief: "Second is the stage of birth. That is to say, [the rising line] is [like] a single wave of transitory existence arising on the formless, tranquil empty sea of [Dharma] Nature. Master Tsao-po's commentary, 'There is no wind on the Nature Sea, yet of itself a golden wave shimmers on its surface,' expresses this concept."

This passage introduces a major doctrinal issue that this study has not yet considered directly: origination, or the analysis of how phenomenal entities come into existence. In Mahayana Buddhism, the orthodox doctrine of origination is *engi* (C. *yüan-ch'i*, S. *pratītyasamutpāda*), "conditioned arising." The workings of cause and effect are exhaustively analyzed to demonstrate the interdependent nature of all sense perceptions and the resulting object consciousness. Since both the self and all dharmas arise only through contingent causes, which in turn are based on other contingent causes, and so on, they are free of any self-nature or permanent, discrete identity. However, the engi theory does not account for any functional relationship between the relative and absolute. Even the doctrine of shinnyo zuien discussed above relies upon the engi conception (represented by the *en* of *zuien*) to explain origination. Suchness is said to "encounter conditions"; these conditions, which are unrelated to Suchness in any ontological sense, are the immediate causes of individual dharmas.

In contrast to engi, the later doctrine of *shōki* (C. *hsing-ch'i*)[30] or nature origination, states that all phenomena are ultimately grounded in "nature"—a synonym for Dharma Nature, One Mind, Suchness, or the Dharmadhātu. The term itself was borrowed by Fa-tsang from one title for chapter 32 of the 40-chapter *Avataṃsaka Sūtra*, "Ju-lai hsing-ch'i" (The appearance of the nature of the Tathāgata), although its meaning in the sutra is unrelated to any theory of origination.[31] Chinul (1158–1210), a major figure in Korean Son (J. Zen) who was strongly influenced by Hua-yen, explains the rationale of nature origination as follows: "Phenomena are all devoid of essence or nature, for originally they are nondual and their essences are indistinguishable. Since they all arise from the nonproductive conditions of the own-nature of the Dharmadhātu, the conditions and the characteristics of these conditions all arise from that nature. That nature itself is the Dharmadhātu; there is no inside, outside, or in between."[32]

Of particular interest is Chinul's appropriation of the ocean symbol to represent this nature: "Buddhas and sentient beings manifest illusorily

---

[30] As this doctrine was first formulated in China, there is no Sanskrit counterpart for *shōki*.

[31] See Tamaki Kōshirō, "Kegon no shōki ni tsuite," in Miyamoto Shōson, ed., *Indo tetsugaku to Bukkyō no shomondai* (Tokyo: Iwanami shoten, 1951), 281–309.

[32] *Wondon songbŭllon*, in Sim Chae-yŏl, ed. *Pojo pŏbŏ*, 366–67; translation in Buswell, *Chinul*, 205.

from the Nature Sea of the fundamental wisdom of universal brightness. Although the form and functioning of sentient beings and buddhas seem to be different, they are entirely the form and functioning of the fundamental wisdom of universal brightness. . . . This corresponds to the tenet of nature origination."[33]

The treatise that contains these remarks is Chinul's response to the views of Li T'ung-hsüan (635–730), a layman who, in his several commentaries on the *Avataṃsaka Sūtra*, was the most vigorous proponent of nature origination within the Hua-yen tradition. His works were largely ignored in China by the later Hua-yen patriarchs, but they eventually gained wide influence in Korean Buddhism due to Chinul's promotions. In Japan they served as an inspiration to the most famous Kegon figure of the Kamakura period, Kōben, mentioned earlier in this chapter. It is due to Kōben that Li's writings became popular in Japan,[34] and Shigyoku's *Gokyōshō kenmon* contains several references to them.[35] Recent commentators have noted that, in Li's view, nature origination provides a more direct path to enlightenment, because it bypasses the elaborate "conceptual apparatus" that encumbers the various theories—particularly those of Fa-tsang—based upon the dependent origination doctrine.[36]

Li's views are relevant to the present discussion because Shigyoku cites him as a source for the lines "There is no wind on the Nature Sea, yet of itself a golden wave shimmers on its surface." Again the term "Nature Sea" appears, a sure indication of the implicit shōki doctrine. But there are two unusual features of this sentence. First, unlike the waves of the *Awakening of Faith* ocean metaphor, these are described as golden. Second, there is no wind. These deviations from the norm are crucial to an understanding of the originality of the rokurin ichiro system.

Unfortunately, neither I nor the Japanese commentators have been able to locate the original passage in Li's extant works.[37] However, an almost identical phrase, with no attribution, appears in Shigyoku's own *Gokyōshō kenmon*, as a definition of nature origination: "There is no wind on the Nature Sea, yet *all waves* seethe of themselves."[38] The only difference is that the almost identical character *zen* 全 (all) appears in place of *kin* 金

---

[33] Ibid.

[34] See Robert M. Gimello, "Li T'ung-hsüan and the Practical Dimensions of Hua-yen," in Gimello and Peter N. Gregory, eds., *Studies in Ch'an and Hua-yen* (Honolulu: University of Hawaii Press, 1983), 350–59, for a discussion of Li's influence on Kōben.

[35] For example, in *kan* 5.

[36] For example, see Steve Odin, *Process Metaphysics and Hua-yen Buddhism* (Albany: SUNY Press, 1982), 63–64.

[37] Omote is silent on the origin of the passage. Takamine identifies the *zenpa* version (see discussion below) as an innovative feature of Shigyoku's thought. Takamine, *Kegon shisō shi*, 447. He does not mention Li as a possible source.

[38] *Kenmon, kan* 5.

(golden). The *Ki* version may simply be miscopied, perhaps an error committed by Anki.[39] Let us ignore this possibility for the moment. As it stands, the *Kenmon* version is likely the statement of a Hua-yen commentator; "all waves" is easily understood as a symbol for the interrelated web of the phenomenal realm. *Kinpa*, on the other hand, introduces an alien element to the analogy. Of itself the word usually means the reflection of the moon on the ocean's surface. This suggests the presence of the moon in the metaphoric seascape, a common symbol for Buddha Nature or enlightenment in Buddhist literature. At the very least, a kind of transcendent purity is expressed by the image of *kinpa*, lacking in the more conventional and conceptual *zenpa*.

Judging from the evidence of the *Kenmon*, where the phrase appears twice, it is most likely that Shigyoku originally wrote *zenpa*, not *kinpa*. It is my hypothesis that *kinpa* in the *Ki* manuscript is not a simple scribal error, but that it was unconsciously—or even deliberately—modified by Zenchiku when he assembled the *Ki* into its present form. This is because the *kinpa* version of the passage also appears in a syncretic Buddhist-Shinto work composed by Jihen (d. 1347?), the *Toyoashihara shinpū waki*,[40] which he utilizes in the writing of later rokurin ichiro treatises. That text will be discussed in chapter 6. Furthermore, Zenchiku uses the identical phrasing in his *Kabu zuinō ki* to symbolize the portrayal of "fundamentally tranquil things that temporarily become rough and disordered."[41]

The second unusual feature here is the fact that there is *no wind*. In the *Awakening of Faith* configuration described earlier, the wind of ignorance is the direct cause of the wave formations. From the standpoint of dependent origination, if there is no wind, no dependent phenomena should form on the surface of Mind; its true nature as tranquil, formless Suchness should be evident as a waveless surface. But here, Li suggests that just as even a calm, glassy sea undulates in subtle, constant motion, so does the enlightened mind exhibit activity; enlightenment does not mean total extinction of the phenomenal realm. Furthermore, the ebb and flow of conditioned existence is not simply driven by deluded ignorance, it is the natural expression of its true Nature. This modification of the stock *Awakening of Faith* metaphor, whether conceived by Li or by Shigyoku, is among the most powerful and affecting expressions of the nature origination doctrine in the Hua-yen/Kegon corpus.[42]

[39] See chapter 1 for a discussion of the various extant manuscripts.

[40] In *Zokuzoku gunsho ruijū*, 1:124; see chapter 2, note 14, for more details.

[41] *KKSS*, 138.

[42] There is a startling contemporary parallel to Shigyoku's language in the following lyric from the 1970 popular song "Ripple," composed by Robert Hunter and Jerry Garcia: "Ripple in still water—when there is no pebble tossed, no wind to blow." This refrain is presented as a metaphor for music "played on the harp unstrung," for "a fountain . . . not made by the hands of men." The Grateful Dead, *American Beauty* (Warner Bros. WS 1893).

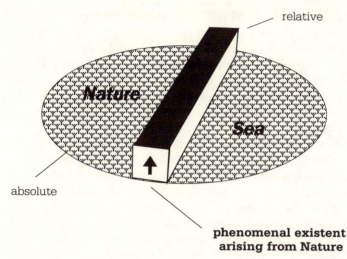

FIG. 4-6. Nature Origination

Figure 4-6 is essentially a three-dimensional representation of Zen-chiku's own Circle of Height drawing. One aspect of Zenchiku's original has been altered. He speaks of the "*tachinoboru ten*," the vertical line that rises from the bottom to the top edge of the circle as it appears on the page. Here, the entire line rises upward in the third dimension, representing the emergence of an individual phenomenal entity from the ground of Such-ness, in the spirit of nature origination. This representation preserves the three-dimensional perspective used in the previous diagrams.

The reader might object that the shōki doctrine presented here is little more than a restatement of the dōsei ichigen configuration discussed in the previous section. It is true that they share the conception of a creative, dynamic Dharmadhātu that is the origin of all manifest reality. However, in addition to the fact that these two doctrines have different historical roots, it should be noted that dōsei ichigen emphasizes the common source—the ichigen—of the mental processes of delusion and enlighten-ment, whereas shōki seeks to explain the arising (*ki*) of the phenomenal plane. It is these two aspects—origin and arising—that Zenchiku's first two circles represent.

THE CIRCLE OF ABIDING: AT EASE IN THE DHARMA POSITION

"Abiding" is a term with rich connotations in the Buddhist tradition. It has already been discussed here as one of the Four Characteristics, but most commonly it describes a mental attitude. In the context of pre-Mahayana

Buddhism, the practitioner is admonished against "abiding" in—being attached to—the material world. In the Mādhyamika teachings, a one-sided abiding in Emptiness is criticized as nihilistic and a violation of the Middle Way. As often happened with traditional terminology,[43] later Mahayana thought reverses the usage of the term, although not the final import of the doctrine: abiding becomes a positive quality, meaning to be at ease (as in the expression *anjū* used here by Shigyoku), attached neither to form nor to emptiness.

One sees this affirmative meaning of abiding in the passage from the *Lotus Sutra* cited by Shigyoku: "Dharmas abide in their own dharma positions; the forms of this world are eternally abiding." These words would shock an orthodox Theravāda practitioner. To declare that the forms of the world are eternal is a flagrant contradiction of the fundamental doctrine of impermanence. Tendai commentators, however, interpret the phrase *hōi* not as "the position of phenomenal existents," but rather as "the locus of the Law" or Suchness.[44] Thus the *Lotus* passage comes to mean that all forms are eternal because they are nondually unified with Suchness. The enlightened attitude represented here is a kind of equanimity, "abiding in the Dharma position," which permits the calm observance of individual dharmas arising and disintegrating.

The *Awakening of Faith* ocean metaphor appears yet again in Shigyoku's remarks, in a citation from Fa-tsang's *Wang-chin huan-yüan kuan*: "Deluded views are exhausted, the mind clears and myriad images appear together." An examination of the original text indicates Shigyoku's motivation for including it—the occurrence of the term *jōjū*:

> Grounded on [the pure and perfectly bright essence of the self-nature], two functions are produced. First is the constantly abiding (J. *jōjū*) function of the ocean-seal of all phenomena. "Ocean-seal" means the original enlightenment of true Suchness. When falseness is extinguished and the mind is purified, myriads of images will appear together. It will be like clear seawater; there are no images

---

[43] One of the most astounding examples of this is the transformation of the "four upside-down views" (*viparyāsa*). Originally these form the basis of ignorance: (1) to regard what is impermanent (*anitya*) as permanent (*nitya*), (2) to regard what is suffering (*duḥkha*) as blissful (*sukha*), (3) to regard what lacks self (*anātman*) as having self (*ātman*), (4) to regard what is impure (*aśubha*) as pure (*śubha*). In later Mahayana texts, beginning with the *Nirvāṇa Sūtra*, these very same qualities—permanence, bliss, selfhood, and purity—are enumerated as *positive* attributes of Nirvana! These are the Four Qualities enumerated by Tsung-mi in the passage cited by Kaneyoshi; see chapter 2, note 69. Nevertheless, the net effect of the teachings has not changed: it is delusion to attribute these qualities to an entity that exists within the cycle of samsara.

[44] Thus taking *dharma* to mean "the Law," rather than "phenomenal entity." There is another possible interpretation, however: "all things in the world abide in a fixed order, which itself is permanent."

that do not reflect. *The Awakening of Faith* calls it "the sea of the dharma-nature's Suchness which is a store of immeasurable qualities."[45]

We have returned to the conventional view, that the winds of ignorance are the immediate cause of the arising of phenomena. But rather than dwelling on the ontological relationship between waves and water, Fatsang emphasizes the reflective quality of the ocean's surface. The tranquil mind is able to reflect all objects "together"; that is, without attachment or aversion to any particular forms. The simile of the mind as a mirror occurs frequently in Chinese Buddhism, particularly in Ch'an texts, where the nature of mind and its functions are exhaustively treated through such analogies.

Figure 4-7 is a depiction of the Circle of Abiding. Zenchiku's original exhibits only one short line, but I believe it represents a continuous pulsation: the line "appears and disappears, like thoughts in the mind," as Zenchiku remarks in the *Kichū*. To emphasize that "the myriad dharmas" appear here, several individual lines have been depicted.

This examination of Shigyoku's remarks on the first three circles reveals his ingenious vision of the rokurin ichiro categories. His opening remarks enable one to see the six circles as a totality: six discrete stages, the Four Characteristics bracketed by the two empty circles, together representing a complete process. But when one looks at each circle individually, this linear progression collapses. From up close, each circle encompasses the entire system, each illustrating the totality of the absolute and relative planes from a different perspective. The jurin represents the potentiality and completeness of the Absolute; the shurin demonstrates the arising of phenomena on the ground of Suchness; and the jūrin demonstrates how the tranquilly abiding mind embraces all phenomena equally like a reflecting mirror. Each circle is complete in itself, a functioning soteriological paradigm. The six circles are like the different facets of a jewel, each reflecting all others and the totality itself. This is the One in All, All in One, All in All doctrine of Hua-yen par excellence. At the same time, this initial group of three circles is an analogue for the tripartite doctrine of Suchness (jurin as creative Suchness) Following (shurin—locus of origination) Conditions (jūrin—dharmas abiding peacefully).

THE CIRCLE OF FORMS: THE REALM OF CONSCIOUSNESS-ONLY

At the end of the Circle of Abiding section, an interesting shift in diction occurred. The term *banpō* (myriad dharmas), which first appeared in

---

[45] *T* 1876.45.637b, trans. Buswell, *Chinul*, 215.

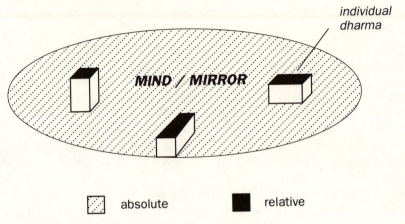

FIG. 4-7. Abiding in the Dharma Position

Shigyoku's introduction and was repeated at the beginning of the section, suddenly shifted to *banshō* (myriad images) in the Fa-tsang passage. *Banpō* is a Sino-Buddhist term that emphasizes certain uniform structural aspects of all phenomena: each is a dharma, an entity that exhibits the set characteristics of dependent origination, impermanence, and so on. In contrast, *banshō* is a native Chinese expression that alludes to the infinite variety of appearance among the things of this world. In a sense, *banpō* emphasizes the essential sameness of all phenomena, whereas *banshō* highlights their differences. And so this shift in language within the jūrin section foreshadows a transition from discourse on the structural relationship between the absolute and phenomenal aspects of reality in the first three circles, to the representation of diversity within the world of phenomenal characteristics in the Circle of Forms.

Here in the zōrin section one sees a recurrence of the reflected images mentioned in the previous Fa-tsang passage. However, now the circular form no longer represents a mirror: it functions as the One Mind that itself "transforms" into the myriad images of the phenomenal plane. Shigyoku writes, "Grasses, trees, and domains all are transformations of 'consciousness-only': the One Mind transforms, and all things are manifest."

Here Shigyoku has introduced terminology from the Yogācāra tradition of Mahayana thought. Derived from Vasubandhu's famous "Consciousness-Only Treatise," the term *wei-shih* (S. *vijñaptimātra*, J. *yuishiki*) is an alternative designation for the Fa-hsiang School founded by Hsüan-tsang (596–664), the most enduring Yogācāra school in China. It survives in Japan as the Hossō Sect, headquartered at Kōfuku-ji in Nara.

Yogācāra doctrine maintains that all perceived reality is actually the fruition of seeds (*bīja*) that have been planted by past experience in the *ālaya-vijñāna*, a "storehouse consciousness" in some sense analogous to the unconscious. These seeds are stored over a period of many lives; as each matures it generates a karmic effect upon the ideating consciousness, the *manas*. Enlightenment is achieved when the pure seeds planted by Buddhist teachings eventually cause all the tainted seeds to be purified, and the *manas* experiences *prajñā*, the wisdom that transcends dualistic consciousness. Yogācāra is generally characterized as an idealist philosophy, in the sense that it considers all perceived reality to be a projection of the mind, generated by prior conditions.

The *ālaya-vijñāna* is usually discussed in terms of the functioning of the individual mind. Each human being maintains a discrete area of "memory" within a larger "data bank" of reality. However, Hua-yen thought does not generally treat "mind" as the individuated human mind. As discussed earlier, its focus is speculation on the pseudo-ontological entity of One Mind, in contrast to the analysis of psychological function found in many earlier schools. Here Shigyoku borrows the term *tenpen* (S. *parināma*) from the Yogācāra—where it usually represents the transformation of latent mental forms into the projection of external reality[46]—and designates it as a function of the One Mind, as in the sentence quoted above: "Since grasses, trees and domains are all manifestations of 'consciousness only,' the One Mind transforms, and all things (*banshō*) are manifest."

Thus, through this model of transformation, the absolute plane has vanished from our awareness. The previous three circles all symbolize configurations that in some sense represent both the absolute and relative aspects of existence, but here only the myriad forms of the phenomenal realm, distinct and luminous, are present. This new perspective is diagramed as in figure 4-8. The underlying plane of One Mind is represented only in outline; it has transformed into the upper circle.

The characterization of the Circle of Forms as "change," the third of the Four Characteristics, requires little comment. In this context it means "differentiation," in the sense that the One Mind appears as individually differentiated forms. As was the case with Shigyoku's previous applications of the Four Characteristics, this is a novel but expressive use of the traditional term.

The passage Shigyoku attributes to the *Avataṃsaka Sūtra* ("The essential nature of the Dharmadhātu makes no distinctions; the myriad images of all

---

[46] The mechanism by which the eight consciousnesses of Yogācāra—the *ālaya*, the *manas*, the *mano* (*vijñāna*) that organizes sensory input, and the five senses—interact is termed the "threefold transformation." See *SBCP*, 371 ff.

It should be noted that within the Hua-yen School, *The Awakening of Faith* was valued in part because it connects the *ālaya-vijñāna* with Suchness, in contrast to conventional Yogācāra doctrine.

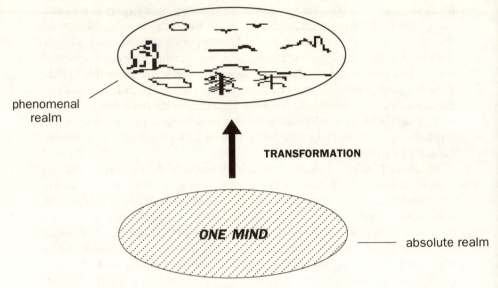

FIG. 4-8. Realm of Consciousness-Only

existence are none other than the Buddha's body") is not to be found in that text. This is not surprising; such Sinitic expressions as *shinra banshō* (C. *sen-luo wan-hsiang*, the myriad images of all existence) are more likely drawn from a Chinese commentary. In any case, the passage expresses the perfect nonduality of the absolute and the relative. This is not simply because they are functionally interrelated in a yin–yang configuration, nor because each is logically implicit in the other. The forms of the world, *as is*, are the body of the Buddha. This radical affirmation of the phenomenal world is a distinguishing feature of East Asian Buddhism, expressed in many forms. Here, that affirmation is based on a theory of *transformation*.

The nature of this transformation can be explained by further exploring the metaphor of the mirror. In the case of the Circle of Abiding, the emphasis is on the reflecting surface of the mirror (the placid ocean). The images are subordinate. In the Circle of Forms, however, attention is shifted to the reflected images themselves, to the degree that all awareness of the mind's existence disappears. This distinction can be experienced easily in symbolic form by gazing at an actual mirror. If the eyes are focused at the mirror's plane, the images it reflects will be blurred. When one refocuses on the reflected images, the physical surface of the mirror— demarcated by a scratch or other imperfection—cannot be seen. In the first instance, one is aware of both planes simultaneously, as in the Circle of Abiding where both noumenon and phenomenon are present. Only blurry outlines of the reflected objects are visible, however, reminiscent of the emphasis on formal structure of dharmas in the third circle. After re-focusing, the mirror effectively disappears, "transformed" into phenom-enal reality. Nevertheless, the very existence of these clear images depends upon the invisible functioning of the underlying mind/mirror.

Incidentally, this notion of the forms of creation as reflected images (zō) is implicit in Zenchiku's original term zōrin; an alternate translation might be "Circle of Images."

THE CIRCLE OF BREAKING: HUMAN DESIRE
AS THE BUDDHA REALM

As the stage of cessation, the fifth circle, the Circle of Breaking, provides the anticipated disintegration of phenomenal existence. This is fore-shadowed by the impending presence of the formless Circle of Emptiness; the process of birth-and-death must cease to enable entry into Nirvana.

Within Shigyoku's commentary, the character ha (to break) appears only in the final quoted passage, from The Awakening of Faith: "Because one's wisdom is pure and clear, he breaks through the compound con-sciousness, puts an end to the deluded mind of successive forms, and manifests the Dharmakāya." This "deluded mind" is the web of interde-pendent phenomena perceived as a coherent, seamless, external reality. It can be considered a kind of mental motion picture, projected from the unconscious. While appearing real, it is actually synthesized from a rapid succession of images created by karmic residue—sense impressions and ideations of the past and present. One must break through this harmo-nious but deluded picture.

The previous paradigms introduced by Shigyoku suggest that the at-tainment of enlightenment entails the onset of tranquility. Within the Awakening of Faith ocean metaphor, the wave patterns of deluded form vanish when the violent winds of ignorance abate; in dōsei ichigen, en-lightenment is the process of sei itself. But here, the process of enlighten-ment is paradoxically described as the violent disruption of a harmonious process. To invoke the mirror metaphor of the previous section, the invis-ible mirror that underlies the myriad images of the zōrin must be shattered: both mind and its objects must drop away.

In a sense, the harin represents the reemergence of the classic Buddhist attitude toward the realm of conventional experience. It is an illusion that must be dismantled. While the previous zōrin functions primarily as a paradigm which at least provisionally affirms the phenomenal world, as explained above, it also provides a symbolic equivalent for the realm of samsara. Therefore the zōrin-harin progression (and its final result, the

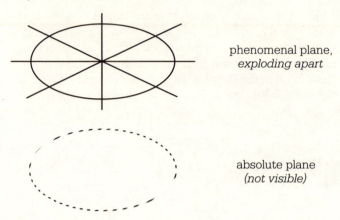

phenomenal plane,
exploding apart

absolute plane
(not visible)

FIG. 4-9. Breaking the "Mind of Successive Forms"

kūrin) provide an excellent representation of the ruten genmetsu process as a whole, as suggested by figure 4-4.[47]

Figure 4-9, a revision of Zenchiku's original harin diagram, illustrates how the shattering of the phenomenal world reveals the underlying absolute plane.

One important feature of Shigyoku's harin commentary is his emphasis on mental attitudes, in contrast to the external forms of the previous circle. For example, he states that within the harin, "even worldly desires (*bonnō*) appear as bodhi"; further on in the quotation from "the Great Master of T'ien-t'ai," he records "Vairocana's body and domain do not surpass a single thought (*ichinen*) of the ordinary man." The use of the term *ichinen*, drawn from a Tendai source, immediately recalls the Tendai doctrine of *ichinen sanzen* (C. *i-nien san-ch'ien*; three thousand worlds in a single thought), an ingenious symbolic representation of mental interdependence.[48]

According to this teaching, a sentient being dwelling in any of the ten realms of existence[49]—from Buddhas and bodhisattvas down through

[47] Several Japanese commentators have voiced reservations about Shigyoku's use of the term *metsu* to describe Zeami's ran'i, the major performance concept represented by the harin, on the grounds that the kūrin would be more appropriate. See Itō, *Komparu Zenchiku no kenkyū*, 156–57. However, Shigyoku uses the term to imply the shattering of deluded consciousness, rather than a final extinction into Nirvana. Furthermore, disintegration is surely a component of ran'i.

[48] The term *ichinen sanzen* itself is not used in Shigyoku's text; however, it does appear in Zenchiku's *Yūgen sanrin*, in conjunction with the same citation from "the Great Master of T'ien-t'ai." *KKSS*, 264.

[49] The ten realms of existence are the realms of buddhas, bodhisattvas, *pratyekabuddha* (those who have awakened to the nature of conditioned origination), *śrāvaka* ("hearers" of the Dharma), devas, asuras, human beings, animals, hungry ghosts, and hell-dwellers.

human beings, animals, and hell-dwellers—actually resides within each of the ten. This is often described in psychological terms: for example, when human beings are greedy, they manifest their animal nature; when they act out of selfless compassion, they are instantaneously "reborn" in the bodhisattva realm. Since each of the ten is unified with ten realms, this yields a product of one hundred. This is again multiplied by ten because each exhibits Ten Aspects of existence: form, nature, substance, force, action, condition, effect, reward, cause, and ultimate state.[50] The final factor of three represents three separate divisions of each of these thousand worlds: the living being, his five skandhas, and the space he occupies. Through the functioning of dependent origination, when "one thought" arises, it simultaneously embraces this macrocosm of the "three thousand worlds."

Historically, this doctrine predates the Hua-yen categorization of "the interpenetration of all phenomena" (C. *shih-shih wu-ai*, J. *jiji muge*),[51] which it resembles in some respects. Here I simply wish to emphasize the most obvious distinction: the Tendai doctrine addresses the nature of [human] thought, rather than the ontological categories of "principle" and "phenomena." Although decidedly metaphysical in its implications, the psychological foundation of the *ichinen sanzen* doctrine echoes the experiential emphasis of traditional Buddhist meditation and philosophy. It begins with the everyday, every-instant experience of every person—a random thought, a daydream, a flash of anger. And that very thought is

---

[50] The translations for the terminology used here are from Kenneth K. S. Ch'en, *Buddhism in China* (Princeton: Princeton University Press, 1964), 311–12n.

[51] The last of the four views of the Dharmadhātu (J. *shihokkai*), perhaps the most central of all Hua-yen teachings. These may be summarized as follows:

1. The Dharmadhātu of Phenomena (J. *ji hokkai*). This is the conventional view of reality, where phenomena are accepted as they appear to the senses, as independent existences. When viewing the "ocean" of the Dharmādhatu from this perspective, one sees only waves that appear as discrete forms.

2. The Dharmadhātu of Principle (J. *ri hokkai*). This is reality perceived as a formless Absolute, as Emptiness. The ocean is perceived only as an undifferentiated mass of water.

3. The Dharmadhātu of the Noninterference of Phenomena and Principle (J. *riji muge hokkai*). Here it is understood that water assumes shapes to form waves, yet its identity as water is not lost. Conversely, the waves are understood to be constituted of water. Thus the total interpenetration of the absolute and relative—noumenon and phenomenon, principle and facts, Suchness and ignorance—is realized.

4. The Dharmadhātu of the Noninterference among Phenomena (J. *jiji muge hokkai*). This is the realization that all phenomena are mutually interpenetrating, functioning as a harmonious whole without losing their individual identities. One perceives the ocean as patterns of infinitely overlapping and mutually informing waves.

This is the Hua-yen paradigm most widely implemented to illustrate various aspects of the absolute/relative relationship. Shigyoku, however, does not even allude to it, probably because its categories are not well suited to the six-circle structure.

instantaneously interfused with all worlds, including the highest realm of an enlightened Buddha. As quoted by Shigyoku, "Vairocana's body and domain do not surpass a single thought of the ordinary man."

In the zōrin, the function of the circle motif was seen to shift from a symbolic representation of the Absolute, as found in the first three circles, to an expression of the completeness and harmony of the phenomenal realm. It is this harmony, perhaps even complacency, that is shattered in the harin. The resulting dissolution is not merely the slow disintegration which occurs at the end of a biological life cycle; rather, it is precipitated by a strong force, depicted by the eight lines that emanate from the center of Zenchiku's diagram. From the perspective of Shigyoku's commentary, this force is the mental energy of one thought, breaking through its illusory shell of self-identity to penetrate the three thousand worlds.[52]

In a more general sense, the power of the Circle of Breaking is clearly related to the theme of strong emotional energy, as represented by the term bonnō ("even worldly desires appear as bodhi"). Of the six circles, only the harin alludes to the binding forces of deeply seated human attachment—the realms of desire, greed, and hatred. In traditional Buddhist practice, these passions must be extinguished, or allowed to cool of themselves. However, in certain Mahayana schools—most notably those influenced by tantrism—the purifying function of strong emotion is keenly observed and utilized. This is forcefully expressed in the iconography of the esoteric sects, where beatific bodhisattvas instantaneously transform into wrathful deities, representative of the cleansing power of fire to consume all attachment.

This paradoxical relationship between human desire and spiritual attainment, often expressed in terms of Mādhyāmika-derived radical nondualism, is a major theme of Zenchiku's age. It is at the heart of such noh plays as Eguchi, Sotoba Komachi, and Yamamba. Its very personification is the great Zen master Ikkyū, whose famous love poetry emits sparks of erotic passion and enlightened wisdom. It is worth noting that Ikkyū is celebrated as "the priest who violates the precepts" (hakai no bōzu)[53]—a connotation of the graph ha perhaps relevant to the harin.

[52] Zenchiku, on the other hand, identifies this force as the power of inner tranquility of the master actor. In the Hichū (Bunshō bon) he writes that the destructive power of the harin "arises from the tranquil heart that functions harmoniously. When a tranquil nature is temporarily rough, it is like a golden wave on the Nature Sea. [In contrast,] a rough nature that is temporarily quiet only calms down a little. It is like a tiger lying down." KKSS, 257.

Note this new implementation of the "golden wave" motif that appeared in Shigyoku's shurin analysis, and also in Zenchiku's own Kabu zuinōki (KKSS, 138).

[53] For a discussion of Ikkyū's infamous behavior and its relation to Zenchiku's aesthetics, see Haga, Higashiyama bunka, 597 ff.

THE CIRCLE OF EMPTINESS: FREE AT LAST

Shigyoku's remarks on the Circle of Emptiness require little comment. This final stage is not an abstract principle such as the symbolic One Source of delusion and enlightenment represented by the Circle of Longevity. Rather, it is Emptiness experienced directly, as all mental obscurations drop away. In terms of the previous harin diagram, the upper plane of phenomenal reality has disintegrated, and the underlying empty circle reappears. This is the final extinction of Nirvana, and yet it is also a new beginning, as a new set of six circles appears.

ONE DEWDROP: GLINT OF SWORD

For Zenchiku, the ichiro symbolizes an underlying "spirit" (seishin) that connects the six circles.[54] But how can the ichiro be implemented as an explicitly Buddhist symbol?

In fact, the Buddhist tradition utilizes dew as a symbol in many ways. It is most familiar to students of Japanese poetry as an emblem of the evanescence of life. In the nomenclature of esoteric Buddhism it is used to represent amṛta, the ambrosia-like substance that is the essence of prajñā, or transcendent wisdom. In meditation practice, this is often visualized as a thick, white liquid secreted from a buddha seated on the adept's head. It slowly enters his body through the "Brahma opening" at the crown, purifying defilements and bestowing wisdom. Also, in the iconography of Japanese Buddhist sculpture, this "sweet dew" (kanro) fills the flower vase held in the left hand of the Eleven-Headed Kannon. The specific image of a single dewdrop is reminiscent of the bindu, a single "point" which, in Shingon doctrine, symbolizes the final consonant м, and thus the realm of ultimate Emptiness.[55] More generally, the bindu is a white drop of amṛta that is visualized at different locations within the body. Like a seed, or perhaps a drop of semen, it is cultivated through yogic practices to generate wisdom.

For Shigyoku, too, the dewdrop symbolizes prajñā. But he chooses to represent it with another image of potency traditionally associated with transcendental wisdom: the sword. The wisdom sword of Mañjuśrī and the blade of Acalanātha that cuts off ignorance at its root are wielded to

[54] See the Kichū translation in chapter 2.
[55] See chapter 2, note 12.

"clear away the six gates" of the six circles, lest any reader become attached to these provisional, abstract symbols. Here the profound mistrust of verbal description and conceptualization, found in most forms of Mahayana Buddhism and so prominent in Zen, reasserts itself. For Shigyoku, the glint of this One Blade (*ikken*) is his final symbol for the realm of the inexpressible, the razor's edge between form and no-form where the enlightened mind freely enters. Zenchiku himself adopted the term *ikken* as a synonym for the One Dewdrop, and an upright sword, drawn in the formal iconographic style of esoteric Buddhist painting, is its graphic representation in all of the rokurin ichiro manuscripts.

There is an interesting postscript to Shigyoku's use of the ichiro symbolism. A phrase meaning "one dewdrop" (written *itteki no tsuyu*, however) appears prominently in his own *Gokyōshō kenmon*. He quotes a fragment of a poem by the Kegon priest Zenni (d. 1325), who studied under Gyōnen: "[The doctrine of] stained yet not stained is [represented in the poem of] the third elder of this cloister, Zenni Daitoku, 'The white dew . . . ,' etc. The one drop of dew is the One Mind. The red [flowers] are sentient beings; the whiteness is buddha[hood]. The essence, which is white, appears to be entirely red."[56] Unfortunately, it is impossible to understand this passage completely without the full text of the poem. Takamine Ryōshū points to this fragment as an illustration of the mutual identity of the Three Natures as expounded in Kegon: the dependent nature of One Mind, the perfect nature of buddhahood, and the disoriented nature of sentient beings are all present within a single thought.[57] At the very least, it indicates that within the Kegon tradition at Tōdai-ji, the image of "one drop of dew" was associated with the concept of One Mind, nondually identified with the stained redness of sentient beings and the perfect whiteness of buddhahood. The image of white dew resting on red blossoms also recalls that the character *rin*, and thus the circle symbol itself, can be used as a counter for flowers; thus, on one level, the rokurin represent six varieties of Zeami's hana.[58] It is tempting to hypothesize an influence upon Zenchiku's conception of the ichiro, but the evidence is insufficient.

[56] In *kan* 2.

[57] Takamine, *Kegon shisō shi*, 446. The Three Natures are *etashō*, which represents the dependent nature of all existents; *enjōshō*, their perfect nature, the incipent cause of buddhahood; and *hengeshō*, their disoriented nature, which results in the delusion of sentient beings.

[58] One can see this conception of the six circles as flowers, covered by the dew of the ichiro, in the following poem by Zenchiku, appended to the Hachiemon manuscript of the *Kichū* (*KKSS*, 221): "On the heart of the Six Circles— Jewels form / on ephemeral leaves and grasses: / when the blossoms fall, / these return to their fundamental state, / the white dew below."

CONCLUDING THOUGHTS

The above analysis treats Shigyoku's argument step by step. Yet his commentary is not merely a dry explication of static meanings; it embodies a dynamic of four succeeding views of Zenchiku's symbolic construct. In the first view, the circles are divided into two groups of three, representing the two patterns of Suchness-Following-Conditions and Samsara-and-Its-Extinction, respectively. These correspond in a general sense to the centrifugal and centripetal categories defined in the previous chapter. The entire six-circle sequence is then immediately reconfigured as a continuous cycle, divided 1–4–1: a phenomenal entity arises from the ground of Emptiness, and eventually returns. From this second, distant perspective, the first and sixth circles represent the absolute, the middle four, the relative; these two levels are functionally codependent. Natural process is perfect and complete, an expression of Mahayana nonduality. In this fashion, the law of impermanence, whereby all provisional existences must expire, becomes a metaphor for the process whereby delusion arises temporarily from a ground of original enlightenment, and inevitably returns, as in figure 4-10.

Shigyoku then zooms in for a closer view, focusing on each individual circle. The previous conception of the middle four circles as ignorance, as unreal, is negated: each in its own way is affirmed as a complete, functional paradigm of Mahayana nonduality.[59] Each circle has a relative and absolute aspect, represented in the diagrams by an upper and a lower plane. (In the last circle, these two planes are merged.) Thus, as mentioned earlier, the microcosm of each circle contains the totality of the six, embodying the Kegon notion of All in One, One in All, All in All: all existences are mutually reflecting, interrelated like the jewels of Indra's Net. At this level, not just the general pattern of natural process, but the individual forms of this world are affirmed as nondual entities. Furthermore, once each symbolic, conceptual model is established, it is demolished at the succeeding stage; the succession of discrete soteriological paradigms prevents one from becoming attached to any particular doctrine. In this fashion, the reader experiences the dynamic, ongoing negation typical of Mahayana discourse.

Shigyoku then moves still closer, negating even this level of insight. Within Zenchiku's system, the Absolute is adequately represented first by the Circle of Longevity and the Circle of Emptiness, and also by the absolute aspect of the middle four circles. These remain relativistic con-

---

[59] There is an interesting precedent in *The Awakening of Faith*, which presents each of the Four Characteristics—in reverse order—as a means to actualize enlightenment. See Hakeda, *The Awakening of Faith*, 38–40. However, the doctrines represented differ from Shigyoku's.

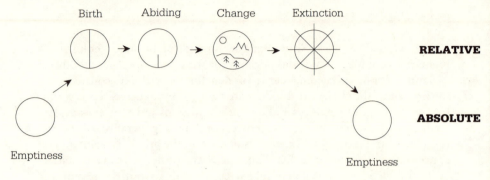

FIG. 4-10. Six Circles: Relative and Absolute

ceptions, however, insofar as they incorporate interaction with the relative plane. The ichiro, on the other hand, is a truly transcendental locus seemingly beyond the centrifugal/centripetal cycle; it is utterly beyond the conceivable. The final One Dewdrop, then, "is the ultimate, most profound stage, just as rain and dew, frost and snow vanish, collecting into a single dewdrop." At first, one sees the ichiro as absolute, the six circles as relative; the One Dewdrop appears to be a symbol of the One within the Many. But this dualistic distinction collapses once again, as the dewdrop—a delicate image of distilled essence—transforms into the forceful One Blade. So thin that it has no sides, utterly tranquil yet always in motion, this sword cuts away the deluded consciousness that attempts to grasp it as a conceptualized, static object. This process is diagrammed in figure 4-11.

In this chapter, it has been shown how Shigyoku coopts Zenchiku's symbolic system for his own ends. Largely ignoring its practical signifi-

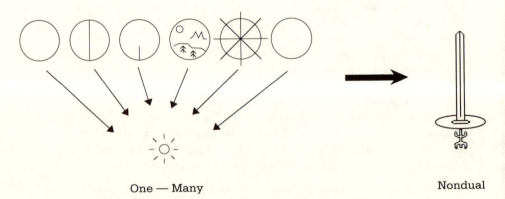

FIG. 4-11. One Dewdrop Becomes One Blade

cance for the art of sarugaku, he treats it as a text to be decoded in accord with the hermeneutics of his own tradition. Shigyoku explicates Zenchiku's group of seven symbols as an embodiment of Buddhist spiritual ideals, of Buddhism's views on the true nature of things, and as a procedural guide to personally experience these truths. Of course, the correlations between the six circles of performance and Shigyoku's characterizations provide a new level of insight into the aesthetics and training of sarugaku. His interpretations of the individual circles broaden our understanding of an underlying Buddhist dimension of the individual performance effects—jo–ha–kyū and the like—that they represent. But we must make the connections on our own.

Surprisingly, Shigyoku's analysis, taken as a whole, does not support the medieval ideal of michi, the path of artistic cultivation and growth. Unlike the Buddhist typologies mentioned in chapter 1, his six-circle sequence does not represent ever higher levels of attainment. For Shigyoku, natural process, represented by the middle four circles, is the endless cycle of birth and death, the numbing futility of samsara—hardly an auspicious vision of the maturation process. To arrive at a cogent view of artistic cultivation, Kaneyoshi's Confucian commentary must be examined.

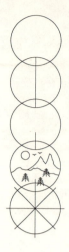

Chapter Five: Kaneyoshi's Commentary
—The Confucian Response

Iᴄʜɪᴊō Kᴀɴᴇʏᴏsʜɪ (or Kanera)[1] was reknowned as the greatest scholar of his time, indeed as "the greatest of the past five hundred years"—by his own account, more worthy of respect than Sugawara Michizane.[2] His accomplishments in many fields of learning are indeed astonishing. Whatever the circumstances surrounding the composition of Kaneyoshi's rokurin ichiro commentary, Zenchiku could not have wished for a more erudite proponent of the Confucian point of view.

ICHIJŌ KANEYOSHI AND MEDIEVAL SCHOLARSHIP

Kaneyoshi's father Ichijō Tsunetsugu was actually born the third son of Nijō Yoshimoto (1320–1388), the illustrious poet who had tutored the young Zeami (ironically, Tsunetsugu's mother was descended from the Sugawara). However, the head of the Ichijō line of the Fujiwara clan, Tsunemichi, was without an heir, and so Tsuneyoshi was adopted to succeed him.

[1] Although the reading "Kanera" appears more frequently in Western accounts, and indeed in many older Japanese sources, recently a clear preference for "Kaneyoshi" has emerged. Steven Carter, who is preparing a biography of Kaneyoshi (and who now prefers that reading), has said that "Kanera" first became prevalent in the renga tradition.

[2] Sugawara Michizane (845–903), the great scholar enshrined at the Kitano Shrine, now revered as a deity of the literary arts. His portrait, as Tenjin, was hung at renga gatherings. Kaneyoshi is said once to have angrily torn down the image above his head, reciting three ways in which he surpassed Michizane's accomplishments: he had risen to a higher office at court, was of a better family, and was more knowledgeable because he lived in a later age when there were more Chinese texts to study! Nagashima Fukutarō, *Ichijō Kanera* (Tokyo: Yoshikawa kōbunkan, 1950), 97–98. The following account of Kaneyoshi's life is based upon this volume; Fukui Kyūzō, *Ichijō Kanera* (Tokyo: Kōseikaku, 1943), Kokumin seishin bunka kenkyūjo, ed., *Nihon shoki sanso* (Tokyo: Meguro shoten, 1935), i–xii; Wajima Yoshio, *Chūsei no jugaku* (Tokyo: Yoshikawa kōbunkan, 1965), 157–62; and Fukui Kyūzō, *Ichijō Kanera* (Tokyo: Kōseikaku, 1943).

Kaneyoshi—born in 1402, when his father was forty-five and serving as regent (*kanpaku*)—actually was not the eldest son, but he became the offical heir when his elder half-brother Tsunesuke took Buddhist vows at a time of serious illness. Kaneyoshi himself was promoted to the office of regent in 1447 at age forty-six, after a long dispute with his political rival Konoe Fusatsugu. He ceded the position to his eldest son Norifusa in 1453 but was reappointed in 1467 and served until 1470.

Kaneyoshi's four younger brothers also became Buddhist priests. Of greatest interest to us, however, is his half-brother Ikkyō (or Ikkei) Unshō (1386–1463), a Zen priest who served as abbot at Tōfuku-ji and Nanzen-ji. He studied the teachings of Sung Neo-Confucianism under Giyō (or Kiyō) Hōshū (1363–1424), a priest of the Rinzai Sect and the foremost scholar of Sung learning of his time.[3] It is recorded that through Giyō, Kaneyoshi was exposed to the writings of Chu Hsi, including his commentaries on the *I ching*—an experience that had a strong influence on his subsequent literary activity. For example, Kaneyoshi wrote extensively on the *Tahsüeh*, designated by Chu Hsi as one of the Four Books, and he frequently cites Chu in the *Nihon shoki sanso* (ca. 1472), his greatest achievement of Shinto scholarship. This work, and its relationship to his rokurin ichiro commentary, will be discussed in chapter 7.

Kaneyoshi was the author of more than ten works on ancient court practices and customs, a fact indicative of his fundamental conservatism. His library, with vast holdings estimated at more than 35,000 volumes,[4] was destroyed by fire during the Ōnin Wars, and many of his papers were lost, including the manuscript for an imperial waka anthology he had secretly been commissioned to compile, to be called the *Shingyokushū*. After this misfortune he fled to Nara in 1468, living with his son Jinson (1430–1508), who had become an influential cleric, the superintendent of Kōfuku-ji, residing at the Daijō-in.[5] Kaneyoshi spent ten years in the Nara region, lecturing on the classics of Japanese literature and writing steadily. Among his best-known works from this period is the *Kachō yozei* (1472), a commentary on the *Genji monogatari* that promotes the Heian classic as a treasury of waka.

Kaneyoshi finally returned to the capital in 1477, reportedly at the in-

---

[3] Giyō was reportedly an acquaintance of Zeami, and Nishi Kazuyoshi suggests he is responsible for Zeami's extensive allusion to the Chinese classics in *Shūgaku shūdō fūken* and *Goi*. Nishi Kazuyoshi, *Zeami: hito to geijutsu* (Tokyo: Ōbaisha, 1985), 69–73. Giyō was probably the first in Japan to lecture on Chu Hsi's commentaries on the Four Books.

[4] As estimated by Motoori Norinaga. Nagashima, *Ichijō Kanera*, 96.

[5] The diary of Jinson, the *Daijōin jisha zōjiki*, is considered one of the most important historical sources of the age. It records Zenchiku's participation at a renga session in 1457 at the residence of Keikaku, former abbot of the Daijō-in. It was Keikaku who administered Buddhist precepts to Kaneyoshi in 1473. Itō, *Komparu Zenchiku no kenkyū*, 25, and Nagashima, *Ichijō Kanera*, 55.

sistence of the shogun Yoshimasa's wife Hino Tomiko, with the understanding that the Ichijō house would be restored to its former status. She became a frequent companion and later engaged him as a tutor for her son, the young shogun Yoshihisa. Kaneyoshi was in demand in the capital as an authority on court literature and also the Chinese classics; for example, he lectured on the *Genji* for the emperor Go-Tsuchimikado in 1478 or thereabouts, and he was often asked to expound on the writings of Mencius, perhaps for the political wisdom contained therein. Kaneyoshi was respected both by the nobility and the warrior class; it is recorded that he once lectured on the *Genji* to these two groups on successive days.

Perhaps sensing the legacy of Yoshimoto, Kaneyoshi was a central figure in renga circles for decades; for example, he wrote an important revision of Yoshimoto's rules of composition, *Shinshiki kon'an*, in 1452[6] and the preface to Sōgi's *Chikurinshō* in 1476. He served as teacher to a whole generation of waka and renga poets, and refereed at many important poetry gatherings.

Kaneyoshi's eldest son Norifusa moved to Tosa in Shikoku, and it was decided that Fuyuyoshi (or Fuyura)—a son born in 1464—would be raised by Norifusa and become the official family heir. In fact Kaneyoshi outlived Norifusa by one year, dying in 1481 at the age of eighty. Fuyuyoshi went on to a successful scholarly career, while all of Kaneyoshi's remaining sons had entered the priesthood.

Kaneyoshi was an assiduous, prolific scholar, evidently supremely confident in his own talent. At first glance, however, his writings generate little excitement: the poetry seems unexceptional, and the majority of his works are plodding (and sometimes excessively ornate) commentaries on earlier texts. But Kaneyoshi is best viewed as a pioneer whose critical perspective on the native literary tradition laid the groundwork for the more influential (and ideological) scholarship of Motoori Norinaga and the other Nativist figures of the Tokugawa period. Without his efforts, which helped to disseminate the classics of court literature to the warrior elite, many of these works might have been buried in the cultural and social upheaval of the sixteenth century. Kaneyoshi is described by Steven Carter as the "last courtier"—the last important figure of the *kuge* who openly promoted the courtly values of an aristocratic culture that was vanishing before his own eyes.

Kaneyoshi's accomplishments in "Chinese learning" are equally significant. The study of the Chinese classics had been the province of the *kuge* since the Nara period, but Kaneyoshi was among the first of the aristocratic scholars radically to recast his views of the classics in accord with the

---

[6] See Steven D. Carter, *The Road to Komatsubara* (Cambridge: Council on East Asian Studies, Harvard University, 1987), 35–37.

new teachings of the Sung masters. Many historians rigidly distinguish the "heterodox" Neo-Confucian scholarship undertaken by the Zen priests of the Muromachi period—Kaneyoshi's initial contact—from the "pure" Chu Hsi school of the Tokugawa period. However, this view is too simplistic. Such scholar-monks as Giyō considered themselves transmitters of Sung culture in a general sense, rather than narrow partisans of Zen only. Their enthusiasm for Ch'eng I and Chu Hsi is unmistakable. Furthermore, there are important links between the two groups. For example, Kaneyoshi's son Norifusa established a branch of the Ichijō family in Tosa, a locale that later became an important center for Tokugawa Confucian studies. And the purity of orthodox Tokugawa Neo-Confucianism itself has been called into question by recent critics.[7]

As with Shigyoku, the exact circumstances that prompted the writing of Kaneyoshi's rokurin ichiro commentary are unknown. There is an almost twelve-year gap between the completion of Shigyoku's text and the appearance of the final *Ki* document in 1455, the date of Nankō Sōgen's postscript. Itō Masayoshi speculates that Kaneyoshi was not asked to write his commentary until 1454 or 1455, when he encountered Zenchiku and discussed the matter.[8] One other document written by Kaneyoshi contains mention of Zenchiku: the *Sarugaku kōshō ki*, dated Bunmei 3 (1471).[9] Written after Zenchiku's death, it praises his performing skills and records that, at his request, Kaneyoshi wrote a play entitled *Sagoromo*. It also mentions a friendly encounter with Zenchiku's son Sōin, a relationship that seems to have continued for some years.[10]

KANEYOSHI'S COMMENTARY

The concluding section of Shigyoku's commentary presents a variety of religious symbols and literary anecdotes that expound the soteriological value of song and dance. Similarly, Kaneyoshi's text begins with a series of quotes from the Confucian classics that praise the efficacy of music for moral cultivation. The views of the two men on this topic will be examined in chapter 7.

The foundation of Kaneyoshi's Confucian interpretation of the rokurin ichiro system, however, is his analysis of Ch'ien (The Creative), the first hexagram of the *I ching*. At first glance, the categories set forth do not seem

---

[7] For example, see Wm. Theodore DeBary's introduction to Wm. Theodore DeBary and Irene Bloom, eds., *Principle and Practicality* (New York: Columbia University Press, 1979), 31.

[8] Itō, *Komparu Zenchiku no kenkyū*, 23–24.

[9] This work is reproduced in *KKSS*, 567–71.

[10] See Itō, *Komparu Zenchiku no kenkyū*, 25.

to mesh well with the rokurin ichiro structure. For example, there are only five cognate principles available—Ch'ien itself and each of its Four Qualities (C. *ssu-te*, J. *shitoku*). After apportioning these, Kaneyoshi introduces the Neo-Confucian metaphysical categories of the Great Ultimate (C. *t'ai-chi*, J. *taikyoku*) and the Ultimate of Nonbeing (C. *wu-chi*, J. *mukyoku*) to account for the concluding Circle of Emptiness and One Dewdrop. In such a scheme, the sense of the sixth circle representing a cyclical return to the first is lost. Nevertheless, Kaneyoshi's categorizations furnish a host of illuminating insights into new aspects of Zenchiku's system.

The immediate inspiration for Kaneyoshi's selection of Ch'ien and the Four Qualities is Shigyoku's use of the Four Characteristics typology to categorize the middle four circles. Kaneyoshi cites as his authority a Buddhist source, a commentary to the *Perfect Enlightenment Sutra* written by the fifth Hua-yen patriarch, Tsung-mi.[11] As noted earlier,[12] Tsung-mi rhetorically links the Four Qualities of Ch'ien to the Four Qualities of Nirvana, not the Four Characteristics. Nevertheless, this citation provides Kaneyoshi with a transition from a Buddhist to a Confucian context. Let us now consider in detail the nature of the Four Qualities.

THE FOUR QUALITIES OF THE CREATIVE

The early history of the *I ching* is at best obscure. Although what we call the "text" (as opposed to the *Ta chuan* or *Wen-yen chuan*, for example, which are clearly commentaries) has traditionally been treated as a monolithic entity, twentieth-century scholarship has uncovered multiple layers of various origins. According to Iulian Shchutskii, there are four basic strata:

1. The name of the hexagram
2. The Four Qualities (*ssu-te*: viz., *yüan*, *heng*, *li*, *chen*)
3. The Judgment (*kua-tzu*)
4. The lines (*yao-tzu*).[13]

Here we are concerned only with the first and second categories. The *I ching* as we know it came into existence when the system of sixty-four hexagrams and their names were established; thus, the first layer is the foundation of the text. In contrast, the second layer, comprising what we now call the Four Qualities, is a fragmentary layer. One or more of the four terms *yüan*, *heng*, *li*, and *chen* appear in only thirty-two of the sixty-

[11] See chapter 2, note 69.
[12] See chapter 4, note 43.
[13] This discussion of the Four Qualities is based on Iulian K. Shchutskii, *Researches on the I Ching* (Princeton: Princeton University Press, 1979), 132–65.

four hexagram texts. These are probably formulaic responses received in divination, remnants of an earlier system. It is likely that this system contained responses for all sixty-four hexagrams, utilizing other terms that have been lost. One indication of the differing origins of these layers is that, in most cases, the four terms are not syntactically related to the surrounding text. For example, hexagram 9: "Rearing of the small. Accomplishment (*heng*). Dense clouds from our western region."[14] In this respect these mantic formulas resemble the expressions *chi* (good fortune) and *hsiung* (misfortune), which also appear in the text and are still widely used in Chinese and Japanese divination.

Shchutskii summarizes the available archaeological and philological evidence and makes the following comments on the meanings of the four graphs *yüan*, *heng*, *li*, and *chen*:

1. *Yüan* 元. The upper two strokes represent the present-day *shang* 上 (above); the lower two function as *jen* 人 (person). Thus, it originally connotes the upper part of the body, the head. *I ching* commentators, including Chu Hsi, often provide the gloss "great" (*ta* 大), but it is best understood as impulse or initiative, in reference to the first moment of creation.

2. *Heng* 亨. Probably originally formed from the characters *kao* 高 (tall) and *jih* 日 (sun, rather than the current *liang* 了 —the filled sacrificial cup), its original meaning is "to make sacrificial offerings to the spirits on high." In a cultic context, the priest who makes the offering is understood to unite with the deity; thus the meaning "to penetrate" (*t'ung* 通, the most common gloss) or "completion." The final meaning is "development and completion" of what was undertaken by the initiative of *yüan*.

3. *Li* 利. This is a combination of the characters *ho* 合 (harmonious combination) and *tao* 刀 (knife, to divide). According to Shchutskii, the notion of two objects that are at once contiguous and yet distinct generates a meaning of determination or formation of an object's identity. The harmonious connotations extend this to "corresponding," "suitable," and finally "favorable," its general meaning in the *I ching*.

4. *Chen* 貞. Composed of the characters *pu* 卜 (to divine, to consult an oracle) and *pei* 貝 (shell), the latter said to be an abbreviation for *chih* 贄 (gift or offering). The present form of *chen* is equivalent to the character *ting* 鼎 (tripod). In the sense that the decision of an oracle was considered something correct and reliable, *chen* came to mean "steady."

The opening sentence of the *I ching* contains these four terms in succession. A basic rendition might be "Creation (*ch'ien*). Beginning, penetration, definition, stability." However, there is a natural tendency to link the individual characters syntactically. Because the pairs *yüan* and *heng* and *li*

---

[14] Adapted from Wilhelm and Baynes, trans., *The I Ching*, 40.

and *chen* appear separately in several hexagram texts,[15] it is reasonable to group these pairs and interpret the text as "Creation: great accomplishment, steadiness is favorable." Some commentators have even treated the five characters as a single syntactical unit. For example, the Wilhelm/Baynes translation reads, "The Creative works sublime success, furthering through perseverance."[16]

Whatever the original syntax of the text, later Chinese commentators began to interpret each of the individual characters as an abstract quality, each an attribute of the Creative. These came to be known as the Four Qualities of Ch'ien. This interpretation is questionable, since these four characters also appear in hexagrams 2 (with an extra character inserted), 3, 17, 19, and 25. Nevertheless, it came to dominate *I ching* scholarship. The most important text in the establishment of this tradition is the *Wen-yen chuan*, the seventh of the "Ten Wings" (*shih-i*) traditionally attributed to Confucius. This text, which contains comments on the first two hexagrams only, begins,

> Of all that is good, sublimity (*yüan*) is supreme. Succeeding (*heng*) is the coming together of all that is beautiful. Furtherance (*li*) is the agreement of all that is just. Perseverance (*chen*) is the foundation of all actions.
>
> Because the superior man embodies humaneness, he is able to govern men. Because he brings about the harmonious working together of all that is beautiful, he is able to unite them through the mores. Because he furthers all beings, he is able to bring them into harmony through justice. Because he is persevering and firm, he is able to carry out all actions.[17]

At the stage represented by the *Wen-yen*, then, each quality is experienced individually by man as an attribute of the Creative; the relationships among the four are not explored. My preferred English equivalents for the Four Qualities (as they are applied in Kaneyoshi's commentary) are initiative, flourish, advantage, and perseverance (see figure 5-1).

There exists within the very nature of the *I ching*, however, an impulse to systematize the Four Qualities even further. In its present form, the text represents a vast system of interrelated cycles of yin and yang: cosmic process and the cycles of nature are tightly interwoven. For example, individual hexagrams often represent specific points in the agricultural and astronomical year (hexagram 24—*Fu*, "Return"—represents the winter

---

[15] *Yüan* and *heng* appear in hexagrams 14, 18 and 46; *li* and *chen* appear in 26, 30, 31, 34, 58, and 62.

[16] Wilhelm, *The I Ching*, 4. Some of the frequently used English glosses for the Four Qualities are (1) *yüan*, sublimity, origination, initiative, beginning; (2) *heng*, success, flourish, development, penetration; (3) *li*, furtherance, advantage, determination, definition; (4) *chen*, perseverance, steadiness, stability.

[17] Ibid., 376.

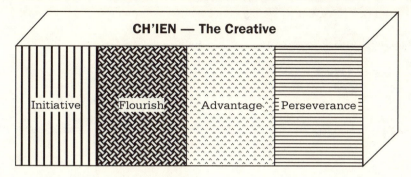

FIG. 5-1. Four Qualities of Ch'ien

solstice, etc.). The commentators of the Han dynasty correlate the eight trigrams with the eight directions of the compass.[18] There are countless examples. The leading figures in Sung thought focused much of their energies on the renewed study of the *I ching*, and thus the Four Qualities underwent a similar transformation.

Shao Yung (1011–1077), best known for his interest in numbers, is a good example. In his view of the universe, the Great Ultimate produces yin and yang, which constitute spirit (*shen*); spirit in turn generates number, number generates form, and form generates things. In particular, there is a strong emphasis on groupings of four, reflecting the categories of major and minor yin and yang in the *I ching*. For Shao, there is a correlation between the workings of Heaven, which causes things to come to completion, and the development of the human being, which results in the sage's perfection. This process is represented in his cycles of "four treasuries" (*ssu-fu*), by which the subcategories given in figure 5-2 are grouped.[19] In this fashion, the Four Qualities are correlated with the four seasons, implying a developmental progression.

Chu Hsi's views on the *I ching* are often described as a synthesis of Shao Yung's emphasis on form and image and Ch'eng I's focus on moral principle. Thus, as the Four Qualities of Ch'ien are correlated with seasonal cycles and stages of the biogenetic process, they come to represent the development of specific moral virtues of the sage. Utilizing the language of the *Wen-yen*, Chu writes in his *Chou-i pen-i*,

> "Initiative" is the onset of living things; among the qualities of heaven and earth, none is before this. Therefore, among the seasons it is spring; in man it is benevolence, the highest of all virtues. "Flourish" is the penetration of living

[18] For a discussion of the Han commentaries, see Douglass White, "Interpretations of the Central Concept of the *I Ching* during the Han, Sung, and Ming Dynasties" (Ph.D. dissertation, Harvard University, 1976).

[19] As enumerated in Birdwhistell, *Transition to Neo-Confucianism*, 134–38.

HEAVEN: FOUR SEASONS	spring	summer	autumn	winter
FOUR DIRECTIONS	east	south	west	north
MAN: FOUR CLASSICS	Book of Change	Book of History	Book of Songs	Spring and Autumn Annals
FOUR STAGES OF LIFE	birth (sheng)	growth (chang)	maturity, harvest (shou)	death, being hidden (ts'ang)
FOUR QUALITIES OF CH'IEN	initiative	flourish	advantage	perseverance

FIG. 5-2. Four Treasuries

things; when they arrive at this state, everything is beautiful and virtuous. Therefore, among the seasons it is summer; in man it is propriety. It is the coming together of all that is beautiful. "Advantage" is the achievement of living things, the harvest; every thing has its proper place, not interfering with any other. Among the seasons it is autumn; in man it is righteousness. It is harmony of the separate parts. "Perseverance" is the completion of living things. True principle is present, following in accord with each [thing's] needs. Therefore, among the seasons it is winter, in man it is wisdom. And it is the foundation of all things.[20]

The above discussion of the Four Qualities is at best a short summary of its long history. No attempt has been made to trace developments in the work of such commentators as Wang Pi, or to treat the views of the Sung Neo-Confucianists in any detail. Perhaps most important of all is the antiquity and ultimate obscurity of this terminology. The Four Qualities do not submit to facile interpretation; later commentators often seem frustrated, unable to categorize neatly or explain away these fragments of an earlier stage of Chinese civilization. Yet this very obscurity is the appeal of the Four Qualities, their poetic life, for they function as a linguistic correlative for the mystery and mythic stature of the Age of Antiquity. It is impossible for us, and for the Sung commentators as well, to understand how these words were originally used, or what power they wielded in the minds of those who used them. But they are experienced by our own minds as symbols of an idealized mode of being: the mantic. Stripped of the conventional functionality we associate with words, the Four Qualities linger in the Chinese consciousness as remnants of the numinous age of Fu

[20] *Chou i pen-i*, 1:5.

Hsi, legendary originator of the trigrams; an age in which man dwelt in intimate contact with the force of Heaven.

Kaneyoshi's implementation of the Four Qualities follows closely Chu Hsi's comments presented above. As mentioned earlier, Kaneyoshi's rationale for the utilization of these terms is the precedent of Shigyoku's Four Characteristics. The link is the temporal progression found in each: the sequence of stages in a human lifetime in the Buddhist system, and the seasonal cycle of one year, of the botanical life cycle, as portrayed in the Confucian paradigm. Once the underlying system is recognized, most of Kaneyoshi's remarks on the individual circles are self-evident. The correlations among the seasons and four of the five phases (*wu-hsing*) and five virtues (*wu-te*) are standard in the canons of yin–yang theory established in the Han dynasty. They are shown in figure 5-3. Kaneyoshi also cites the *Wen-yen* texts for three of the Four Qualities, and corresponding sections of a *Shu ching* passage that suitably illustrate the behavior of man and beast in the various seasons (see figure 5-4).

These sets of correspondences impart a sense of consistency and clarity to Kaneyoshi's commentary that is lacking in Shigyoku's remarks. As demonstrated, the Buddhist commentary constantly shifts its perspective and mode of analysis. Kaneyoshi's system, however, seems to lack the creative insight shown by Shigyoku. The latter chooses widely from different sources and schools within the Buddhist tradition, whereas Kaneyoshi latches onto a single idea (the Four Qualities) and mechanically recites all the established associations for each category. Nevertheless, a closer examination of Kaneyoshi's terminology as it applies to each circle will reveal many impressive features.

THE CIRCLE OF LONGEVITY: THE CIRCULATION OF THE CREATIVE

In utilizing Ch'ien as the cognate for Zenchiku's Circle of Longevity, Kaneyoshi sets the tone for a truly Confucian interpretation. It could be

Circle	Quality	Season	Phase	Virtue
Height	initiative	spring	wood	benevolence
Abiding	flourish	summer	fire	propriety
Forms	advantage	autumn	metal	justice
Breaking	perseverance	winter	water	wisdom

FIG. 5-3. Correspondences of the Four Qualities

Circle	Quality	Wen-yen	Shu ching
Height	initiative	Of all that is good, initiative is supreme.	People part company, birds and animals raise their young and mate.
Abiding	flourish	Development is the coming together of all that is beautiful.	—
Forms	advantage	—	Birds and animals prepare themselves for winter by growing additional fur.
Breaking	perseverance	Perseverance is the foundation of all actions	People gather together; birds and animals have thick coats.

FIG. 5-4. Literary Equivalents for the Four Qualities

argued that the Great Ultimate is a more appropriate equivalent for the Absolute that this first circle represents. Kaneyoshi, however, chooses a less abstract symbol associated directly with the power of generation. As suggested above, Ch'ien represents an earlier, less philosophical period of Chinese history, a period characterized by the worship of Heaven as an anthropomorphic deity. At this stage, the abstract concept of a formless Absolute that precedes the impersonal interaction of yin and yang forces has not yet emerged. Ch'ien embraces the most potent symbols available to this culture: the majesty of the heavens, the life-giving warmth of the sun. And despite subsequent Chinese forays into more abstract metaphysical speculation, the expressive power of Ch'ien is a constant motif in Confucian thought, reflecting a fascination with life-force, with the power and mystery of the biogenetic process. In this sense, Ch'ien is a fitting symbol for the felicitous, life-bestowing nature of the Circle of Longevity.

Kaneyoshi's remarks on the Circle of Longevity contain several elements not found elsewhere in his commentary. He writes,

The first [circle, the] Circle of Longevity, is the so-called Circle of the Creative. The wheel of Heaven revolves day and night without stopping for the interval of a single breath; the four seasons run their course, and various things are born. Is this not [due to] the power of the Creative? Thus, constant sincerity is called the Creative. The Creative is health, and health without end is the heart of the Circle of Longevity.

Here, the jurin is described as a wheel of Heaven that revolves. This is the only occasion in the Ki where this second meaning of the character rin is utilized.[21] The constant motion of the heavens—the sun, moon, and stars, as well as meteorological phenomena—are a basic symbol of change as portrayed in the *I ching*; in particular, the cycle of day and night commonly represents the alternation of yin and yang.[22] But the Creative is not simply the source of the circulating generative energy, it is the energy itself, even when manifest on earth. The essence of Ch'ien is its revolving nature, which causes things to grow and reproduce. Within this process, the two poles of yin and yang material force (*ch'i*) interact and alternate in dominance, but Ch'ien itself is the pervasive energy that keeps this process going. In this sense, it is the underlying force that propels the four seasons, which, as explained earlier, are represented by the middle four circles. This process is represented in figure 5-5.

The relationship between the revolving wheel of Heaven and the Four Qualities—that is, between the Circle of Longevity and the middle four circles—is not the substance/function (*t'i/yung*) dichotomy found in Shigyoku's dōsei ichigen paradigm. In fact, Ch'ien itself is best understood as function—a function of Heaven. In the words of Ch'eng I, "The heavens are the substantive form of Heaven; the Creative is its nature and feeling."[23] Ch'ien is the circulating function of Heaven, and each of the Four Qualities is the state it assumes in a different season. Thus, the Circle of Longevity is the *totality* of Ch'ien, and the four middle circles are its *appearance* in the four seasons. This relationship is indicated by the placement of the four middle circles on the rotating perimeter of the jurin.

Two other phrases used by Kaneyoshi emphasize the nature of Ch'ien as an ongoing process. The first is "absolute sincerity without end," echoing a famous passage in the *Chung-yung*.[24] This quality of sincerity (*ch'eng*), one of the central ideals of Neo-Confucianism, is essentially an emotional or spiritual attitude experienced by man. Yet by describing it as ceaseless, the Confucianists endowed it with cosmic attributes: it is a transcendental virtue that circulates constantly like the movement of the heavens, flowing through the human heart. Conversely, through the cultivation of sincerity man attunes himself with the workings of Heaven.[25] Similarly, the expression "health without limit," probably borrowed from Ch'eng I,[26] cosmicizes the essentially human value of health and also recalls the concept of

[21] However, Zenchiku himself later presents the circles as wheels of karma, suggesting the endless cycles of samsara. See chapter 6.

[22] For example, in the *Ta chuan*: "The firm and the yielding are images of day and night." Wilhelm, *The I Ching*, 289.

[23] For reference, see chapter 2, note 75. This also appears in Chu Hsi's *Chin-ssu lu*, the famous Neo-Confucian anthology.

[24] See chapter 2, note 74.

[25] Tu Wei-ming insists on this perspective, to guard against anthropomorphizing Heaven. Tu, *Centrality and Commonality* 2d ed. (Albany: SUNY Press, 1989), 71–74.

[26] See chapter 2, note 75.

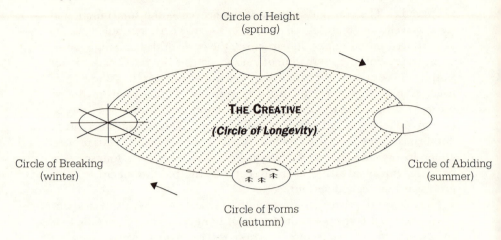

FIG. 5-5. The Circulation of the Creative

longevity. In sum, in his remarks on Ch'ien as the Circle of Longevity, Kaneyoshi has consciously emphasized the anthropocentric nature of Confucianism.

THE CIRCLE OF HEIGHT: THE PRIMACY OF INITIATIVE

Of greatest interest here is Kaneyoshi's perplexing statement, "The material force of the One Origin (*ichigen no ki*) is the beginning of the birth of all things." In a general sense, the term *ichigen* means the single essence or origin of all things. Therefore, as it stands, Kaneyoshi's sentence seems to mean that the material force (*ki*) emanating from this essence is the impulse that gives rise to all phenomena. This is a reasonable statement. In terms of the six circles, the impulse depicted in the Circle of Height would correspond to the *ki*, and the ichigen would have to be the Circle of Longevity (note that in Japanese pronunciation, this ichigen is homophonous with the "One Source" in Shigyoku's dōsei ichigen).[27]

The general topic under discussion here, however, is *yüan*, which, as one of the Four Qualities, differs considerably from ichigen (C. *i-yüan*). I think that Kaneyoshi was careless. His intended meaning emerges if the character *ichi* is dropped: "The material force of initiative (*gen no ki*) is the beginning of the birth of all things." When the text is emended in this fashion, *gen* and *ki* are in apposition, rather than in a genitive relationship, and so both refer to the Circle of Height.

But why does this term ichigen appear at all? Omote simply cites Chu

[27] See chapter 4.

Hsi's commentary on Ch'ien presented above, but it does not contain *i-yüan*, only *yüan*. I suspect that Kaneyoshi is cribbing from a different Chu Hsi passage: "Heaven and Earth have no other business except to have the mind to produce things. The *material force of one origin* (C. *i-yüan chih ch'i*, J. *ichigen no ki*) revolves and circulates without a moment of rest, doing nothing except creating the myriad things."[28]

The appeal of this passage for Kaneyoshi is the appearance of the circulation motif, utilized earlier in his characterization of Ch'ien. It is even possible that this passage inspired that conception. Kaneyoshi associates the infusion of material force with the initiating power of yüan, and so, due either to misunderstanding or to carelessness, he misreads *i-yüan*, which, as Wing-tsit Chan notes, here actually represents the Great Ultimate.[29]

In light of the emphasis on creation within Ch'ien, it is not surprising that yüan is the most highly praised of the Four Qualities. It is the initial stage at which Heaven directly infuses the earthly world with its creative life-force. In "A Treatise on Jen," Chu Hsi writes, "The moral qualities of the mind of heaven and earth are four: initiative, flourish, advantage, and perseverance. And the principle of initiative unites and controls them all. In their operation they constitute the course of the four seasons, and the vital force of spring permeates all."[30] The primacy of yüan among the Four Qualities is represented in figure 5-6.

Note that the generative force of Ch'ien is input directly into the first stage of initiative; it is then circulated to the three succeeding stages, without further interaction with Ch'ien. This implies that the biogenetic process is programmed into the initial stage, just as a seed contains the potential form of the mature plant. As the plant develops, its ration of yang-energy is gradually depleted.

Perhaps the most radical expression of this theme is found in the writings of Ch'eng I. He rejects the notion of material force returning to its source:

> When a thing disintegrates, its material force is forthwith exhausted. There is no such thing as material force returning to its source. The universe is a like a vast furnace. Even living things will be burned to the last and no more. How can material force that is already disintegrated still exist? Furthermore, what is the need of such a disintegrated material force in the creative process of the universe? It goes without saying that the force used in creation is vital and fresh.[31]

In the Chinese context, this might be interpreted as a veiled attack upon the alleged passivity of Taoists, who embrace the notion of return to a

---

[28] *SBCP*, 642–43.
[29] *SBCP*, 643.
[30] Translation modified from *SBCP*, 594.
[31] *SBCP*, 558.

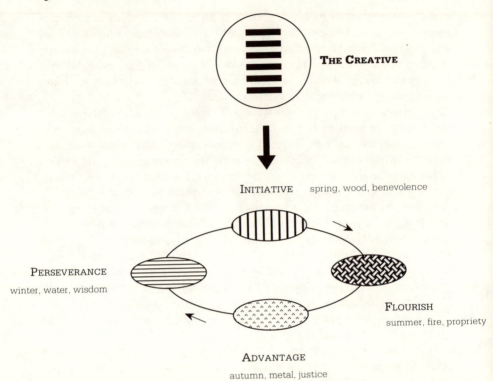

THE CREATIVE

INITIATIVE   spring, wood, benevolence

PERSEVERANCE
winter, water, wisdom

FLOURISH
summer, fire, propriety

ADVANTAGE
autumn, metal, justice

FIG. 5-6. The Primacy of Initiative

quiescent state of nonbeing, and also upon the Buddhist concept of re-incarnation. But this statement underscores the dilemma of Kaneyoshi's commentary mentioned earlier. Ch'ien is not an all-embracing symbol of the Absolute: it represents only its creative aspect, and so it is incompatible with the Circle of Emptiness. Kaneyoshi must provide a cognate for the kūrin that resolves this problem.

THE CIRCLE OF ABIDING: THE FLOURISH OF SUMMER GRASSES

The Circle of Abiding presents a challenge to the Confucian commentator. Of the six circles, only the jūrin and kūrin are named with explicitly Buddhist terms. Although not so annoying as the "nihilistic" concept of emptiness, the term "abiding" is not attractive to the Confucianist. Indeed, the original meaning of *jū* as one of the Four Characteristics—the stage of young adulthood during which one's physical appearance is stable—is antithetical to the doctrine of constant change derived from the

I ching and extolled by Neo-Confucianism. It was vigorously criticized by Ch'eng I on these grounds.[32]

Abiding as represented by Zenchiku, however, is actually a state of mental calmness, to be cultivated while observing the constant ebb and flow of phenomena. While Kaneyoshi's commentary does not explicitly treat mental attitudes of any kind, it does furnish a truly affecting objective correlative for this sense of abiding: the flourishing of summer grasses and trees, the peaceful activity of birds and animals. They come and go freely, with no sense of anxiety or impending hardship. In Japanese poetry, the swift growth of summer grasses is frequently a symbol of indiscreet passion, tinged with a Buddhist sense of delusion. But here, the uninhibited celebration of growth and vitality is freely embraced: "Flourish is the coming together of all that is beautiful." Such is the delight of the Kaneyoshi commentary. Although his remarks are predictable, the individual juxtapositions of his categories with the more elusive sequence of Zenchiku's original six circles, and with the Buddhist symbols provided by Shigyoku, generate surprising effects.

THE CIRCLE OF FORMS: FRUITS OF THE HARVEST

Kaneyoshi's characterization of the Circle of Forms is also successful in these terms. The Buddhist commentary emphasizes the unity of Mind and the diverse world of phenomena, thus offering a provisional affirmation of conventional reality. The Confucian point of view is less restrained: the quality of "advantage" (*li*) celebrates the utility and mutual benefit of the world's diverse forms. Utility, in the sense of accomplishing work or growing food, is an excessively worldly value incompatible with the spiritual goals of Buddhism. For the Buddhist, at best the forms of the world are the stuff of consciousness, and the correct understanding of consciousness is the key to liberation. But the Confucian perspective can account for the essential goodness of the natural world: here, the generative powers of Ch'ien are present in the fruit of the autumn harvest.

An equally important aspect of *li* is its meaning of "determination" or "definition." In autumn, the fruit has formed, and the component parts

[32] For example, in the following passage: "The Buddhists talk about formation, remaining in the same state, deterioration, and extinction. This indicates that they are ignorant of the Way. There are only formation and deterioration but no remaining or extinction. Take plants, for example. When they are first produced, they are already formed. As they approach the highest point of growth, they immediately begin to decay. The Buddhists think that in the life of plants, they grow until they reach maturity, remain in that state for some time, and then gradually deteriorate. But nothing in the world remains in the same state. Any day added to the life of an infant means a day spent. Since when can one stay in the same state?" SBCP, 564–65.

of the plant are differentiated; at this stage, the infinite variety of plants is fully manifest. This meaning strongly echoes Zenchiku's own vision of the Circle of Forms, the art of *monomane* that depends upon the clear mimetic representation of varying roles.

THE CIRCLE OF BREAKING: INNER STATURE

The Circle of Breaking is an inherently difficult and complex symbol created by Zenchiku. Its most obvious feature is the destruction of the circular form, which represents completeness and harmony. As seen earlier, Shigyoku's Buddhist interpretation amplifies the transcendental aspect of a psychological process in which human desire, at its moment of greatest intensity, generates a climax that shatters the conventional world of human perception. This is seen as a kind of enlightenment experience. But what is an appropriate Confucian response to the Circle of Breaking?

Kaneyoshi again ignores the mental aspect, instead relying upon his organic model of change. Rather than positing a self-destructive psychological mechanism, he depicts disintegration as the result of the natural process embodied in the three previous circles. In this context, the winter symbolism is easily understood: the forms of organic life wither and die, animals hibernate, and everything returns to a state of dormancy, awaiting the renewal of spring.

However, the assertion that "this stage is the foundation of all actions"[33] is at first confusing. While perseverance is easily understood as the foundation of all action, its correlation with winter is questionable. Kaneyoshi presents one possible interpretation: winter is a foundation in the sense that it is the transitional stage between two life cycles: "[The Circle of Breaking] is the cause of the next stage of initiative. . . . [It] expresses the quality of the foundation of perseverance which governs the continuous cycle of all things." In other words, the forms of the world circulate in a closed loop of the middle four circles, without returning to the absolute stage of the Circle of Emptiness. More specifically, firmness can be seen in the persistence of the life process, which survives the adversity of winter.

But one puzzle remains. How is one to reconcile the quality of firmness with the original name and diagram of Zenchiku's circle? It is an oxymoron—firmness that in some sense breaks or disintegrates.

The problem arises from structural differences in Zenchiku's original symbol and Kaneyoshi's interpretation. As discussed earlier, the harin is composed of two elements: the circle and the expanding contents that

---

[33] In fact, this statement is taken directly from the Chu Hsi text previously cited. By equating this stage to Zenchiku's harin, however, Kaneyoshi enters a new dimension of meaning—and difficulty—not implicit in the original Chu Hsi context.

shatter it. In the Shigyoku commentary, the symbolism of both the circle itself and its contents are consistently addressed, through the representation of such dichotomies as mind and matter, absolute and relative, and so on. But up to this point, Kaneyoshi has ignored the symbolism of the circle. In the case of the jurin, its symbolic function as a wheel was emphasized, the wheel of the Creative which revolves. But for the middle four circles, only the general meaning of their contents has been analyzed. Therefore, one appropriate reading of the firmness/breaking paradox— that it represents a firmness of character, an inner strength that shatters or transcends external form—is not expressed in Kaneyoshi's remarks. Although this idea exists implicitly in the structure of Zenchiku's original symbol, Kaneyoshi has not implemented the dichotomous structure necessary to represent it. To be consistent, "breaking" must describe an objective quality, not an inner, mental state.

The full effect of Kaneyoshi's harin interpretation is best measured by comparing it to Zenchiku's remarks. Zenchiku states that the Circle of Breaking represents the ran'i, the stage at which the aging actor performs in unorthodox styles to uncanny effect.[34] In such a context, the performer's stature as a master comes to dominate any external characteristics of his performance, like a kind of spiritual presence. This presence allows him to go beyond the formally correct styles of the Three Roles, to incorporate unorthodox tricks that would appear inelegant if performed by others. Zeami compares this art to the towering, august *sugi*. While less appealing to the casual observer than a cherry tree in bloom or the crimson leaves of a red maple, its impact is more profound, generated by inner stature rather than external beauty.

In this sense, the aspect of the harin revealed by Kaneyoshi is highly expressive. The "firmness" of the aging actor's inner stature is accompanied by a dissolution of orthodox style. Yet this is a stage where external actions are not important, because the inner emotion is so refined and deep. In the *Kichū*, written after Kaneyoshi's commentary, Zenchiku cites the famous *Analects* passage to describe this state: "At seventy I could follow my heart's desire without transgressing moral principle." This axiom from the *Analects* brings into perfect focus the contrasting Buddhist and Confucian interpretations of the Circle of Breaking. Shigyoku sees the harin as one of many soteriological paradigms available within the Buddhist repertoire: inner turmoil that shatters external convention. The Confucian model is the very opposite: superficially disruptive, inharmonious behavior that preserves, or perhaps reveals, inner tranquility.[35] This latter circumstance occurs due to the cumulative effect of chronological aging

---

[34] For a more complete discussion of Zeami's ran'i, see chapter 3.

[35] Zenchiku uses Shigyoku's golden-wave metaphor to represent this quality; see chapter 4, note 52.

and the accompanying physical deterioration. As external appearance shows irregularity and imperfection, the underlying strength, the "foundation of all actions," emerges as the dominant feature. Surprisingly, this Confucian interpretation is closer in spirit to Zeami's ran'i.

It should be noted that, unlike his Confucian counterparts in China, Kaneyoshi is not hostile to Buddhism. Indeed, he openly supports the "unity of the three creeds" as an ideal. Therefore, he is not averse to using Buddhist terminology to further his ends. In this harin section there is an interesting occurrence of the term *chi* (wisdom), one of the five virtues, traditionally associated with winter. But it is also the Sino-Buddhist equivalent for *prajñā*, or transcendental wisdom, and so it provides a convenient bridge back to Kaneyoshi's words, "Again breaking its shape and returning to formlessness, it changes in the same manner that worldly desires become bodhi." As mentioned earlier, the notion of a return to formlessness is not directly supported by the Four Qualities. But the occurrence of "wisdom" at this point in Kaneyoshi's remarks is a key component in his transition to the final Circle of Emptiness.

WISDOM AS HIDDEN AND STORED

Among the Confucian four stages of life (birth, growth, maturity, and death),[36] the last is *ts'ang* (lit., being hidden). In the "four treasuries" of Shao Yung mentioned earlier, it is aligned with winter, wisdom, and perseverance. In light of the previous discussion, the stage of winter is easily understood as "hidden": life force lies dormant in winter, "persevering" in an unmanifest state. In what sense, however, is the virtue of wisdom "hidden"?

According to Okada Takehiko, in his later years, Chu Hsi gave considerable attention to the notion of "wisdom as hidden and stored" (*chih-ts'ang*).[37] Following Mencius, he argued that when the four virtues of benevolence (*jen*), justice (*i*), propriety (*li*), and wisdom (*chih*) are manifest as human feeling, they take the form of commiseration, complaisance, shame and dislike, and a sense of right and wrong, respectively. Of these, only the last does not imply direct involvement in human affairs; in

---

[36] Slightly different from the Buddhist Four Characteristics, perhaps reflecting an underlying agricultural orientation.

[37] Okada Takehiko, "Chu Hsi and Wisdom as Hidden and Stored," in Wing-tsit Chan, ed., *Chu Hsi and Neo-Confucianism* (Honolulu: University of Hawaii Press, 1986), 197–211. This theme is also explored in Rodney L. Taylor, *The Confucian Way of Contemplation* (Columbia: University of South Carolina Press, 1988), 146–52; this volume is a study of Okada as a contemporary Confucianist. In Japan, this conception was emphasized in the school of Yamazaki Ansai (1612–1682).

this sense, wisdom is hidden. Furthermore, insofar as wisdom is furthest removed from human feeling, it is closer to the realm of pure principle (*li*).

Of the four virtues, wisdom is the most passive, exhibiting the greatest yin component. For Chu, benevolence is the most important of the four, but wisdom is second to it because, just as the yang energy of spring follows the peak of yin in winter, so does benevolence emerge from wisdom. At the winter solstice, the most subtle yet potent yang energy emerges. Furthermore, one can best engage in reflection and self-cultivation in the tranquil solitude of winter, when all that has come before is stored and can be examined.

This notion of wisdom as hidden and stored is important in Kaneyoshi's system for two reasons. First, it provides an explicit mechanism by which the moral virtues represented by inner four circles form a continuous cycle. Chu Hsi himself spoke of a circle of the four virtues.[38] But even more important, if the fifth circle, as wisdom, represents a retreat to the hidden, the unmanifest, it provides a potential exit point from the four-stage cycle to the sixth Circle of Emptiness. Wisdom thus becomes a precondition to the experience of the formless.[39]

THE CIRCLE OF EMPTINESS: THE GREAT ULTIMATE

For Kaneyoshi, the sixth Circle of Emptiness is the absolute state lacking in the previous five circles. He describes it as the Great Ultimate, which in turn is:

a. Supreme truth
b. The greatness of heaven and earth, arising from principle
c. Tao
d. Mind
e. Possessed by all things
f. At one with all things

At first glance, these statements seem strung together in an offhand fashion that discourages coherent analysis. They seem to be spontaneous exclamations, expressing delight at reaching the absolute realm. However,

---

[38] As quoted in Ying-shih Yü, "Morality and Knowledge in Chu Hsi's Philosophical System," in Wing-tsit Chan, ed., *Chu Hsi*, 241: "Mencius himself was speaking of a circle (of the four virtues, rather than a mere list). In fact, humanity, righteousness, and propriety are all stored in intelligence (*chih*). You can act in a certain way only when you know it."

[39] As Okada emphasizes, this notion of wisdom is consistent with Sung aesthetics, which emphasize surface simplicity that conceals inner richness and "unrevealed significance." Okada, "Chu Hsi," 198. In chapter 7 similar Japanese aesthetic ideals associated with the *harin* will be examined.

perhaps this is the point—as exclamations, they reinforce the epistemological dimension that is an important aspect of the Circle of Emptiness, which represents the Absolute experienced directly. The famous quote from Shao Yung—"Mind is the Great Ultimate"—may be significant in this sense.

The fundamental issue here is whether it is meaningful to assign the Great Ultimate to the Circle of Emptiness. To decide, one should first compare the Buddhist and Confucian representations of the Circle of Longevity. As the "one source of motion and stillness," the Buddhist *jurin* is a symbol of absolute unity. On the other hand, Ch'ien is an image of yang creative force, the opposite of K'un, the Receptive. In the early *I ching* commentaries such as the *Wen-yen*, Ch'ien and K'un are discussed as concepts of equal importance. Therefore, Kaneyoshi's conception of the Circle of Longevity as Ch'ien has dualistic implications and is not entirely appropriate as an Absolute. But what of the Circle Emptiness?

Here it is instructive to reconsider Chou Tun-i's *T'ai-chi-t'u shuo* (*Explanation of the diagram of the Great Ultimate*), the basic text of Neo-Confucian metaphysics cited by Kaneyoshi in his opening remarks. This work is the explication of the central portion of figure 5-7.

In the standard Confucian interpretation, the diagram is read from top to bottom, as a depiction of the creation of the material world. In this sense, the Great Ultimate is clearly a generative entity, reflecting its original meaning in the "Appended Remarks" of the *I ching*.[40] There is ample evidence, however, that this diagram originates in the Taoist tradition, where it represents a meditation technique.[41] The adept withdraws from the outer sensory world of things, perhaps through a discipline of sexual yoga, to extract *ch'i* from seminal essence (*ching*). Within the body five varieties of *ch'i* are visualized, located in the five associated internal organs (water–kidneys, wood–liver, earth–spleen, fire–heart, metal–lungs). These vital energies are fused in an internal cauldron, initially located in the solar plexus; in a process of inner alchemy, they are refined to extract the more primary forces of *k'an* and *li* (trigrams equivalent to water and fire). These are subsequently merged to form spirit (*shen*), which finally dissolves into the Fundamental Vacuity of the Tao. When read from bottom to top, the diagram represents this meditation process.

In a general sense, Kaneyoshi's Circle of Emptiness can be seen as a similar withdrawal to the formless Tao. The individual retreats from the

[40] "Therefore in the system of Change there is the Great Ultimate. It generates the Two Modes [yin and yang]. The Two Modes generate the Four Forms [major and minor yin and yang]. The Four Forms generate the Eight Trigrams. The Eight Trigrams determine good and evil fortunes." *SBCP*, 267.

[41] See Feng Yu-lan, *A History of Chinese Philosophy* (Princeton: Princeton University Press, 1952), 2:438–42.

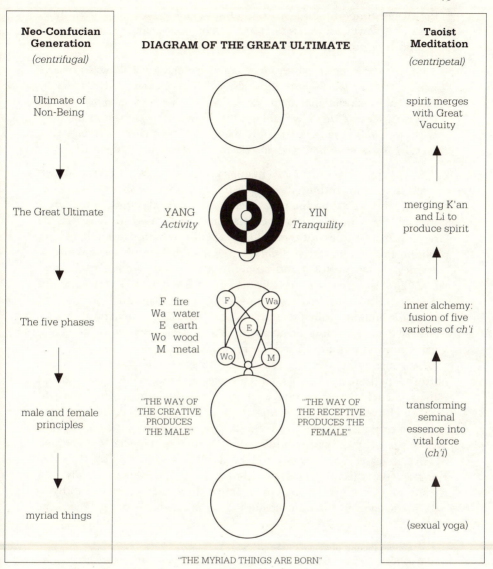

DIAGRAM OF THE GREAT ULTIMATE

| Neo-Confucian Generation *(centrifugal)* | | Taoist Meditation *(centripetal)* |

Neo-Confucian Generation *(centrifugal)*:
- Ultimate of Non-Being
- The Great Ultimate
- The five phases
- male and female principles
- myriad things

Center:
- YANG *Activity* — YIN *Tranquility*
- F fire / Wa water / E earth / Wo wood / M metal
- "THE WAY OF THE CREATIVE PRODUCES THE MALE"
- "THE WAY OF THE RECEPTIVE PRODUCES THE FEMALE"
- "THE MYRIAD THINGS ARE BORN"

Taoist Meditation *(centripetal)*:
- spirit merges with Great Vacuity
- merging K'an and Li to produce spirit
- inner alchemy: fusion of five varieties of *ch'i*
- transforming seminal essence into vital force *(ch'i)*
- (sexual yoga)

FIG. 5-7. Diagram of the Great Ultimate

fourfold cycle of circulating *ch'i* in the middle circles to the formless sixth circle. However, this interpretation seems to negate the orthodox Confucian conception of the Great Ultimate as a generative entity. Can the Great Ultimate be described as an *experiential* Absolute?

A solution can be found in Chu Hsi's notion of principle (*li*). As is widely known, the dichotomy between principle and material force (*ch'i*) is the cornerstone of Chu Hsi's thought. *Li* and *ch'i* are coexistent in all forms of the world, and yet *li* can be said to be antecedent in an ontological sense. For example, he writes,

> Throughout the universe there are both principle and material force. Principle refers to the Way, which exists before physical form [and is without it] and is the root from which all things are produced. Material force refers to material objects, which exists after physical form [and is with it]; it is the instrument by which things are produced. Therefore in the production of man and things, they must be endowed with material force before they have physical form.[42]

Thus, "Principle is one, but its manifestions are many"[43]; it is that which gives each individual thing its own identity, that which shapes its *ch'i*. At the same time, the supreme principle,[44] shared by all things, is the Great Ultimate. For Chu Hsi, however, principle as such—and therefore the Great Ultimate—does not create: "*Li* has neither emotion nor will; neither planning ability nor creative ability. . . . *Li* is a thoroughly clean world of emptiness; it has no form and no ability to create anything."[45] That is, while Chu Hsi sometimes pays lip service to Chou Tun-i's conception of the Great Ultimate when discussing his famous diagram,[46] in his own system of thought, principle is not, strictly speaking, a generative entity. The above description of principle bears a striking resemblance to Kaneyoshi's conception of the Circle of Emptiness.

When discussing the creation of all things, of constant growth and nurturing in the natural world, Chu Hsi accords Heaven the highest role. It is the mind of Heaven to produce things. Similarly, human beings strive to emulate Heaven through the constant development of benevolence (*jen*): "Heaven operates ceaselessly. When the sun goes down, the moon rises. Winter passes by and summer follows. . . . All these take the Way for their essence, and are in motion day and night without stop. And so, the superior man takes this for his model and makes ceaseless efforts to aspire after the sublime."[47] Thus, through the practice of self-cultivation, the individual "participates in the onto-cosmological process that brings about the

---

[42] *SBCP*, 636.

[43] A famous dictum of Ch'eng I; *SBCP*, 544.

[44] According to some scholars, for Chu Hsi the Great Ultimate is simply another name for principle; the qualification "supreme principle" is unnecessary. See Yu Yamanoi, "The Great Ultimate and Heaven in Chu Hsi's Philosophy," in Wing-tsit Chan, ed., *Chu Hsi*, 79–92.

[45] Quoted in ibid., 86.

[46] My argument here is based on ibid., 79–92. Not all scholars would accept Yamanoi's limiting definition of the Great Ultimate; but at the very least, he provides evidence within Chu Hsi's writings that supports Kaneyoshi's views.

[47] Quoted in Chiu Hansheng, "Zhu Xi's Doctrine of Principle," in Wing-tsit Chan, ed., *Chu Hsi*, 124.

completion of the Great Ultimate"[48]—that is, the realization of pure principle. As one's own individual endowment of *ch'i* is increasingly purified, purged of turbid, selfish desire, the immanent Heavenly principle (*t'ien-li*) shines ever brighter.

Surely it is this process that Kaneyoshi's commentary represents. His Circle of Longevity is functionally equivalent to Heaven; the Circle of Emptiness represents the personally realized absolute principle; and the middle four circles contain the element of material force, as the Four Qualities of Ch'ien. After many cycles of natural development, self-cultivation, and purification, the mature practitioner achieves the realization of "wisdom as hidden and stored" at the harin and breaks through to the final stage of the kūrin. Figure 5-8 illustrates this process.

ONE DEWDROP: NEITHER SOUND NOR SMELL

The final One Dewdrop is described as the Ultimate of Nonbeing, the complement of the Great Ultimate. Kaneyoshi states that the Ultimate of Nonbeing is beyond the dualism of principle and material force, thus subtly setting off the ichiro from the previous six circles and preserving the spirit of Zenchiku's original conception. The Ultimate of Nonbeing is the most transcendental metaphysical category available within the Neo-Confucian repertoire, and in fact it was ignored by many of the Sung thinkers for this very reason. Functionally, it has little bearing on the paradigm of self-cultivation depicted above.

The "neither sound nor smell" phrase cited by Kaneyoshi from the *Chung-yung* is in fact used by Chu Hsi to explicate Chou Tun-i's dictum, "The Ultimate of Nonbeing and then the Great Ultimate": "The operation of Heaven is devoid of sound or smell. It is indeed the pivot of creation and the ground of everything."[49] In other words, when the essence of the universe cannot be grasped as an object, it is called the Ultimate of Nonbeing; when perceived as the pivot point of creation, it is called the Great Ultimate, which is principle. In this sense, the kūrin and ichiro are paired. This seems to have appealed to Zenchiku, who frequently treats them as a unit in his later treatises.[50]

Again, Kaneyoshi resorts to Buddhist language: "The Ultimate of Non-

---

[48] This eloquent formulation by Tu is found in a discussion of Chou Tun-i, but it applies equally to Chu Hsi. Tu Wei-ming, *Humanity and Self-Cultivation* (Berkeley: Asian Humanities Press, 1979), 72.

[49] Translated in Tomoeda Ryūtarō, "The System of Chu Hsi's Philosophy," in Wing-tsit Ch'an, ed., *Chu Hsi*, 158.

[50] For example, see the *Yūgen sanrin* passage translated in chapter 3.

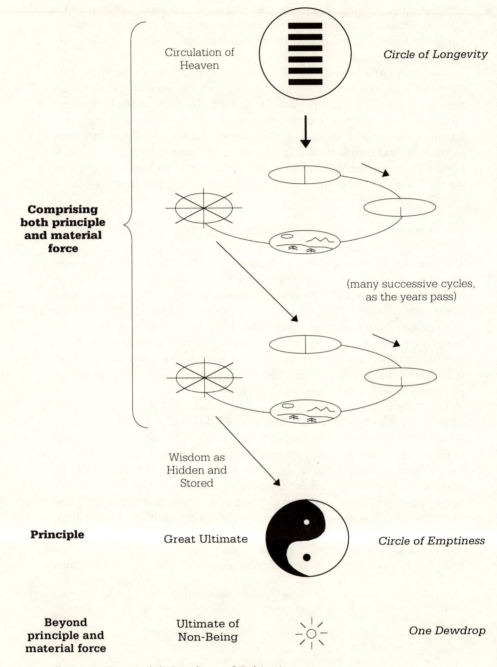

Circulation of
Heaven

Circle of Longevity

**Comprising
both principle
and material
force**

(many successive cycles,
as the years pass)

Wisdom as
Hidden and
Stored

Principle

Great Ultimate

Circle of Emptiness

**Beyond
principle and
material force**

Ultimate of
Non-Being

One Dewdrop

FIG. 5-8. Kaneyoshi's Paradigm of Cultivation

being departs from the word-based distinction of being and emptiness; it does not lie within the realm of contemplation." This notion of nonduality is reinforced by the subsequent allusions to the *Analects* and other Confucian classics—the "one thread," "Tseng-tzu's 'yes,'" and so on—which represent some of the transcendental glimmers within this generally humanistic tradition.

CONCLUDING THOUGHTS

In evaluating the vision of self-cultivation implied by Kaneyoshi's commentary, we should take account of a debate between Chu Hsi and Lu Hsiang-shan.[51] For Chu, principle is inherent in human nature. To activate principle, however, an individual must work through the mechanism of the mind, which is composed of both *li* and *ch'i*, or nature and human feeling. The process of self-cultivation, then, is a process whereby the *ch'i* of the mind is gradually refined, ever approaching the principle that lies within. In other words, Chu consistently sees a division between mind and principle. Lu Hsiang-shan opposed this view, arguing that mind and principle are one: every human mind is an authentic manifestation of principle, identical to the mind of the sage. Self-cultivation, then, is directed at uncovering this inherent mind, which emerges in a simple, direct act of transformation. The contrast between Chu and Lu here strongly echoes the ongoing debate in Chinese Buddhism, especially Ch'an, between proponents of gradual and sudden enlightenment.

Kaneyoshi's comments do not clearly favor either position. On the one hand, he embraces Shao Yung's statement, "The Mind is the Great Ultimate," which, in its original context,[52] accords with Lu's views. In general, the Buddhist rhetoric used by Kaneyoshi supports the "sudden" position: for example, the Circle of Breaking is said to "change in the same manner that worldly desires become enlightenment." At the same time, however, he insists that the dualism of *li* and *ch'i* is present in all of the six circles. I interpret this to mean that the first five circles contain material force, while the final Circle of Emptiness, as the Great Ultimate, is pure principle (see figure 5-8); only at this final stage can sagehood be realized. Thus the gradualism of Chu is also supported.

In fact, Zenchiku's original six circles of performance contain both sudden and gradual components. The individual performance effects, the spontaneous appearance of hana at various stages, all suggest that the supreme levels of art are immediately available. At the same time, the

[51] As summarized in Tu, *Humanity and Self-Cultivation*, 77–79.
[52] "The mind is the Great Ultimate. The human mind should be as calm as water. Being calm, it will be tranquil. Being tranquil, it will be enlightened." *SBCP*, 493.

following of the Way, the cultivation process of michi, is essentially a gradual process that occurs over the course of the performer's career. In this sense, the Way is analogous to principle, realized in its fullest form at the Circle of Emptiness, the "style of the young voice" executed by the aged master performer. The accomplishment of the artist is measured by the degree of harmony he has achieved with the workings of Heaven; at the same time, the primal energy of Heaven propels his refinement and development. At age seventy, the effect is effortless.

A. C. Graham has pointed out that the correlative mode of thinking implicit in the Chinese cosmology of the five phases and yin–yang is protoscientific. That is, while it attempts to link disparate events and qualities in order to explain the order of things and predict future occurrences, this mode of thought is human-centered. It depends on the experience of the observer, on one's ability to perceive similarity and correspondence. In contrast, true analytical, scientific thought is more detached: it assumes that the natural world operates independently of the human ability to perceive it, responding to invisible laws of causality.[53]

From our perspective, however, the anthropocentric nature of correlative thinking is perhaps its greatest strength. In particular, it is fundamentally compatible with aesthetic experience. Just as the cosmologist seeks similarity to explain and predict events, the perception of beauty largely derives from an experience of harmony. The artist and his audience resonate with the perceived outer world, reestablishing a sense of the interrelatedness of all things, of self and other. Similarly, to the extent that the artist sees a correlation between cosmic process and his own development, he is following the Way. Earlier in this chapter I criticized Kaneyoshi for the deliberate, mechanistic quality of his categorizations of the six circles. Yet through this sense of organic inevitability, through the immanence of Heavenly principle in natural process, he manages to represent the developmental aspect of michi that is lacking in Shigyoku's commentary. The latter's discrete soteriological paradigms, individually perfect and complete, can account for sudden moments of transcendence, but not for the ongoing evolution of the performer's art.

Following Shigyoku's precedent, Kaneyoshi does not comment on the practical significance of his commentary. To be sure, his various categorizations do enhance our understanding of the individual performance effects these circles represent; for example, it has been seen how Zenchiku's notion of the Rank of the Sublime (ran'i) is perhaps Confucian

---

[53] A. C. Graham, *Disputers of the Tao* (La Salle, Ill.: Open Court, 1989), 319–25.

at heart. Still, like Shigyoku, Kaneyoshi treats the middle four circles as one unit, a grouping that is incompatible with Zenchiku's original conception. For a precise analogue to the centrifugal process represented by the first three circles—the onset of vocalization, jo–ha–kyū, and the like—we must turn to Zenchiku's own implementation of medieval Shinto terminology in the *Kichū*.

Chapter Six: Zenchiku and Medieval Shinto

IN MOST ACCOUNTS of medieval Japan, Buddhism is accorded a position of overwhelming domination in the religious, cultural, and intellectual spheres. Certainly Shinto experienced a period of occlusion during the Heian period, when the native religion—although hardly defunct—was obscured by the grandeur of Buddhism's spiritual profundity, its vast cosmology and advanced technologies. At the onset of the medieval age, however, Shinto begins to forge a new, more focused identity in response to the Buddhist hegemony. In this chapter I shall trace some of the developing patterns of medieval Shinto as they manifest in the cultural microcosm of the rokurin ichiro texts.

THE EMERGENCE OF ISE SHINTO

The history of Buddhist-Shinto relations begins in the sixth century, when Buddhism was first introduced to Japan. After an initial period of strong political tension between the custodians of the native religion (the term Shintō does not appear before the *Nihon shoki*) and the patrons of Buddhism, individual shrines managed to coexist with the Buddhist establishment for many centuries, usually in a subservient role, providing local protection for temple precincts. But although their ritual observances maintained a strong identity, Shinto proponents made little effort to develop anything resembling a systematic body of doctrines. Only in the eleventh century[1] does a formal debate take shape that compares the qualities of the two belief systems.

[1] It is difficult to date the beginnings of the phenomenon of Buddhist-Shinto amalgamation (*shinbutsu shūgō*), since many of the key texts are medieval forgeries attributed to earlier figures such as Gyōgi, Saichō, and Kūkai. Certainly, syncretic beliefs can be traced back to the importation of Buddhism. In this chapter, however, the concern is the evolution of formal theories of *shinbutsu shūgō*.

In fact, supporters of both Shinto and Buddhism had strong motivation to establish such a theoretical link. The Buddhists endeavored to demonstrate that native deities were a localized, delimited manifestation of their more universal pantheon: thus the well-known theory of *honji-suijaku* (original ground–trace manifestation) emerged. This theory enabled them to co-opt, rather than confront, local beliefs. At the same time, Shinto proponents were willing to adopt Buddhist concepts and symbolism, to create a more articulate vision of their faith.

For the purpose of this study, the first important school of Buddhist-Shinto syncretism is Dual Shinto (*Ryōbu Shintō*), developed by members of the Shingon Sect in the Ise area. Perhaps motivated by a desire to ally themselves with the dominant religious institution of the region, these Buddhist priests established an elaborate set of correspondences between esoteric doctrine and the symbolism of the Ise Shrines. Most notably, the sun goddess Amaterasu was paired with the cosmic buddha Mahāvairocana (J. Dainichi Nyorai), and the Inner and Outer Shrines were proclaimed a Japanese manifestation of the dual mandalas of Shingon doctrine, the Womb and Diamond Realms.

This line of reasoning had an important side-effect: in theory, it elevated the status of the Outer Shrine to virtual parity with the previously dominant Inner Shrine, the sanctuary of the sun goddess. Traditionally, the god of the Outer Shrine, Toyo'uke (or Toyuke)-no-ōkami, was considered a grain deity who provided sustenance to the sun goddess. By traditional account first located at a site on the imperial palace grounds, his sanctuary had been moved to Manaihara in Tamba Province before arriving at Ise during the reign of Emperor Yūryaku. To justify an enhanced status for Toyo'uke, the Watarai family, hereditary custodians of the Outer Shrine, began to develop their own Shinto-oriented doctrines. By the end of the thirteenth century, they had created a canon of five apocryphal "classics," subsequently known as the *Shintō gobusho*. These works represent a significant advance in Shinto cosmology, systematically incorporating elements from both esoteric Buddhism and Chinese yin–yang theory. They exerted widespread influence on later schools of Shinto thought.

In the Muromachi period, the most widely circulated work of Ise Shinto (also often called Watarai Shinto) was the *Ruijū jingi hongen*, compiled by Watarai Ieyuki (1256–1351) and dated 1320. Divided into fifteen chapters, it is largely a compilation of passages from the *Gobusho*. Certainly the most important section is the first chapter, on the topic "The Division of Heaven and Earth" (*tenchi kaibyaku*). In their efforts to achieve doctrinal parity with the Buddhists, Shinto proponents of all schools consistently resort to the famous cosmogony at the beginning of the *Nihon shoki*, because it is the closest thing to an explicit native cosmology, a model that explains the origin and order of things. In his first chapter, Ieyuki begins by providing multiple Chinese prototypes and parallels for the "division of heaven and earth," culled from a wide range of sources. Excerpted works include *Lao Tzu*, various *I ching* commentaries, *Lieh Tzu*–derived works, *Chuang Tzu*, the *Huai-nan Tzu*, works of five-phase theory, and, most significantly, a collection of Sung writings that quotes from Chou Tun-i's *Explanation of the Diagram of the Great Ultimate*—Ieyuki includes the diagram itself. The second part of the chapter adds material from native sources, grouped into official government, Shinto, and Buddhist sections. While this material is presented in disjointed, bombastic fashion,[2] it provides a fascinating glimpse into the intellectual horizons of this fourteenth-century Ise priest. Furthermore, Ieyuki's compendium would serve later generations as an anthology of both Chinese and native thought.

I am convinced that the *Ruijū jingi hongen* played a pivotal role in the formation of the rokurin ichiro texts. First of all, Kaneyoshi seems to have relied on it for a number of his key citations from Chinese sources. The most obvious of these is the passage from Tsung-mi's commentary to the *Perfect Enlightenment Sutra* that provides the rhetorical connection between Shigyoku's categorizations and his own.[3] The likelihood that both men would independently excerpt this obscure and, for Tsung-mi, parenthetical remark is quite small. In addition, many of the themes of Ise Shinto will resurface in Zenchiku's own appropriation of Shinto symbols.

The first task is to examine Zenchiku's incorporation of Shinto terminology in the *Kichū* and later rokurin ichiro drafts. Of course, this is not the first appearance of Shinto motifs. Both Shigyoku and Kaneyoshi allude to the divine origins of sarugaku in the rock-cave myth. Kaneyoshi also introduces other pseudohistorical connections between Shinto mythology and sarugaku and proclaims the "unity of the three creeds" to introduce his Confucian commentary. But in the *Kichū*, Zenchiku goes one step further, responding to Kaneyoshi's rhetoric by providing his own set of cognates from the Shinto tradition, based on the "division of heaven and earth" paradigm.

THE DIVISION OF HEAVEN AND EARTH

The opening of the *Nihon shoki* delineates a process whereby a state of undifferentiated formlessness (C. *hun-t'un*, J. *konton*) undergoes transfor-

[2] Herman Ooms discusses the implications of this style of presentation in his *Tokugawa Ideology* (Princeton: Princeton University Press, 1985), 93–97.
[3] See Chapter 2, note 69.

mation: yin and yang polarize and divide, eventually coalescing into matter. This is the formation of heaven and earth:

> Of old, heaven and earth were not yet separated, and the yin and yang not yet divided. They formed a chaotic mass like an egg which was of obscurely defined limits and contained germs. The purer and clearer part was thinly drawn out, and formed heaven, while the heavier and grosser element settled down and became earth.
>
> The finer element easily became a united body, but the consolidation of the heavy and gross element was accomplished with difficulty.
>
> Heaven was therefore formed first, and earth was established subsequently. Thereafter divine beings were produced between them.
>
> Hence it is said that when heaven and earth first opened into being,[4] the soil of which lands were composed floated about in a manner which might be compared to the floating of a fish sporting on the surface of the water.
>
> At this time a certain thing was produced between heaven and earth. It was in form like a reed-shoot. Now this became transformed into a god and was called Kuninotokotachi-no-mikoto.[5]

This cosmogony was originally adapted—almost word for word in places—from the *Huai-nan Tzu*, the influential Chinese Taoist work of the second century B.C. (However, the Chinese prototype makes no mention of "divine beings," who, in the *Nihon shoki* account, are the progenitors of the Japanese archipelago and the ancestors of the imperial clan.) There are numerous related descriptions in the Chinese tradition, some of which use the terms *i-ch'i* (J. *ikki*) or *yüan-ch'i* (J. *genki*)—"primal pneuma"—to describe the contents of the cosmic egg. The significance of this genesis in the Japanese tradition is far-reaching. Most important, it depicts one smooth continuum of being, underscoring the divinity of the imperial family and the Japanese nation.

Zenchiku enumerates three distinct stages of this creation process: the state before polarization, the act of division, and a stabilized state of differentiation. He aligns them to his first three circles, as in figure 6-1. The logic of these categorizations is compelling. In the Taoist tradition of self-cultivation, this creation paradigm is frequently played back mentally *in reverse*, as the adept attempts to return to the Great Beginning, a formless

---

[4] *Tenchi kaibyaku* here is read in the Japanese fashion, *ametsuchi hiraku(ru)*. (Translation suggested by Susan Matisoff.) Note that in the original account, it is yin and yang that divide, while heaven and earth form subsequently; strictly speaking, the translation "division of heaven and earth" is inaccurate. In the later tradition, however, the phrase *tenchi kaibyaku* denotes the entire process of bifurcation, as depicted in the opening passage.

[5] *NKBT* 67:76; translation modified from Aston, *Nihongi*, 1–3.

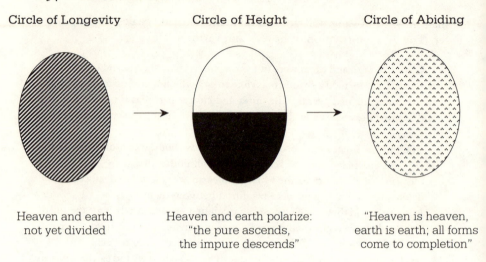

Circle of Longevity	Circle of Height	Circle of Abiding
Heaven and earth not yet divided	Heaven and earth polarize: "the pure ascends, the impure descends"	"Heaven is heaven, earth is earth; all forms come to completion"

FIG. 6-1. Division of Heaven and Earth

state of perfection "before yin and yang have divided."[6] Thus Konton is not merely "primeval chaos," as it is often translated, but a privileged state of perfect tranquility and infinite potential—a fitting parallel for the Circle of Longevity. The second stage, at which Primal Pneuma polarizes into yin and yang, echoes the various origination paradigms utilized by Shigyoku and Kaneyoshi, all of which represent a shift to duality. The third Circle of Abiding can easily be understood as homeostatis, in which the forms of the material world regenerate regularly.

In fact, this is not the first appearance of the tenchi kaibyaku motif in Zenchiku's writings. In *Go'on sangyoku shū* he applies this grandiose mythic imagery to the microcosm of musical rhythm within a performance: "Concerning interval and beat. All actions should be executed in the interval. If they are performed on the beat, they have little effect. The state when heaven and earth have not yet divided is the interval; the division is the beat. [The manifestation of] all things comprises arising from this interval."[7]

For Zenchiku, the empty spaces between the musical beats are intervals

[6] See N. J. Giradot, *Myth and Meaning in Early Taoism* (Berkeley: University of California Press, 1983), 134 ff. This process resembles the meditation described in the previous chapter; see figure 5-7.

[7] *KKSS*, 184. For a complete translation of this passage, see chapter 2, note 131. The topic is also discussed in the *Hichū* (*Bunshō bon*); *KKSS*, 261.

of creative tension, and the performer must begin his movement during these intervals in order to generate the maximum effect. The emphasis, then, is on the potential energy compressed within the state of commingled yin and yang: when polarization occurs, the act of division unleashes great kinetic force. Within a performance, the silence before the energy is released is beyond time, insofar as the beat is indeterminate; yet such intervals provide a psychological tension that heightens the effect of subsequent movement, when discernible form appears.

This interpenetration of mythic time in one instant of performance we have encountered before: in Zeami's interpretation of the rock-cave incident, analyzed in chapter 3. Indeed, it is not difficult to see a parallel between the state before the polarization of yin and yang—of light and dark—and the anticipation generated by the sun goddess' seclusion in the heavenly rock cave. In Zeami's paradigm, the flash of light represents the process of reception: the arising of feeling in the minds of the audience. For Zenchiku, the division of heaven and earth represents the act of expression: the appearance of movement and rhythm. In both cases, the Shinto analogies provide a sense of potential energy, a kind of gestating force that explodes as blinding yang energy, the activating force. As the yin force of consolidation then emerges, the individual notes take their shape, and material form is perfected.

Although the tenchi kaibyaku motif is not present in the original *Ki* manuscript, its importance cannot be overstated. Both Kaneyoshi and Shigyoku break up the six circles into groups of 1–4–1; but in fact the natural division from the perspective of performance is 3–3, as frequently implied by Zenchiku himself through his grouping of "the first three circles" (*jōsanrin*).[8] Thus the tripartite tenchi kaibyaku model is the most cogent symbolic representation for such centrifugal principles of performance as jo–ha–kyū, the Miraculous–Flower–Fascination, and First Pitch–Second Breath–Third Voice. Furthermore, rather than depicting the manifestation of relative form on an absolute ground, the "division of heaven and earth" represents the bifurcation of Primal Pneuma into two complementary, equal entities, which then interact to generate the forms of the world. Thus this ontology represents a *temporal*, rather than metaphysical, process—more appropriate for stage effects that occur in "real time."

Zenchiku makes no attempt to find Shinto cognates for the second group of three circles. However, there are several Shinto precedents for the One Dewdrop.

[8] See chapter 3.

PRIMAL WATER

Although the One Dewdrop is a prominent image in the *rokurin ichiro* texts, Zenchiku has surprisingly little to say of it. His most extended discussion is found in the *Go'on sangyoku shū*, a work on vocalization styles and other performance matters. The topic is the "flavorless flavor":

> The water of wisdom (*chisui*) that has no taste is an important matter in song and dance. People have their own preferences among the five flavors. There are those who like bitterness, those who like saltiness, those who like sweetness. Such preferences are inherently changeable. These five flavors originate from [the flavorless ground of] Primal Water (*issui*). The taste of water has no fixed flavor; the five flavors are added to it in accord with [individual] preferences. Therefore it is important to know the original "flavorless flavor."
>
> This is also the case in song and dance. If one flavor receives too much emphasis in a passage, there will be those who like it, and those who dislike it: they will not agree. If the water-like passages are sung in a flavorless style, however, with no undue emphasis, [the effect] will be agreeable to all. Furthermore, it is possible to mix in "flavored" elements in accordance with the preferences of the host [in attendance], for as long as the moistness of the basic water is present, the sense of the five flavors is light in character, in harmony with the natural state of the mind. Thus a feeling of interesting flavor results without undue emphasis. In both dance styles and vocal performance, if one does not overemphasize external qualities (*sugata*), the effect will be like flowing water. In this fashion, both the role and its flavor are endowed with the power of Primal Water (*issui no toku*). Water takes shape from its vessel.[9] [Thus] there is no need to worry when an emotional flavor that accords with a personal preference for one of the five flavors is generated by a role in noh. Since the three components of skin, flesh, and bone[10] arise from this Primal Water, mountains, rivers, and the great earth, all grasses and trees, all things are comprised of this water-essence. I have written a volume about learning the Way, "Six Circles and One Dewdrop." This [conception] also [utilizes] the form of the water circle. The One Dewdrop is the inception of Primal Water (*issui no hajime*), the bone of a sharp sword's power. Thus it is essential that study begin with these three components [of skin, flesh, and bone]. Water takes shape by flowing and gets its life from a lack of flavor. [Similarly,] music gets its flow from the meander of the singing, and produces the quality of "no-flavor" from a lack of heaviness. Dance gets its flow from the

[9] Similar statements are found in *Han Fei Tzu*, section 32 (Shinshaku kanbun taikei, 12:500), and in *Hsün Tzu*, section 12 (ibid., 5:346). See *KKSS*, 182, n. 2.

[10] This terminology is found in Zeami's *Shikadō* (*ZZ*, 116–17). Most generally, skin (*hi*) represents external, graceful beauty, flesh (*niku*) is the skill developed from mastery of the essentials of song and dance, and bone (*kotsu*) is the artist's natural ability. In singing, the three terms are also equated with a beautiful voice, an interesting melody, and proper breathing technique, respectively.

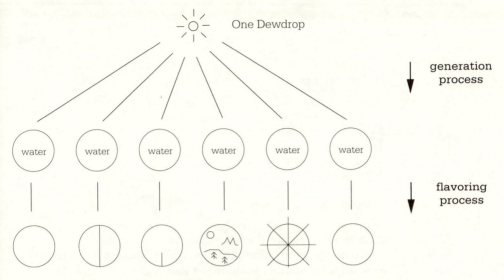

FIG. 6-2. One Dewdrop Generates Primal Water

beautiful, ordered progression of movement in accordance with jo–ha–kyū, and derives its no-flavor from a lack of heaviness in appearance. Everything is like this. The color of water is also empty[, without inherent characteristic]. Through reflection it manifests color, and this color is not stationary: "Through having no place to abide, the mind is born."[11] This must be kept secret; it is concealed wisdom. Do not transmit it to anyone, even for a thousand pieces of gold.[12]

Symbols from the native Chinese and the Buddhist traditions are freely mixed in this rather disjointed passage. Zenchiku begins his exposition with the Buddhist expression *chisui*, in which water symbolizes the inherent purity of *prajñā* and its ability to wash away defilements produced by ignorance. To emphasize the principle of formlessness that he values, Zenchiku then introduces a term derived from five-phase theory, the five flavors (*gomi*). Each flavor is said to exist as a kind of modulation of an underlying ontological "stuff," termed "Primal Water" (*issui*). This relation is represented in figure 6-2.

In fact, this *issui* conception is not to be found in the orthodox system of five flavors. Water is one of the five phases, a cognate of the salt flavor; however, it is in no sense an underlying essence, or even the central component. Earth (sweetness) is the element of the center, although only in the sense that it represents a neutral, balanced state, neither yin nor yang.

[11] From the *Diamond Sutra*. T 235.8.749c.
[12] *KKSS*, 181–82.

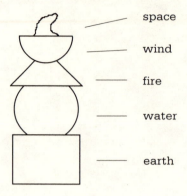

FIG. 6-3. Five-tiered Stupa

The use of water as a symbol for the lack of characteristic, then, seems to be derived exclusively from the Buddhist conception *chisui*, reinforced at the end of the passage by additional Buddhist language.

Next the rokurin ichiro motif is introduced, as a further illustration of the water metaphor. An associative link between water and the circular form is established through the use of yet another set of symbols: the geometric shapes that represent universal elements depicted in Buddhist cosmologies. There are systems of four, five, and six elements.[13] Unlike the previously introduced five phases from the Taoist/Confucian tradition, which are best understood as five varieties of *ch'i* in constant flux, these are fundamental, static "elements" that comprise the universe. In Japan the most common of these groupings is the five-element system, symbolically depicted by the ubiquitous five-tiered stupa (*gorin tō*). Each element is represented by its own geometric shape, termed *samaya-gyō* in the esoteric sects, as shown in figure 6-3.

The *samaya-gyō* for water is the circle (*suirin*), hence Zenchiku's statement "This [circular form] is the shape of the element water."[14] In other words, the circle symbolism in the rokurin ichiro context is said to represent water. Furthermore, through juxtaposition the six circles are associated with the concept of *issui*, which Zenchiku has implemented to represent a basic, flavorless essence. Again, this *issui* conception is in fact incompatible with the original doctrinal content of the Buddhist *samaya-gyō* system, where water is only one of five equally important elements. Still, this rather sloppy chain of associations is of interest because it pro-

[13] See chapter 2, note 6.

[14] Zenchiku benefits from a fortuitous linguistic coincidence. As noted, the term for the water symbol is *suirin*, but in fact the *rin* component does not refer to its circular shape: it simply means "realm," derived from the Sanskrit *maṇḍala*. This is demonstrated by the expression *gorin*, and the names of the other four shapes: *jirin, karin, fūrin,* and *kūrin*.

vides a clever semantic link between the symbolism of the six circles, as water, and the One Dewdrop.[15]

To be sure, this passage should not be interpreted as a missing key to the secrets of the rokurin ichiro structure, for the simple reason that these associations do not appear in any of the rokurin ichiro treatises themselves. It is likely that this conceptual link between the dewdrop and the six circles—mentioned during the explication of a largely unrelated topic— occurred to Zenchiku some time after the rokurin ichiro structure was established. At first glance, his links seem both innovative and illogical. The above analysis, however, treats only Zenchiku's explicit argument. To understand the broader significance of this conception, it is necessary to turn to its subtext—the world of medieval Shinto, where precisely this kind of associative thinking is the norm. In Ise Shinto, the water motif, and even the term *issui*, are found in many contexts.

It was noted earlier that in traditional five-phase theory, water is neither the central nor primary component. In the *Huai-nan Tzu* and related texts, however, water does have an antecedent position: "The hot pneuma of accumulated yang generates fire, and the embryonic essence of the fiery pneuma makes the sun; the cold pneuma of accumulated yin makes water, and the embryonic essence of the watery pneuma makes the moon; the embryonic essence left over from forming sun and moon makes the starry chronograms."[16] Water and fire, then, are often singled out as representative of yin and yang. This terminology frequently appears in the texts of Ise Shinto, due to the obvious association of the sun goddess with fire. And if Toyo'uke is the equal of Amaterasu, then naturally enough, he must be identified with the moon, and with water. For example, he wields the "power of Primal Water" (*issui no toku*), bestowed by Amenominakanushi-no-kami to "give birth to the propagation of life."[17] This link is "proven" by the fact that an alternate name for Toyo'uke is Miketsu-no-kami, and the word for water, *mizu*, is said to be a contraction of *miketsu*.[18] In fact, since water conquers fire in traditional five-phase theory, the Outer Shrine is arguably of higher status; and occasionally Toyo'uke is even identified with Amenominakanushi himself, the central deity of the cosmos at the

[15] *Issui* can also mean "one drop of water," although not in the Primal Water passage translated above.

[16] Section 3:1 (Shinshaku kambun taikei, 54:131). Translated in Edward H. Schafer, *Pacing the Void* (Berkeley: University of California Press, 1977), 43.

[17] *Zokuzoku gunshō ruijū*, 1:25, 94–95. The latter passage is also reproduced in *NST*, 19:132.

[18] See the passages cited in the previous note. When associated with water, Miketsu is written with the second character "pneuma," rather than the more customary "food" or "food offering."

opening of the *Kojiki*.[19] Water thus becomes a central motif in the texts compiled by the Watarai family.

The *Ruijū jingi hongen* presents the following argument from a Chinese source that uses the graph for water to "prove" its primacy:

> It says in the *Compendium of Primordial Life*,[20] "Water represents flowing: yin transforms into wetness, and circulates widely. Therefore when the graph [for water 水] is written, two people [人 , 人] join around one [vertical] stroke: what emerges from within is water. One is the first number, and the two people are like man and woman: when yin and yang commingle, they produce one. [Thus] water is the first of the five phases, the congealed liquid of Primal Pneuma (*genki*).[21]

Through this line of reasoning, water is the first *product* of the union of yin and yang, which have commingled to produce the material world through the mechanism of the five phases. Due to its flowing nature and its identity as Primal Pneuma, it circulates freely and propagates life.

In another section, drawn from the *Yamato Katsuragi hōzanki*—a late Kamakura text of Dual Shinto falsely attributed to Gyōgi, the charismatic Buddhist monk of the Nara period—water *precedes* heaven and earth and functions as a nurturing force: "Water is the source of the Way—flowing, it becomes the father and mother of the myriad things. Therefore it nurtures and makes grow the myriad forms of creation. Know this—since the distant past when water transformed, dividing into heaven and earth, on the High Plain of Heaven there was a single numinous entity. Its form was like that of a reed-shoot."[22]

In a later chapter of the same work, Ieyuki recounts a startling connection, based on sound, between the first sprouting reed (*ashikabi*) on the High Plain of Heaven (which, in the *Nihon shoki* account, subsequently transforms into Kuninotokotachi-no-mikoto) and the letter A (*A-ji*) of esoteric Buddhism, a symbol for the fundamentally unborn nature of all phenomena. This equivalence, which first appears in earlier *Gobusho* works, serves to amplify the inherent purity of the Shinto creation paradigm: the emergence of manifest form, of the gods, is fundamentally

---

[19] For example, see *Zokuzoku gunshō ruijū*, 1:47.

[20] "Yüan-ming pao," one of the twenty-eight sections of *Ch'un ch'iu wei*, a Han dynasty work of divination and prophecy.

[21] *NST*, 19:93.

[22] *NST*, 19:103; for the original passage, ibid., 63–64. The passage goes on to identify this deity as Brahma, whose vajra staff is eventually transmitted to earth and becomes the "mind/heart pillar" (*shin no mihashira*) of the Ise shrine.

The *Yamato Katsuragi hōzan ki* in fact begins with a similar creation account that depicts the transformation of water into heaven and earth, and the subsequent emergence of Vishnu. Brahma then manifests from a lotus within Vishnu's navel, and in turn gives birth to the Japanese gods. Ibid., 58.

unborn—untainted, pure. This is one of many passages devised to demonstrate that the relatively simple Shinto creation accounts are replete with esoteric significance, just as Shingon proclaims countless secret meanings within the exoteric sutras. Stringing together excerpts from various texts, Ieyuki goes on to argue that a crescent moon resembles a floating reed, and thus the letter A; furthermore, the yin-essence of the moon is water, which in turn is like the mind, reflecting all things.[23]

These interwoven patterns of association (water / reed / letter A / moon / mind) explain many of Zenchiku's symbolic equivalences. For example, in the *Go'on sangyoku shū* he states, "The impurity of the five organs arises from Primal Water. The emerging point of Primal Water is the single thought of the letter A."[24] This statement surely results from his exposure to these Shinto texts, rather than from orthodox Buddhist treatises, where these elements are not found in this configuration. In the symbolic discourse of medieval Shinto, physical resemblance, functional similarity, and perceived etymological and phonetic connection are used to erect a self-evident universe of correlative truth. While this mode of thought may be disturbing to some modern readers, it is common in the esoteric and "occult" traditions of many cultures, and in a different sense, in the language of poetry. Most perplexing to this reader is not the "illogical," unscientific nature of medieval Shinto, fusing what we consider unrelated aspects of reality, or its "refusal to recognize man as a source of initiative other than for action confirming [the stated] general order,"[25] but rather its blatant disregard for the pedigree of its appropriated motifs, symbols, and doctrines in their original Chinese or Buddhist contexts. This is another example of the "fracture of meaning" that occurs in Japan's absorption of continental culture, as discussed by David Pollack.[26] Nevertheless, as Shinto discourse develops in the medieval era, its transformational rules become increasingly focused and identifiable.

Most important, the above evidence demonstrates that the term *issui* as used by Zenchiku was absorbed from Shinto sources. It is often functionally equivalent to *ikki* (or *genki*), "primal pneuma." As A. C. Graham notes, despite its original (and still fundamental) connotation of breath, of "energetic fluid which vitalizes the body," the term *ch'i* was "adapted to cosmology as the universal fluid, active as yang and passive as yin, out of which all things condense and into which they dissolve."[27] This fluid is the content of the egg-like shape in the *Nihon shoki* cosmogony, and, as water,

---

[23] For this passage, see ibid., 119.

[24] *KKSS*, 170.

[25] Ooms, *Tokugawa Ideology*, 95.

[26] This is the basic theme of his *The Fracture of Meaning* (Princeton: Princeton University Press, 1986), especially as it manifests in a Japanese-Chinese (*wakan*) dialectic.

[27] Graham, *Disputers of the Tao*, 101.

is the bestower of life. This function of water is implicit in the phrase *issui no toku*, used above by Zenchiku to describe the powerful effect of the "flavorless flavor." In the following passage, the subliminal associations of Primal Pneuma with semen (and thus dew), and then water, can be discerned:[28] "At the time when heaven and earth opened into being, the primal divinity, a transformation of seminal pneuma (*seiki*), looked down below the heavens. He regulated the seasons by instructing the heavenly gods to shine upon the realm between heaven and earth, and furthered (*ri*) the growth of living things through the power of Primal Water (*issui no toku*)."[29]

One need hardly mention that Zenchiku uses the masculine symbol of the sword for his One Dewdrop, both in the rokurin ichiro texts and in the passage above ("The One Dewdrop is the inception of Primal Water, the bone of a sharp sword's power"). While in the Buddhist context the sword is a symbol for cutting away ignorance, in the above passage the graph that represents its sharpness (*ri*) has the potent meaning of "to benefit" or "to further"—and of course *ri* is none other than the Chinese *li* (advantage), one of the Four Qualities of the Creative.

In addition, the term ichiro itself also appears in Shinto writings. The character *ro* can also mean "to appear," "to manifest" (as in the native reading *arawaru*); thus it may mean "a single manifestation," as in "The Inner and Outer [Shrines] are not two, they are eternally of one substance; the heavenly and earthly deities are one manifestation (*ichiro*)."[30] This usage explains Tokiwa Gishin's ingenious rendition of Zenchiku's ichiro, "Oneness disclosed."[31]

There are many other associations of water in the Buddhist tradition that resurface in medieval Shinto: for example, the water metaphor underlying the Four Wisdoms,[32] and the conception of the Dharmadhātu as a

---

[28] Indeed, the masculine qualities of water shown here support the male gender of the god Toyo'uke of the Outer Shrine (despite the traditional yin associations of water, and of the moon).

[29] *Jinnō jitsuroku*, in *Zokuzoku gunsho ruijū*, 1:211–12.

[30] *Ruijū jingi hongen*, kan 8; *Zokuzoku gunsho ruijū*, 1:52.

[31] In the English edition of Hisamatsu Shin'ichi, *Zen and the Fine Arts* (Tokyo: Kodansha International, 1971), 101.

[32] For the Four Wisdoms, see chapter 2, note 45. Konishi Jin'ichi sees the *Five* Wisdoms of esoteric Buddhism (the fifth is *hokkai taishō chi*, the Wisdom of the Essential Nature of the Dharmadhātu) as a prototype for Zenchiku's six circles. He cites as evidence the water symbolism of the *Go'on sangyoku shū* passage discussed above, and Zenchiku's appropriation of Mirror-like Wisdom in the *Kichū* (see chapter 2). Konishi, *Nōgakuron*, 250 ff. However, I agree with Itō's position that Zenchiku's immediate source is the canon of medieval Shinto, which has both absorbed and reconfigured the esoteric symbolism. For example, the appeal of the Mirror-like Wisdom to Zenchiku is the *mirror* metaphor, as it appears in Shinto; he never mentions the other four wisdoms. On the other hand, Konishi's linking of Zeami's

vast ocean in *The Awakening of Faith*, discussed in chapter 4. In the latter context, the term *issui* sometimes signifies "one body of water," representing the One (emptiness, principle, etc.) that is functionally nondual with the Many.[33] In Shinto contexts, however, the One is the temporal, genealogical source for the Many, and this is the most prominent meaning of *issui/ichiro* symbolism used by Zenchiku.

In the native literary tradition, the image of dewdrop as generative seed appears frequently. Perhaps the most prominent example is in the Chinese Preface to the *Kokinshū*: "Poetry grew as a cloud-brushing tree grows from a wispy seedling, or a heaven-reflecting billow from a dewdrop."[34] Both the cloud/wave imagery and the phrase "heaven-reflecting" link the realms of sky and sea, of heaven and earth, in a manner reminiscent of the following: "The pneuma of water changes form. Thus heavenly pneuma falls [as precipitation], and earthly pneuma rises [as mist]; heaven and earth commingle, and grasses and trees sprout. Is this not due to the power of water?"[35] Not only is water the source of all life, but in the natural world it is constantly separating and reunifying. Like Japanese poetry itself,[36] water thus has the power of *harmonizing* yin and yang, of reunifying heaven and earth.

The importance of esoteric Buddhism in the formulation of the symbolic discourse of medieval Shinto cannot be overemphasized. It is true that much of the rhetoric of Buddhist-Shinto relation is based on the exoteric essence/trace metaphor, which emphasizes the mutuality, the codependence of paired symbols—and thus their inherent relativity, their emptiness. But Shingon takes the opposite position: its symbols are absolute, esoteric Truth. The Dharmakāya has form, it preaches directly (*hosshin*

---

musical theory to *shōmyō*, the liturgical chant of Japanese Buddhism, suggests a highly plausible medium of indirect influence. Konishi, 251.

[33] For example, in Kūkai's *Hizō hōyaku*: "The great space, being vast and tranquil, embraces all phenomena within itself; the great ocean, being deep and serene, contains in its vast body of water (*issui*) countless beings (*senbon*). As the cardinal number one is the mother of one hundred and one thousand, so is emptiness the root of all provisional existences." *Kōbō Daishi zenshū*, 1:452. Translation modified from Hakeda, *Kūkai*, 201, following the glosses in *Kōbō Daishi chosaku zenshū*, 1:179. This passage is also quoted in the *Ruijū jingi hongen*; *NST*, 19:105.

[34] *NKBT*, 8:335–37; Helen McCullough, trans., *Kokin Wakashū* (Stanford: Stanford University Press, 1985), 257.

[35] Quoted in Jihen's *Shinpū waki*. *Zokuzoku gunsho ruijū*, 1:119. This also appears in *Jinnō jitsuroku*, ibid., 212.

[36] Cf. the Kana Preface: "Poetry it is which without effort moves heaven and earth, touches with pathos the unseen gods and demons, makes tender the bonds between men and women, and comforts the hearts of valiant warriors." *NKBT*, 8:93; translated by Edwin A. Cranston.

seppō) through the symbolic language of the Three Mysteries—mudrā (Body), mantra (Speech), and meditation (Mind). Thus when *mikkyō* symbolization is absorbed into Ise Shinto, the absolute divinity of such traditional symbols as mirror, sword, jewel, and pillar is implicitly affirmed.

Most important of all, the esoteric ideal of secrecy, of inner truth, seems to give ontological priority to that which is within—the mind/heart.[37] In Shingon, the body is a microcosm of the universe; the adept visualizes an internal stupa, comprising the Six Elements. The most widely practiced visualization is the "contemplation of the letter A" (*a-ji kan*): a lunar orb forms within the heart, embodying emptiness and the clarity of the en-lightened mind. On the face of the moon is visualized the letter A, repre-senting the fundamental nonbirth of all phenomenal existents. Through the chain of association just described, in Shinto discourse the heart/moon becomes the divine mirror, the inner palace of Konton whence the first reeds of being/feeling sprout.[38] In this fashion, the gradual shift in Shinto dogma from a traditional insistence on external, ritual purity to an increas-ing emphasis on inner, spiritual purity is accelerated through extended interaction with esoteric Buddhism.

JIHEN AND YOSHIDA SHINTO

The Shinto sources examined to this point were generated in the Ise re-gion, but the capital was also an important center of medieval Shinto. Of the traditionally powerful Shinto families of the nobility, the Urabe—diviners at court and, from the mid–Heian period, hereditary custodians of the Hirano and Yoshida Shrines—emerged as the most influential. The family branched into two, and the Yoshida faction spawned the most enduring of the medieval Shinto schools. Their activity was, at least in part, motivated by political considerations, as the Yoshida scrambled to maintain their prestige in the face of the decay of the *ritsuryō* system.

The first important scholar of the family was Urabe Kanekata (active mid-thirteenth century) who wrote an important early commentary to the *Nihon shoki*, entitled *Shaku Nihongi*. Most influential of all was Yoshida

---

[37] In its original Mahayana context, esoteric Buddhism affirms the nonduality of inner and outer, microcosm and macrocosm, and so forth. When the context shifts to medieval Shinto, however, dualistic tendencies emerge. See chapter 7.

In his summary of pre-Tokugawa Shinto/Confucian hybrid thought, Herman Ooms notes the primacy of theories of mind in Zen, which resonates with Neo-Confucian thought in both China and Japan. Ooms, *Tokugawa Ideology*, 97. I would simply point out that, within medieval Shinto, the emphasis on purity of mind/heart predates Zen influence and can be traced most directly (although not exclusively) to Shingon.

[38] See discussion of Kaneyoshi's *Nihon shoki sanso* cosmogony in chapter 7.

Kanetomo (1435–1511), the founder of the Yuiitsu Shintō (The Only Shinto) movement. He attempted to establish Yoshida Shrine, in the eastern hills of Kyoto, as the center of all Shinto institutions, proclaiming that the divinity of Ise had moved to the new sanctuary (Daigen-gū, Shrine of the Great Beginning) he had constructed in 1484. As might be expected, this campaign infuriated the Ise Shrine establishment. His most important work, the *Yuiitsu Shintō myōbō yōshū* (officially attributed to his ancestor Kanenobu), declares that the Shinto deities are the supreme rulers of the universe. Dismissing the orthodox *honji-suijaku* doctrine as a conventional, exoteric teaching, Kanetomo claims that the esoteric truth, transmitted from antiquity by the deity Amenokoyane-no-mikoto, is the opposite: Shinto is the root, Confucianism the branches and leaves, Buddhism the fruit and flowers. In fact, he uses the Primal Water metaphor to describe the pedigree of his "Shinto of the Original Source":

> From the mysterious beginning when yin and yang were not yet distinguishable, and then from Kuninotokotachi-no-mikoto through to Amaterasu-ōkami, our Way of the Gods was transmitted with an air of profundity and wonder. Amaterasu [in turn] bestowed it to Amenokoyane-no-mikoto. Since then until the present impure, degenerate age, it has drawn from the original water of Primal Pneuma (*ikki no gensui*), not tasting a single drop of the three creeds. Thus there is just one teaching.[39]

For an understanding of Zenchiku, however, a more important figure is Jihen (active mid-fourteenth century). Born into the Urabe family, Jihen was the older brother of Urabe (or Yoshida) Kenkō (1283-1350), the famous author of *Tsurezuregusa*. As a young man he was attracted to Buddhism and studied the Tendai teachings on Mount Hiei; Jihen of course is a Buddhist name. Aware of the gradual decline of Buddhism, however, and inspired by a series of revelatory dreams in 1329 and 1330, he converted to Shinto. His subsequent writings are strongly influenced by Ise Shinto, containing many of the same motifs and symbols discussed above. In fact, the preface to his *Kyūji hongi gengi*, the record of a pilgrimage to Ise, was written by Watarai (Higaki) Tsuneaki. On balance, however, his writings are more political than those of the Watarai family, with an emphasis on Shinto as the Way of the Emperor; in this sense he resembles Kitabatake Chikafusa (1293-1354), author of the *Jinnō shōtōki*. Jihen's views have been seen as an endorsement of the Southern Court, and of the Kemmu Restoration.[40] In addition, he was the originator of the reverse *honji-suijaku* argument later adopted by Kanetomo. His most influential work was the *Toyoashihara shinpū waki* of 1340, a summary of his views along

---

[39] *NST*, 19:239.
[40] Kubota, *Chūsei Shintō*, 159.

with selections from other works, in a format reminiscent of the *Ruijū jingi hongen*. Commissioned by Ano Renshi, mother of Emperor Go-Murakami, it was widely read by influential figures in government.

Several of Zenchiku's later rokurin ichiro treatises quote directly from "a certain Shinto work." Because many of the quoted passages are excerpted in multiple works, the source is not always clear, but Itō Masayoshi has convincingly argued that Zenchiku most frequently turned to the *Shinpū waki*[41] for Shinto material. Aside from its political character, largely irrelevant to Zenchiku, two themes of this work stand out. First, in contrast to Ieyuki, who simply incorporates Buddhist parallels to enhance the status of Shinto symbols, Jihen makes explicit comparisons between the two creeds. Second, the ideals of purity, sincerity, and the like, present in the *Gobusho* and Ieyuki's writings, receive even greater emphasis, particularly in the form of prohibitions against impure behavior. The latter theme is evident in a motif that first appeared in the *Kichū*, the "purity of the three circles."

THE PURITY OF THE THREE CIRCLES

Zenchiku's final major compendium of the rokurin ichiro system, the *Hichū* (*Bunshō bon*) begins,

> The Way of sarugaku and kagura began in the age of the gods. Although the sixty-six entertainments later came into being, they are all governed by *Okina* (*Shikisanba*)—our Way follows Shinto and Buddhist ritual, not personal preference. Still, it is true that [sarugaku] also serves as a vehicle [for the beauty] of flowers and birds, the wind and the moon, an amusement for all under heaven to enjoy. But even if a family of this sacred profession lacks fame, by performing kagura and preserving the Way, it will be blessed by divine protection. Evil conduct which does not accord with the Way incurs sin. Still, there is no obstacle to an individual establishing his own path, utilizing personal strengths. This was the case with my grandfather, and also with Zeami's transmission of his own style.
>
> The heart of the Six Circles and One Dewdrop is the first three circles: these represent the divine art of the "purity of the three circles," the Three Bodies of truth, reward, and transformation,[42] the Threefold Truth of empty, provisional, and mean.[43] It says in a certain Shinto work, "Through activity, the onset

---

[41] Itō, *Komparu Zenchiku no kenkyū*, 171–78. In particular, Zenchiku cites the *Shinpū waki* by name in his *Meishuku shū*.

[42] The three bodies of the Buddha: *dharmakāya* (body of the Law), *saṃbhogakāya* (reward-body), and *nirmāṇakāya* (transformation-body).

[43] The threefold truth of Tendai doctrine: emptiness (*kū*), provisional existence (*ge*), and the mean (*chū*).

of being occurs," and so on. Or, "Since in the beginning there is vital energy, the onset of form occurs." Or again, "At the beginning unshakeable integrity is established." In short, in our profession the foundation of the yūgen of song and dance derives from the the supreme attainment of the purity of the three circles in the three activities of body, speech, and mind; this becomes the spirit of the six sense organs, the Six Circles and One Dewdrop.[44]

Here one sees how Shinto notions of purity and directness have come to dominate Zenchiku's rhetoric. For him, sarugaku is a form of kagura; the ritual performance of *Okina* is the basis of the art, and it results in divine favor. More secular performances that feature "flowers and birds, the wind and the moon" are adjuncts to this religious function. The first three circles, which have been described elsewhere as the foundation of yūgen, now also represent the Shinto ideals of honesty and sincerity. This is the fundamentally pure state of mind that the accomplished performer dwells in, even as he performs in the variety of styles represented by the lower three circles.

In these opening remarks, Zenchiku hints at a new alignment of the six circles. In earlier treatises, the gateway to the profundity of the first three circles is the cultivation of the Three Roles, as the young actor discovers purity within the "secular" forms of *monomane*. Once the essential yūgen of the first three circles is established, he proceeds to perform successfully the roles represented by the Circle of Forms, which are supported by an underlying essence of yūgen (see figure 6-4). In a sense, this paradigm embraces Buddhist nonduality. To be sure, Zenchiku never entirely abandons this conception of training. Nevertheless, in the *Hichū* he implies that the purity and grace of the first three circles are most fully experienced through a devotional attitude, in the ritual performance of *Okina*. This experience enables one to perform the secular roles of the fourth through sixth circles with impunity, but the purity is only fully experienced within the sacred form, not in the relatively tainted, less fundamental art of *monomane*. By comparison, this new vision is implicitly somewhat dualistic.

The unnamed "Shinto work" here is probably the *Jinnō jitsuroku*, another apocryphal work of the same period as the *Gobusho*, where the quoted phrases describe Kuninotokotachi, the first of the *kami* to emerge.[45] In the earlier *Hichū (Kanshō bon)*, Zenchiku uses the same quotations to describe the Circle of Longevity, but here they are applied to the grouping of the first three circles, as the foundation, or "beginning," of the art. A motif found in the *Shinpū waki*, used here and elsewhere, is the "purity of the six sense organs" (*rokkon shōjō*). Zenchiku implies that the spiritual purity of the first three circles transforms the inherently deluded,

---

[44] KKSS, 249. In Buddhist terminology, *sanrin* sometimes denotes body, speech, and mind.
[45] *Zokuzoku gunsho ruijū*, 1:211.

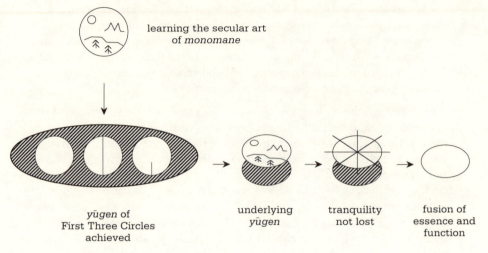

FIG. 6-4. Learning the Six Circles

impure six senses (mind is the sixth), associated by number to the six circles. Zenchiku also aligns the six circles with the six paths of transmigration; as spinning wheels, they are symbols of samsaric attachment. Yet through the spiritual purity of the first three circles, they turn like the Dharma Wheel in praise of the Buddha. In general, the number six is associated with cyclical suffering, which in turn is transformed by various underlying trinities of religious merit.[46]

The expression "purity of the three circles" (*sanrin shōjō*) derives from Miwa Shinto, a late-Kamakura offshoot of Dual Shinto that fuses esoteric Buddhist symbolism with faith in the deity of Mount Miwa. In a famous legend associated with the shrine, retold in the noh play *Miwa*, the priest Genpin makes an offering of a robe to the Miwa deity. In this context, the "three circles" (Miwa and *sanrin* are written with the same character compound) are traditional Buddhist symbols for the alms-giver, the receiver of alms, and the alms given. When almsgiving is practiced without attachment, these three elements are equally pure. In the following passage, Zenchiku explains in very personal terms his own faith in the native gods, attaching a poem attributed to the Miwa deity upon receiving Genpin's offering:

> I have practiced these matters for many years, attaining a mind of faith through constant effort, so there is not a bit of intentionality in my actions. As I

[46] A similar symbolic transformation is depicted in the *Tenchi reiki ki*, a work of Dual Shinto: "Six snakes appear in the sky of the earthly realm, grab their tails in their teeth, and turn into six circles, putting a stop to the samsara of the six paths. These [in turn] manifest the six perfections, and the six circles shine brightly, manifesting the virtue of the Dharmakāya." Here, the number six also has the positive association of the six "perfections" (*pāramitā*) of the bodhisattva. *Kōbō Daishi zenshū*, 5:110.

simply perform with a pure heart, the wondrous effects of the different compositions are present of themselves. The Buddha Nature of the purity of the three circles is like a bright mirror, shining as the moon/mind. Above all, in performing this sacred art I have been blessed with happiness. This is not my doing, it is a favor received from Divinity. He who harbors thoughts of clever words, of erotic pleasure, of confusing people, of getting ahead in the world, will suffer divine retribution. One should simply act in accord with the Way of Heaven that all are endowed with, following its path. To yield to the Way is called Purity, to study without deviation is called Honesty. One should correctly practice the Way through the purity of the three circles, praying for divine favor. The purity of the three circles is a profound teaching of Miwa. Thus the poem:

Miwagawa no	This Chinese robe,
kiyoku mo kiyoki	pure as the purity
karakoromo	of the Miwa River—
kuru to omou na	do not think it given,
toru to omowaji	I will not think it taken.[47]

For Zenchiku, the state of nonattachment extolled in the deity's poem is a perfect analogue for the purity of his own first three circles. He concludes with his own poem, repeating the image of the clear Miwa River:

Expressing my own humble feelings, I write,

Miwagawa no	Pure as the pure
kiyoku mo kiyoki	Miwa River,
minakami wa	the upper courses
arawanu mizu no	are indeed the unmanifest
kokoro narikeri	heart of Water.

This final tanka brings together many of the themes examined in this chapter. To paraphrase, "The upper, unseen waters are pure like the river before my eyes; so too, this pristine heart derives from pure, Primal Water." The allure of the unseen upper courses—analogous to the urge for inner purity, for the age of the gods, for the antecedent state of Konton— presages a new emphasis upon *kokoro*, the mind/heart that denotes the emotional, the intuitive, the unpremeditated, the "sincere." Within the microcosm of Zenchiku's own spiritual evolution, there are hidden currents of medieval culture at work. Just as he no longer insists on the nonduality of Mahayana Buddhism, on a classical balance between emotion and expression in his art, in the late medieval era the aesthetic and spiritual ideals of Japanese culture are moving toward a radical rebirth.

[47] *KKSS*, 246. In the noh play *Miwa* the deity's poem begins *Mitsu no wa wa / kiyoku kiyoki zo*. *Kara* (empty), imbedded in *karakoromo* (Chinese robe) in the third line, denotes a state of nonattachment. Mount Miwa is situated in the Hatsuse region; for the significance of this locale to Zenchiku, see chapter 2, note 166.

Chapter Seven: Conclusion

THIS STUDY has examined the rokurin ichiro phenomenon
from many vantage points. It was introduced as a compendium of dramaturgical principles, written to transmit a body of
knowledge to succeeding generations of performers. In the
ensuing chapters, the responses of Kaneyoshi and Shigyoku
were surveyed to uncover Buddhist and Confucian patterns of
signification. Finally, Zenchiku's own Shinto-derived views
were investigated. This journey has demonstrated the essential
flexibility, or perhaps ambiguity, of the symbols Zenchiku has
created. Like the seven notes of the musical scale, these categories generate resonances in sympathetic regions of Buddhist,
Confucian, and Shinto doctrine. The result is a fascinating
alignment of cognate principles, a result that might not have
emerged under more conventional circumstances. Furthermore, the collective structures implemented—Shigyoku's
Kegon-derived, psychologically oriented interpenetration of
all circles, the revolving cycle of discrete, objective states in
Kaneyoshi's system, and the genealogical stages of creation in
Shinto—denote the differing modes of conceptualization and
discourse prevalent in each tradition.

Considered from the standpoint of the historical genesis of
the *Rokurin ichiro no ki* text, the Zeami-derived material presented in chapter 3 is clearly antecedent. However, to interpret
this performance dimension as the fundamental layer of meaning, and the commentaries as secondary, is to misrepresent the
cultural and intellectual process embodied in the rokurin ichiro
phenomenon. For this monument of seven symbols is the
product of a common cultural environment shared by all three
men, and the interpretations of Shigyoku and Kaneyoshi can
be seen as the articulation of subconscious forces that shaped
Zenchiku's original conception. The most persuasive demon-
stration of this is Zenchiku's wholesale adoption of their
categorizations in his subsequent rokurin ichiro treatises.

The most immediate benefit for the reader of the previous chapters is the correlation of related doctrines from the three traditions, the result of their mutual application to the individual circles. These correspondences reveal some of the implicit cultural foundations of medieval artistic expression. For example, the Circle of Height provides the following:

performance	arising of sound and movement; pattern; feeling; cold, clear singing; experience of the Flower
Buddhist	nature origination
Confucian	primacy of initiative
Shinto	division of heaven and earth

Commentators often associate this appearance of movement or pattern against an empty background in the medieval arts—for example, in monochrome ink painting, or temple gardens—with the form/emptiness dialectic typical of Mādhyamika-derived Zen argumentation. Such a conception is apophatic in tone, emphasizing the insubstantiality and inherent emptiness of material form. However, the rokurin ichiro texts suggest that, in noh, an implicit Buddhist model is nature origination, which portrays the Absolute as a generative matrix. This kataphatic theme is further reinforced by Zeami's tathāgatagarbha-derived theory of music. Similarly, the Shinto metaphor of *tenchi kaibyaku* emphasizes the kinetic force of creation, and the Confucian cognate of *yüan* represents life-force at its most potent, in the spring.

Another example is the notion of jo–ha–kyū, widely regarded as the key structural and rhythmic principle of noh composition and performance. Because Zeami states that "all things of the universe . . . partake of the process of jo–ha–kyū," one is tempted to see this as an aesthetic of impermanence: "all things arise from dependent causes, and eventually vanish." But the alignment of the final kyū stage with the Circle of Abiding, rather than the Circle of Breaking, suggests that, rather than the demise of a transient phenomenon, kyū is the stage at which it is fully delineated, resolved as a discrete entity—what Zeami means by "completion." In the Buddhist sense, each dharma peacefully abides on a lotus-cushion of Suchness, inherently perfect, filling the entire universe. This meaning is reinforced by the Confucian image of flourishing summer grasses, and by the white faces of the gods, individually visible in the effulgence of the sun goddess who has just emerged from the rock-cave.

One can also discover important correlations between, for example, Shinto and Buddhist phenomenologies. As noted, the doctrine of nature origination, aligned to the Circle of Height by Shigyoku, provides that all phenomena originate from the "nonproductive conditions of the nature of the Dharmadhātu"—in other words, from the ground of the Absolute, rather than from dependent causes. But there is also a strong parallel in the Mahayana tradition between the arising of phenomena and the instanta-neous hierophanies of the sutras—for example, the sudden appearance of the Tathāgata, or flowers falling from the sky. This parallel is symbolized by Shigyoku's golden wave, arising on the tranquil Nature Sea: once the state of no-mind is attained, these blissful experiences occur spon-taneously. This theme of origination as hierophany is further highlighted by another Circle of Height correlative, the stage of hana—the delight experienced at the instant when the door of the rock-cave opens. This emphasis on feeling, on subjective experience, on delight, is particularly strong in many of the new forms of Kamakura Buddhism, reflecting a native preference for experientiality over rationality in all modes of re-ligious discourse.[1]

To avoid further tedious explication, readers are invited to draw their own comparisons. Figure 7-1 summarizes the major equivalences dis-cussed in the preceding chapters.

One trend is clearly discernible in the art of Zenchiku's age: an increas-ing emphasis on subjective states, on the mind of both the artist and his audience. This is in marked contrast to early waka treatises, which define only objective styles, and then later, the correct pedagogical sequence. An important factor here is a typically medieval concern with the process of reception, with affective theory, due to the inherently social nature of the dominant literary arts of the age. In renga, a participant must act almost si-multaneously as poet and creative reader, and noh, as a performing art, pro-vides the actor with immediate evidence of the audience response. As Thomas Hare notes, this trend toward theories of mind in art is evident within the development of Zeami's own writings.[2] The early *Fūshi kaden*, considered primarily an explication of his father Kannami's views, describes varying roles in terms of appearance, of external characteristic. But in the *Shūgyoku tokka*, the treatise that had the most direct effect on Zenchiku, almost all topics presented are subjective in some sense. And even within Zenchiku's categories that represent explicit styles—such as *rangyoku* for the harin— the emphasis is on the state of mind of the performer or the psychology of the audience's emotional response. The spiritual and intellectual traditions represented in the *Ki* commentaries both nurture this tendency and also provide principles by which such artistic praxis can be articulated.

As a correlary to this trend, there is an increasing emphasis on music and sound in Zeami.[3] Note that both Zeami and Zenchiku choose to categorize

---

[1] Masatoshi Nagatomi describes this as a consistent Japanese tendency to emphasize *ji* (phenomena, facts, particularity, experience) over *ri* (principle, theory, universality, ab-straction).

[2] Hare, *Zeami's Style*, 29–30.

[3] Also noted in ibid., 30.

	Circle of Longevity	Circle of Height	Circle of Abiding	Circle of Forms	Circle of Breaking	Circle of Emptiness	One Dewdrop
PERFORMANCE	round form of breathing	cold, clear singing	mental ease, abiding in movement & no-movement	three roles	mixing bad technique with good	no-form, no-characteristic	the spirit that joins the six circles
	visual appearance of role, before motion begins	onset of sound, motion	all forms come to completion	*monomane*	rank of the sublime	style of the young voice	
	vessel of *yūgen*	deep feeling arises					
	the wondrous	the flower	fascination				
	jo	*ha*	*kyū*				
	body	speech	mind				
BUDDHIST	true Emptiness	birth	abiding	change	extinction	true Emptiness	wisdom sword; One Blade
	one source of motion and stillness	nature origination	residing in the Dharma position	transformation of One Mind	desire as the Buddha realm	final release of enlightenment (Nirvana)	six circles collect into one dewdrop
CONFUCIAN	The Creative	initiative	flourish	advantage	perseverance	Great Ultimate	Ultimate of Non-being; beyond dualism of principle and material force
	circulation of Heaven	spring, wood, benevolence	summer, fire, propriety	autumn, metal, justice	winter, water, wisdom		
SHINTO	heaven and earth not yet divided	division of heaven and earth	heaven is heaven, earth is earth				Primal Water

FIG. 7-1. Major Correspondences

compositions by their musical qualities (*go'on*, five sounds), while individual *roles* are represented by a visual metaphor (*santai*, three "bodies"). Indeed many of the strongest emotional effects in Zenchiku are associated with singing—for example, the high, clear singing and deep feeling of the shurin. This emphasis underscores the internal, subjective qualities of aural experience, in contrast to the discriminating, objective nature of visual awareness. This distinction is perfectly articulated by the corresponding qualities of the Creative provided in Kaneyoshi's commentary: initiative (*yüan*), the cognate for the Circle of Height, represents the onset of primal, undifferentiated energy that envelops the awareness, while the quality of differentiation (*li*) is the analogue for the Circle of Forms, where variety of appearance is manifest in the roles of *monomane*.

In the remainder of this chapter I will examine three final topics, attempting to situate more precisely the rokurin ichiro texts within the cultural trends of Zenchiku's age.

THE SOTERIOLOGY OF THE ARTS

For Zenchiku, a professional performer, the spiritual value of artistic cultivation is a matter of personal experience. His art—which, despite its secular origins, is associated with a tradition of religious ritual—is a means of self-cultivation that reinforces his own devout nature. In his remarks and those of his commentators, however, we hear echoes of an ongoing medieval debate on the spiritual worth of artistic activity.

The single most important text in this controversy—alluded to by Zenchiku at the opening of his *Kabu zuinō ki*—[4] is a famous remark by the T'ang poet Po Chü-i, who in old age became a devout Buddhist. Fearful that his passion for the secular art of poetry, emblematic of attachment to sensory pleasure and egotistical accomplishment, would be an impediment to salvation, he donated a collection of his poetry to a Buddhist library with the dedication: "I pray that my worldly achievements of this life, my excesses of wild words and fancy language, be transformed in future lives into praise for the Buddhist vehicle, establishing a karmic connection to the turning of the Dharma Wheel."[5]

William LaFleur and others have discussed how such "wild words and fancy language," through a rationale of nonduality, might be seen as extolling the Dharma.[6] Therefore the focus here will be the remarks of the

[4] *KKSS*, 122.

[5] From "Hsiang-shan ssu Pai-shih Lo-chung chi chi," in *Pai Chü-i chi*, chuan 71. ——

[6] See Mezaki Tokue, "Aesthete-Recluses during the Transition from Ancient to Medieval Japan," in Earl Miner, ed., *Principles of Classical Japanese Literature* (Princeton: Princeton

three principals. The modern reader must understand, however, that this issue was a serious concern of the age. While Taoistic spontaneity, in the form of artistic intuition, is often promoted as an ideal in the arts now associated with Japanese Zen, it is important to remember that in the Muromachi period Zen monks were frequently censured for indulging in literary pursuits at the expense of meditation practice.[7] Pressing from the other direction, sarugaku performers in particular were eager to elevate the status of their art, to endow it with spiritual worth and cultural pedigree, for its origins were hardly aristocratic.

Shigyoku justifies music and dance by listing many precedents. First, he announces that it is a divine activity, citing the performance of the gods in front of the heavenly rock-cave and pointing to two groups of bodhisattvas associated with celestial music and dance. Most significantly, in the esoteric tradition the Bodhisattva of Song symbolizes the activity of preaching the Dharma, while the Bodhisattva of Dance represents the playful spontaneity and freedom of the supernatural powers that accompany enlightenment.[8] And even such a "dignified" holy man as the disciple Kāśyapa could not restrain himself, jumping up to dance at the performance of a celestial musician.[9]

The gist of Shigyoku's argument is that "all phenomena of this world manifest Truth." In particular, the statement that "Raising and lowering the feet, all is the mind of Mañjuśrī; seeing, hearing, and understanding, all is the practice of Samantabhadra" suggests that the mental attention directed at performers on stage is a means to realize that every action emerges from, and returns to, the absolute ground of Emptiness, an opportunity to participate in the interpenetration of all phenomena through direct cognition. One might object that this awareness is attainable during any experience, not just the aesthetic. On the other hand, Zenchiku's theories suggest that the art of sarugaku, through a foundation of yūgen, is a more focused, direct manifestation of these truths. In general, this is yet another pronouncement of the nonduality of secular activity and spiritual awareness, accessible at any moment. In this sense, it echoes the "sudden" orientation of Shigyoku's rokurin ichiro commentary.

Most compelling is the faintly humorous story of Prelate Rin'e, who

University Press, 1985), 156 ff.; LaFleur, *The Karma of Words*, 8–9, 80–97; and Pollack, *The Fracture of Meaning*, 93–95.

[7] For example, a famous admonition of the Zen master Musō Soseki (1275–1351), still chanted daily at many Rinzai temples, contains the statement, "As for those students who care about nothing but non-Buddhist books and their own literary reputations, they are nothing more than laypeople with shaven heads." W. S. Merwin and Sōiku Shigematsu, trans., *Sun at Midnight* (San Francisco: North Point Press, 1989), 166.

[8] As described in chapter 2, note 35.

[9] See chapter 2, note 38. This story is also recounted in Kaneyoshi's *Sarugaku kōshō ki* (KKSS, 567–68), suggesting its wide circulation.

had issued a prohibition against the performance of music at Kasuga Shrine because it disturbed his meditations. At the end of a long retreat, the Kasuga deity informed him that music penetrated to the highest realms, pleasing the gods and buddhas; and that, consequently, Rin'e's offerings would not be accepted.[10] Here we see negated the dualistic notion that only restraint and silence are appropriate for the monastic life. Shigyoku interpolates that the offerings of music and dance are even more efficacious than preaching the Dharma in obtaining divine favor.

Kaneyoshi's commentary reveals a different *problematik*. In the Confucian tradition, music is revered as one of the methods of cultivation; it generates feelings of empathy, and is fundamental in the development of *jen*. More specifically, there are correlations between the five phases and the Chinese pentatonic scale, the patterns of dance and the rules of geomancy, and so forth. One sees this in Kaneyoshi's citation, "In dance, one sets the rhythm of the eight instruments and moves in the directions of the eight winds," and in his remark that music nurtures the ears and dance promotes circulation. The performance of music and dance is thus a microcosmic reenactment of, a resonance with, the harmonious interactions of vital energy that comprise the underlying pattern of the natural world—precisely the pattern represented by the inner four circles, as the four seasons, of Kaneyoshi's rokurin ichiro commentary. So the issue is not "music or no music," but rather "What is good music?" In other words, what kind of music is suitable for ritual and self-cultivation?

In the cultural context of Muromachi Japan, Kaneyoshi realizes that the popular entertainment of sarugaku might be dismissed as the equivalent of the "lewd music" of Cheng criticized by Confucius, in contrast to, for example, the more decorous, ancient *gagaku* of court ritual.[11] Consequently, he takes the Mencian position that even contemporary music is valuable and should be performed, because it unifies the ruler and his people. Thus, whenever an audience gathers to share the experience of music—especially a performance sponsored by a ruler such as the shogun—the social aspect of Confucian morality, and the public bond between ruler and subject, is furthered. In the process, distinctions between good and bad, ancient and contemporary, decorous and raucous, are neutralized. Citing the Sung thinker Hu Hung (and distorting his original meaning),[12] Kaneyoshi implies that heavenly music and popular music are identical in function, differing only in emotional tone.

[10] See chapter 2, note 46.

[11] The paradox of sarugaku as a "divine art of beggars" is discussed in Toita Michizō, *Nō: kami to kojiki no geijutsu* (Tokyo: Serika shobō, 1973).

[12] See chapter 2, note 59.

Music, dance, and poetry are so prominent in the native tradition, and in the mythology of the chronicles, that artistic activity requires no justification from the Shinto perspective. It should be noted that all three principals acknowledge the authority of the heavenly rock-cave incident as the ancient and divine origin of contemporary sarugaku. Kaneyoshi adds the precedent of the Sarume, said to be descendants of the goddess Amanouzume who confronted the fierce Sarudahiko and then led him to Ise. Both the presence of "saru" in the name and Amanouzume's role as chief performer in front of the rock-cave reinforce the divine associations of sarugaku. In a similar vein, Zeami notes that when the left-hand radical of the first character of the compound used to write kagura (divine music) is dropped, kami changes to saru, and thus the compound becomes sarugaku.[13] In this fashion, etymology—the linguistic equivalent of cosmogony, and thus a fundamental mode of argumentation in medieval Shinto—is used to establish the divine origins of the art.

The sarcasm of Nankō Sōgen's postscript provides the refreshingly antinomian perspective of Zen. A poet-monk and early companion of Ikkyū, Nankō later left the priesthood to became a professional poet.[14] When asked to respond to Zenchiku's manuscript, he refuses to make more than a few cursory observations. After dismissing Shigyoku as verbose and faintly mocking the morality of Kaneyoshi, he gleefully admits that, when enjoying music and dance, many Buddhist priests indulge in the "backward practice" of wine and women. Nankō then illustrates the proper attitude by alluding to two koans in the Pi-yen lu. The first is case 44:

> Ho Shan imparted some words saying, "Cultivating study is called 'learning.' Cutting off study is called 'nearness.' Going beyond these two is to be considered real going beyond."
> A monk came forward and asked, "What is 'real going beyond'?" Shan said, "Knowing how to beat the drum."[15]

Surely, in this context the implication is that true music transcends the dichotomy of careful study and total spontaneity. Nankō then alludes to dance by mentioning Chin Niu, who appears in case 74:

> Every day at mealtime, Master Chin Niu would personally take the rice pail and do a dance in front of the monks' hall: laughing, out loud he would say, "Bodhisattvas, come eat!"

[13] In the Fūshi kaden; ZZ, 39, trans. in Rimer and Yamazaki, On the Art of the Nō Drama, 33.

[14] Little is known of Nankō's life; he trained at Shōkoku-ji, and he seemed to share Ikkyū's disgust with the Zen establishment. See Pollack, Zen Poems of the Five Mountains, 161.

[15] Translated by Thomas and J. C. Cleary, The Blue Cliff Record (Boulder: Shambala, 1977), 2:312.

Hsüeh Tou said, "Though he acted like this, Chin Niu was not good-hearted."

A monk asked Ch'ang Ch'ing, "When the man of old said, 'Bodhisattvas, come eat!' what was his meaning?" Ch'ing said, "Much like joyful praise on the occasion of a meal."[16]

This incident highlights the tension felt by monks who endeavor to be free of desire, like pure bodhisattvas, yet at mealtime they cannot ignore the pangs of appetite. Chin Niu dances in delight at this paradox, the inseparability of purity and desire in the human realm. Nankō's reference mocks those who suggest that art is devoid of emotional attachment.

Nankō then remarks that an overtly "spiritual" attitude toward sarugaku, as exemplified by the rokurin ichiro system, destroys the vitality of song and dance. He prefers simply to enjoy Zenchiku's performances, rather than daring to augment the erudite comments of Shigyoku and Kaneyoshi. Thus the Zen spokesman gets the last word, and the last laugh, negating Zenchiku's reified, rigid symbols that destroy the subtle life of noh, just as cooking ruins the delicate flavor of the Ai family's pears.[17]

MEDIEVAL SYNCRETIC PARADIGMS

The rokurin ichiro texts are, above all, an artifact of medieval syncretism. Although I have explicated the individual layers of signification, the reader must never lose sight of the larger composite entity. It is a syncretic (rather than comparative or analytic) urge that produced these texts. Once Zenchiku devised the original system, Shigyoku was inspired to interpret his symbols by correlating the performance categories with Buddhist doctrine—categories that, to be sure, were already pregnant with Buddhistic implication. Kaneyoshi in turn provided Confucian cognates (and some generalized Shinto comments), explicitly utilizing the rhetoric of the "unity of the three creeds." Subsequently, Zenchiku himself adopted the syncretist mode, incorporating into later treatises not only his commentators' categorizations, but also his own Shinto and Pure Land cognates, as well as additional typologies from waka criticism.

This phenomenon is essentially an example of correlative thinking, as I have discussed it in the Confucian tradition.[18] That is, to the extent that the various value systems can be shown to correspond, through their mutual application to Zenchiku's seven categories, a deeper level of principle, or truth, is established. The harmonious correspondences among the various

16 Ibid., 3:490.
17 See chapter 2, note 108.
18 See chapter 5.

creeds and principles ultimately serve to enhance each individual component; no favorites emerge. By impartially transmitting all of these viewpoints, Zenchiku endeavors to enhance the prestige and profundity of his art.

In Japan, the most prominent syncretist metaphor is *honji-suijaku*, or "fundamental essence, trace manifestation," briefly mentioned in the previous chapter. This terminology derives from the Tendai interpretation of the *Lotus Sutra*, which divides the scripture into two sections: the fundamental revelation of the Buddha's essence (*hon*) in the second half, and the parables that represent the trace manifestations (*shaku*) of accommodated truth in the first half. As Alicia Matsunaga points out, from the standpoint of Mahayana nonduality, the concrete manifestation is in no way inferior to the underlying essence.[19] It cannot be denied that to the casual observer, however, the widespread practice of pairing buddhas and kami *appears* to give precedence to the buddhas. They represent the hidden, profound essence of their localized, delimited manifestations, the native gods.

This implicitly hierarchical aspect of the *honji-suijaku* doctrine was skillfully appropriated by Shinto apologists. Jihen is a pivotal figure, the first to argue consistently for the innate priority of the kami. In the second half of his *Toyoashihara shinpū waki*, the syncretist work mentioned in the previous chapter, he makes a series of comparisons that explicitly argue for the underlying unity of Buddhism and Shinto, yet implicitly accord the latter a superior position. For example, he cites a work of Dual Shinto: "It says in the *Gyōmon shinshaku*,[20] 'The ground of [Shinto] deities does not accept a single speck of dust; at the gate of Buddhism, not a single dharma is abandoned. On the Nature Sea, there is no wind, [yet] a golden wave dances by itself: Divinity transforms (*ōke*), and Śākyamuni attains the Way.'"[21] In Shinto ritual observances, all impurities, all defilements of the sensory realm, are excluded; in Buddhism, on the other hand, the realm of the senses is not denied, due to its fundamental nonduality with Suchness. The buddhas thus mingle freely with the "dust of the world." Accordingly, it is an easy step to reposition Shinto divinity as the "ground," and the buddhas—particularly Śākyamuni, the historical Buddha—as the temporal, historical manifestation. The traditional *honji-suijaku* order is thus reversed, with Shinto emerging as the fundamental essence, the ori-

[19] Alicia Matsunaga, *The Buddhist Philosophy of Assimilation* (Tokyo: Sophia University, 1969), 224–27.

[20] The wording of the original *Ryōgū gyōmon shinshaku* passage (*Kōbō Daishi zenshū*, 5:151) differs significantly. In particular, it begins with the phrase "the actual ground of *principle* does not accept one speck of dust" rather than "the ground of the truly descended *kami*." However, the following sentence is identical, preserving the comparison between "Divinity" (*shinmei*) and Śākyamuni.

[21] *Zokuzoku gunsho ruijū*, 1:124.

gin. The golden-wave metaphor found in Shigyoku's commentary is then presented as an analogy:[22] just as a golden wave arises spontaneously on the Sea of Dharma Nature, so does the pure ground of Shinto divinity transform in response to the needs of sentient beings and thus the Buddha manifests in the material world. The implicit relation is that of the formless Dharmakāya to the nirmāṇakāya (J. ōjin), the transformed manifestation-body. Because there is "no wind"—no defiling ignorance—the purity of divinity remains unstained. Figure 7-2 contrasts the two symbolic interpretations of the golden-wave metaphor.

This example indicates how medieval Shinto skillfully adopts the principles of *Buddhist* discourse to establish its own superiority. The syncretic movement provides Shinto with what it had previously lacked: a functional mechanism of Buddhist-Shinto relation, by which the two creeds could be compared on equal terms. In my view, *shinbutsu shūgō* represents not merely the amalgamation of Buddhist and Shinto beliefs, but also their polarization. In the Buddhist mode of nonduality, the contrasting qualities of the two creeds are mutually defining, and thus equal; but when the arena shifts, the more dualistic conception of purity typical of Shinto enables the nativists to carve out a position of authority. Moreover, the amorphous quality of the Shinto deities, once a liability, now becomes an advantage as the native conception of divinity becomes functionally equivalent to the formless Dharmakāya.

The Shintoists are even more persuasive when the two creeds are compared in historical terms. Although the honji-suijaku doctrine is based on an ontological relation of essence and trace, because it depicts the appearance of avatars it is also inherently historical. Once the doctrine appears in a Shinto context, it inevitably shifts to the genealogical mode: the ontological priority of essence transfers to the historical precedence of antiquity. For example, Zeami notes that sarugaku originates in the age of the gods, with Amanouzume's performance at the heavenly rock-cave; the precedent for sarugaku he sees in India during the age of the Buddha is clearly secondary in importance, due to its "later" date.[23] Similarly, Jihen states that during the reign of Emperor Suinin, the kami ceded authority to the buddhas, speaking through an oracle.[24] This "permitted" Buddhism to arrive in Japan and quickly rise to a position of dominance in the religious sphere. Once Buddhism in turn declined, however, it was time for Shinto to reassume its rightful position of authority. This argument of course echoes the *mappō* (latter age of the Law) doctrine typical of medieval Buddhism, adapted to show the priority of the native gods. This political

---

[22] See chapter 4.

[23] For the relevant passages, see *ZZ*, 38, and Rimer and Yamazaki, *On the Art of the Nō Drama*, 31–32.

[24] *Zokuzoku gunsho ruijū*, 1:115.

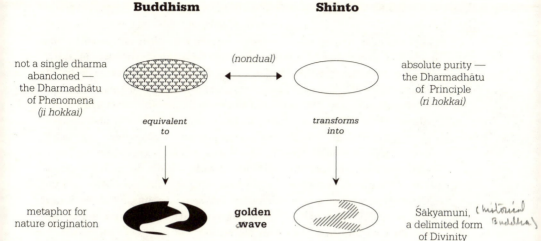

Buddhism   **Shinto**

not a single dharma
abandoned —
the Dharmadhātu
of Phenomena
(ji hokkai)

(nondual)

absolute purity —
the Dharmadhātu
of Principle
(ri hokkai)

*equivalent
to*

*transforms
into*

metaphor for
nature origination

**golden
wave**

Śākyamuni, (historical
a delimited form Buddha)
of Divinity

FIG. 7-2. The Golden Wave

advocacy of Shinto over Buddhism, often utilized to support the Japanese emperor,[25] distinguishes Jihen from his counterparts in Ise Shinto, whose primary orientation is religious.

To gauge the status of syncretist thought in Zenchiku's time, one need look no farther than Kaneyoshi. It is he who introduces the "unity of the three creeds" rhetoric in the *Ki*, and his activities in the cultural sphere are astonishingly diverse. While partly based on lectures given by the Shinto scholar Urabe Kanetsubu, his commentary to the "Age of the Gods" section of the *Nihon shoki*, entitled *Nihon shoki sanso*, draws freely from Buddhist and Confucian sources. It begins,

> The primal pneuma of Konton is harmonious and tranquil, without bound-ary, encompassing the fundamental substance of Divinity and perfecting the true function of the Dharmadhātu. Tranquil itself, it responds to feeling; it is like a mirror that contains images. Moving, it gradually sprouts, like a husk showing a yellow tinge. The pure and the clouded differentiate their positions—this is [the formation of what is] called the material world. Harmonious interaction [between yin and yang] then gives rise to consciousness. In the differentiation that accompanies sentience, the pure preserves the [original] pneuma, joining heaven and earth with one root, while the disordered departs from Nature. Good and evil are visible in differing defilements; consequences unfold and the

---

[25] This theme is particularly evident in Jihen's *Kyūjihongi gengi*; *NST*, 19:157 ff.

three ages [of past, present, future] are differentiated. The six paths [of transmigration] are now clear, extending to both the manifest and invisible realms.

By knowing wrong, one returns to correctness; when instructed by the model of past enlightened ones, one nurtures things and benefits people; mistakes yet to come are predicted by [observing the pattern of] recurring cycles. In praising the wondrous activities of transformed beings, one inevitably approaches the ultimate achievement of sincere faith. But alas, when it comes to matters of the obscure past, how can one record and transmit history? The divine spirit possesses people and makes pronouncements; holy sages take wooden tablets and make records. Using what can be gleaned from the Three Teachings, I have learned the undistorted [truth] of this one book [the *Nihon shoki*]. Although there have been many interpretations since ancient times, I am about to proceed madly, exhausting anew the essential points. My desire is that [these words] circulate widely; by revealing our land to be divine province, I will cause the people to step into a felicitous realm.[26]

The reader will recognize several concepts from the rokurin ichiro system that reappear here. First, the stage of Konton, the primordial amorphous state associated by Zenchiku with the Circle of Longevity, is equated with the Buddhist absolute of the Dharmadhātu. It is inherently tranquil; it reflects feeling like a mirror (recalling the deep feeling that arises from the vessel of the Circle of Longevity at the subsequent stage, the Circle of Height) but is not aroused. Later in the work Kaneyoshi describes Konton variously as the state of One Mind, the palace of divinity, and also as a repository of both principle and material force: its tranquil nature is principle, or substance, while the reflected feelings are material force, or function. This last set of terms clearly derives from the Neo-Confucian thought of Chu Hsi.

At the next stage, motion occurs, and the yang energy contained therein sprouts. This is the stage of differentiation, as the clear and the clouded appear and the material world of heaven and earth gradually form. This onset of activity recalls Chou Tun-i's generative paradigm, as the Great Ultimate begins to move. Of course, in the immediate context of the *Nihon shoki* cosmogony, this is the familiar "division of heaven and earth."

Once the dualism of yin and yang is established, the two forces interact and consciousness is born. In the Shinto creation myth, this is the emergence of the first kami; in a Confucian context, it is the appearance of man, the bridge between heaven and earth. Only at this third stage do good and evil appear. While the pure elements preserve the (primal) pneuma that is the underlying essence of heaven and earth, the "scattered" component departs from Nature. Once again there is a strong resemblance to Chu

---

[26] Kokumin seishin bunka kenkyūjo, ed., *Nihon shoki sanso* (Tokyo: Meguro shoten, 1935), 1.

Hsi's views: the ontological foundation of the cosmos is fundamentally good, but when the activity of knowing gives rise to the duality of good and evil, the impurity within man's individual allotment of material force distracts him from his true nature, which is principle.

At this point the dimensions of time and space unfold: past, present, and future, and the Buddhist six paths of transmigration are established (see figure 7-3). At this third stage, which is the realm of recorded history, man has a choice: he can preserve his pure *ki* by cultivating his Nature, or be led astray by the impurity of disordered *ki*. Implicitly, proper self-cultivation culminates in a return to the primordial state of Konton, the tranquil, lucid state of divinity. This process closely resembles the Taoist meditation practice discussed in chapter 5.

However, Kaneyoshi describes this return not as meditation, but as the study of history. While the process of degeneration is the cause of man's problems, it also provides the solution, for one can examine previous wrongs in order to understand the correct path. Going back through history, one studies the words and actions of the sages, and admires the miraculous functions of (Buddhist) avatars—themselves delimited man-

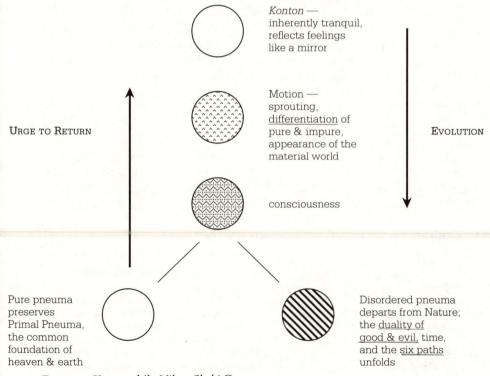

FIG. 7-3. Kaneyoshi's *Nihon Shoki* Cosmogony

ifestations within the material world. Most important, readers of Kane-yoshi's work will discover how the Japanese nation evolved from the gods of the High Plain of Heaven. The historian replaces the meditation master, leading the people back to their divine origins.

Like his rokurin ichiro commentary, Kaneyoshi's *Nihon shoki sanso* is replete with erudite references to the early Chinese classics, the Sung Neo-Confucianists, and many Buddhist texts. Kaneyoshi has a genuine respect for each of the three creeds (four, to include Taoism); he is an independent scholar, with family ties both to a tradition of Chinese scholarship, and to many branches and schools of Buddhism. He was exposed to Neo-Confucianism through the Zen establishment. Thus, although the Ichijō family was a strong influence on the scholarship of Yoshida Shinto,[27] Kaneyoshi is not a spokesman for any particular constituency.

Yet, no less than the Shinto polemics of Jihen, Kaneyoshi's scholarship presages the onset of a Confucian/Shinto hegemony. His creation model depicts a process of delimitation and degeneration, whereby a pristine state of unity is first polarized, then diluted to form the material world. The individual (and collective) solution to human imperfection—return to the primordial state of Konton—is essentially an act of regression, defined in historical terms. This attitude is not only antiquarian, it also reinforces the authority of the primordial ancestral kami and their familial relationships, symbolic representations of the ancient ruling clans of the Yamato period.

These conservative "family values" are precisely the themes within the Japanese tradition utilized by the Tokugawa rulers in their formation of a Confucian ideology. The hierarchy of the four classes, the mandate of the shogun over his vassals—in short, the authoritarian themes of fixed social identity and order—receive far more attention than the ideals of internal growth and egalitarianism implicit in much of Neo-Confucianism.[28] To be sure, in the Edo period there were many followers of Chu Hsi who promoted a personal ideal of sagehood, but they were gradually over-shadowed by the proponents of Ancient Learning (*kogaku*), who advo-cated a return to the social morality of "original" Confucianism. The complexities of Tokugawa intellectual history are beyond the scope of this study, but I would simply note that the Confucian vision of spiritual growth implicit in Kaneyoshi's rokurin ichiro commentary would not

[27] As discussed in Nishida Nagao, *Nihon Shintōshi kenkyū* (Tokyo: Kōdansha, 1979), 5:139–44.

[28] Donald Munro distinguishes three fundametal metaphors in Neo-Confucian thought: family, plant, and stream of water. As seen earlier, Kaneyoshi's rokurin ichiro commentary implicitly draws from the latter two, which represent growth and egalitarianism, respec-tively. Donald J. Munro, "The Family Network, the Stream of Water, and the Plant: Pictur-ing Persons in Sung Confucianism," in Munro, ed., *Individualism and Holism: Studies in Confucian and Taoist Values* (Ann Arbor: Center for Chinese Studies, University of Michigan, 1985), 259–91.

be the only, or even the dominant, Neo-Confucian legacy of the Edo period.

In the eighteenth century a reaction occurred against the perceived rigidity of the "foreign" prescriptions of Confucianism, which, in the popular imagination, was epitomized by the confining code of social obligation, or *giri*.[29] The primacy of *kokoro* in medieval Shinto reappears as an emphasis on emotionalism—*ninjō*[30] in the love-suicide plays of Chikamatsu, and *mono no aware* in the Nativist (*kokugaku*) dogma of Motoori Norinaga. However, this again is quite different from Chu Hsi's inner-directed vision of self-cultivation. Strong emotion and desire are no longer impurities of individual *ki* to be purified, but rather one's untainted, pristine Nature. Despite Motoori's explicit rejection of medieval Shinto's sinitic style of exegesis, its fundamental thrust remains: once again regression, rather than growth, is the dominant paradigm.

As the teachings of the three creeds are apportioned to Zenchiku's seven symbolic categories, one sees these distinctions more clearly. Utilizing an implicit plant metaphor, Kaneyoshi's Confucian interpretation of the six circles presents the cycles of nature as an analogy for the development of the individual, of the artist and his art. Similarly, Shigyoku's commentary utilizes all six circles to embrace directly the entropy of material form in a Buddhist quest for Emptiness. In contrast, the Shinto paradigm of *tenchi kaibyaku* does not extend beyond the first three circles. While the Shintoist's urge to return to the "palace of Konton" can be described as centripetal, it does not follow the asymmetrical, natural process implicit in the middle four circles; its centripetality is simply a process of regression, the centrifugal sequence experienced in reverse. In resisting natural process and the flow of history, it is highly dualistic.[31] And while Nativism's affirmation of spontaneous emotion may seem to sweep away certain dualistic Confucian conceptions of social morality, it simply replaces them with its own dualism that denies moral prescripts and "rationality." Thus the emphasis on cosmogony, on antiquity, on historicism in medieval

[29] David Pollack gives an account of the emergence of the popular conception of *giri*, which is consistent neither with its origins in Confucian thought nor with its significance in Japanese intellectual circles. Pollack, *The Fracture of Meaning*, 199 ff. However, the popular perception is perhaps a more accurate gauge of the overall cultural impact of Confucianism.

[30] Konishi Jin'ichi sees in Yoshida's Kenkō's sporadic resistance to the restricting conventions of medieval art and religion the first glimmerings of *ninjō* as a positive ideal. Konishi, *Michi*, 184–90.

[31] It is frequently remarked that Buddhism's pessimisitic view of history, embodied in the *mappō* doctrine, was an impediment to social and political change. Nevertheless, medieval Buddhism was able to incorporate the perceived decay of society into a powerful vision of individual salvation; the social realities of the age were a means to transcendence, rather than an object of resistence. In contrast, Confucianism and Shinto both draw their legitimacy from a social vision of order and harmony. In the Tokugawa period, this frequently resulted in the rhetoric of return to a primordial, golden age of purity.

Shinto presages both the essential conservatism of Tokugawa political ideology and the radical emotionalism of Nativism.

ZENCHIKU AND "HIGASHIYAMA CULTURE"

In the context of medieval cultural history, Zenchiku is considered one of the major figures of the Higashiyama era. This epoch takes its name from the location of the shogun Ashikaga Yoshimasa's villa, popularly known as the Silver Pavilion (Ginkaku-ji), situated at the foot of the eastern hills of the capital. Yoshimasa's reputation is that of an ineffectual ruler who presided over the eroding authority of the shogunate as the Ōnin Wars broke out in 1467. This series of disturbances resulted in widespread destruction, as many of the physical monuments of *kuge* culture—for example, Kaneyoshi's famed library—were destroyed, and the vestiges of its cultural importance faded.

Perhaps as a distraction from his political misfortunes, perhaps as a contributing factor, Yoshimasa was an enthusiastic patron of the arts, exhibiting a passion for Sung ceramics, monochrome ink painting, sarugaku, and the tea ceremony. His subdued taste is reflected in the intimate Silver Pavilion itself, so often contrasted with the earlier brilliance and self-assurance of Yoshimitsu's Golden Pavilion (Kinkaku-ji) in the northern hills. Certainly one can see a similar contrast between Zenchiku and Zeami, the recipient of Yoshimitsu's patronage and personal attention. During his prime, Zeami was a thoroughly professional artist whose charisma and creativity are reflected in the vitality and variety of his plays. In contrast, Zenchiku seems increasingly absorbed in a world of esoteric, transcendental theories and personal devotion to the ritual side of noh. Such Zenchiku plays as *Teika* are so imbued with the tonal darkness of yūgen that they approach gloomy obsession.

Haga Kōshirō sees in the culture of the Higashiyama era a dialectic of convention (*kaku*) and the shattering of convention (*hakaku*).[32] These terms are of course closely related to the michi paradigm which this study has frequently explored. Through convention, the discipline and standards of the medieval arts are carefully transmitted, yet in time the artist develops to the point that he can naturally break the letter of the law without violating its spirit. If the extreme of convention is found in the conservative attitudes of the Nijō line of waka poets, the epitome of unconventionality is Ikkyū, whose eccentric behavior is considered an emblem of spiritual depth. As shown earlier, in a Buddhist context, the shattering of convention is analogous to the shattering of the "deluded

---

[32] Haga, *Higashiyama bunka*, 752 ff.

mind of successive forms." And indeed, Haga draws the obvious parallel to Zenchiku's Circle of Breaking.[33]

It is instructive to compare Zenchiku's aesthetic theories with the views of Shinkei (1406–1474), the most celebrated linked-verse poet of the age.[34] In his major work of renga theory, *Sasamegoto*, Shinkei consistently emphasizes that conformity to the orthodox rules is the key to the successful training of the beginning and intermediate poet. These rules are likened to the five Confucian virtues and the Buddhist monastic regulations. However, just as Mind is the foundation from which all phenomenal existents arise, the mind/heart of the poet is the origin, the essence of a poem. Therefore, once a master has developed the requisite purity of mind to produce poetry of deep feeling and inner grace, he may occasionally violate the externally imposed rules of renga composition.

In terms of poetic practice, this attitude results in a preference for the style of distant-linking (*soku*), which is more subtle and profound than the obvious close-linking (*shinku*) style. Shinkei disdains the conventional teachings that dictate the appropriate treatment of imagery and demand close links through "words"—*kotoba-zuke*. Intuitive linking by feeling (*kokoro-zuke*), in accordance with the poet's transmundane perception of the preceding link, is favored; overtly explicit syntactical and semantic linking, while frequently appropriate, is accorded less value. In this sense, *shinku* linking, where the formal relationship between verses is obvious, represents the realm of form, while *soku* links are formless.

This emphasis on emptiness of form, and on the foundation of Mind, certainly reflects the attitudes of Zen, arguably the most influential cultural force of the age,[35] and one repeatedly encounters such Zen-derived language in both Zeami and Zenchiku. Yet one should not ignore medieval Shinto's consistent espousal of the primacy of *kokoro*—a phenomenon that, as shown, predates any Zen influence. Shinkei expresses a preference for poetry that is "outwardly flawed but pure within . . . like gold wrapped in shabby cloth."[36] Despite the Zen overtones, the poetic concern here is really the classical dialectic of *kokoro* and *kotoba*. As attention to the merely ornate, entangling "leaves of words" is cast aside, the inner seed of the heart shines ever brighter. In fact, a facade of plain, flawed language may actually imply an inner richness of profound emotion, creating an effect not unlike yūgen.[37]

[33] Ibid., 773.

[34] Although there is no record of their having met, Shinkei does praise Zenchiku's abilities as a performer in his *Hitorigoto*. The passage is reproduced in *NST*, 23:475.

[35] As discussed in Pollack, *The Fracture of Meaning*, 159–60.

[36] Ijichi Tetsuo et al., eds., *Rengaron shū, nōgakuron shū, hairon shū* (Tokyo: Shōgakkan, 1973), 92.

[37] In Kamo no Chōmei's famous definition, yūgen creates an atmosphere that hovers in the background of the poem, generating emotional overtones that the words only hint at. The many various conceptions of yūgen are summarized in Thornhill, "*Yūgen* after Zeami."

Shinkei is best known for his aesthetic ideal of cold, slender beauty (*hie, yase*), as presented in this passage from *Hitorigoto*:

> Indeed, there is nothing of such deep emotion, of such cold purity, as water. At the mention of the water of spring, the image of a woman's face hovers in the mind, inexplicably moving. In summer, the area surrounding a spring of clear water is cool and refreshing. Just hearing the words "the water of autumn," the mind becomes cold and clear. And nothing has so much charm as ice. Thin ice in the morning over a field of harvested rice paddies, icicles hanging from the eaves of an old thatched roof, grasses and trees on a withered field, scenery covered by dew and frost—do not these scenes have interest and charm?[38]

This passage is usually cited as an example of Shinkei's preference for the ethereal beauty of the hibernal landscape.[39] However, it is important to note that the topic here is *water*, praised in *all* its seasonal contexts. The echo of Zenchiku's theory of Primal Water is unmistakable. Although water has no inherent color or form, it appears in various natural forms of great beauty, just as the symbol of the circle, representative of water, takes multiple forms to embody various flavors, styles, and effects.

But what of Shinkei's predilection for coldness? In one sense, this recalls Zenchiku's aesthetic of "cold, clear singing," represented by the Circle of Height.[40] But more generally, Shinkei's *hie* represents a state of detachment: water becomes "cold and clear" in autumn, as the mind becomes dispassionate and penetrating, like that of the solitary priest. Finally, water transforms into ice, a revelation of its internal, jewel-like essence—recalling the diamond symbolism of *prajñā*. Perhaps most affecting is the image of a withered field, covered by dew or frost. Here one sees a close parallel to Zenchiku's Circle of Breaking: the withered, broken grasses of winter follow the perfected fruition of autumn. Yet this is not simply the sad desolation of *sabi*. The whiteness of the dew and frost suggests the glimmer of purity and wisdom found in Zenchiku's One Dewdrop.

In many ways, Shinkei's vision resembles the aesthetic of *kotan*, the plain beauty associated with the Sung style of monochrome ink-painting widely practiced by Zen priests and the professional artists supported by the Ashikaga. Yoshimasa in particular is known as an admirer of this style, which had a great influence on the emerging *wabi* style of tea. Yet this

---

[38] *NST*, 23:469.

[39] Konishi Jin'ichi has researched the origins of *hie* and *yase* as aesthetic ideals in Chinese poetry. Most prominently, they were initially associated with the cold purity of early plum blossoms, and with the slender celestial maidens of religious Taoism. However, although these connotations were current in the *gozan* poetry circles of Shinkei's time, Konishi concludes that Shinkei was unaware of them. Konishi Jin'ichi, "Hie to yase," *Bungaku, gogaku* 10 (November 1957), 12–29. For Shinkei, *hie* and *yase* are colored by an aesthetic of dry, withered beauty; see Pollack, *The Fracture of Meaning*, 176–77.

[40] See chapter 3.

Ashikaga shogun's rejection of Zen as a personal faith, in favor of the Pure Land Buddhism practiced by the nobility, is emblematic of a complex cultural blend. Yoshimasa's lingering attachment to Heian culture indicates that, despite the introduction of newer Chinese models in the medieval era, the aristocratic values of the *kuge* were an important component of Higashiyama culture.

Haga goes on to present the aesthetic of imperfection, embodied in the Circle of Breaking, as a correlative for the breakup of *kuge* culture during the Ōnin Wars. This final stage of dissolution provided moments of creative genius, fueled by the anarchy and freedom of Zen. The intellectual and artistic community in the capital scattered. Some fled to Nara or the surrounding countryside, to gather at Ikkyū's Shūon-an; others like Shinkei traveled to the east or west to seek the support of provincial lords. After the initial disturbances subsided, Kaneyoshi did manage to return to the capital and continue his work, and classical renga would continue as a vital genre into the sixteenth century.

But this brilliance, dependent upon disorder, could not last. It was the afterglow of the long, ethereal night of *kuge* culture, as the dream of elegance came to a close: the "brocade by night" of Tsurayuki's *Kokinshū*, the "autumn evening" of Teika's *Shinkokinshū*, give way to Shinkei's vision of the moon at dawn, shining over withered fields. To present the rokurin ichiro structure as the gyres of history is not Zenchiku's intent, yet as a monument of medieval Japan, it provides a prophetic configuration of cultural forces. If one is to place Zenchiku's age at the juncture of the fifth and sixth circles—to view the social dissolution of Ōnin in Buddhist terms—this disintegration is perhaps a release. At the same time, the final formless stage, symbolized by the Circle of Emptiness, contains the nuance of a new beginning. At the apex of yin, of weakness, the yang energy begins to sprout, just as the voice of the aged actor exudes the faint fragrance of youth. As the priests of the *gozan* temples, the transmitters of Sung learning, also dispersed, the seeds of Neo-Confucian culture were sown in the domains of the provincial lords who were to come to power.

Yet as Japanese culture is reborn under Tokugawa rule, the context is transformed. The centripetal process of self-cultivation is largely replaced by the public Confucian symbolism of state power. Heaven becomes the ruler at the center, the shogun, dispensing vitality to his subjects. And the Shinto ideology that gradually took shape in the medieval period, polished in the discourse of Buddhist-Shinto relation, now eclipses the grandeur of classical Buddhist cosmology. Despite its continuing presence as a practiced religion, Buddhism no longer defines the parameters of intellectual and cultural discourse. The tonal darkness of medieval Buddhism has unwittingly served as a womb for the emergence of brightness and purity, the ideals of the impending Shinto dominance.

Appendix: A Catalog
of Zenchiku's Treatises

AN EXAMINATION of Zenchiku's twenty-three extant treatises reveals three broad categories: (1) works based on Zeami's *go'on* (Five Sounds, or styles of singing and composition) and Fujiwara Teika's *jittei* (Ten Styles of waka) (numbers 1–5); (2) the rokurin ichiro treatises (numbers 6–15); and (3) miscellaneous (numbers 16–23). In the following catalog they are grouped in this manner. Generally speaking, the order within each group is chronological, although firm dates exist only when mentioned. This appendix is based on the catalog of Zenchiku's treatises compiled by Omote and Itō (*KKSS*, 68–84).

1. *Go'on no shidai* is a compilation of passages from various plays, presented as examples of the Five Sounds. These five—*shūgen* (congratulatory), *yūkyoku* (i.e., yūgen), *renbo* (love), *aishō* (sorrow), and *rangyoku* (the sublime)—were formulated by Zeami. He discusses them at length in his *Go'ongyoku jōjō*, utilizing the image of a particular variety of tree (pine, cherry, red maple, a barren winter tree, and cryptomeria, respectively) and a poem to express the essence of each style. In the *Go'on*, a more sketchy work, Zeami utilizes passages from various plays to illustrate the Five Sounds, and it is the format of the latter that Zenchiku imitates here.

Go'on no shidai reads more like a notebook than a finished treatise. There is no introduction. It begins with the names of the Five Sounds, and then a list of technical terms (jo–ha–kyū and others), which then reappear in annotations to the passages included. Brief summaries of Zeami's definitions of the Five Sounds also appear.

2. *Kabu zuinō ki* is the first of Zenchiku's treatises to reveal the deep influence of waka treatises (*karon*). It opens with a formal introduction describing the origins of sarugaku in terms of the heavenly rock-cave myth, alludes to the familiar argument that "'wild words and fancy language" (*kyōgen kigo*) might further the Dharma, and proceeds to state its major theme: that the art of poetry is the essence of the way of song and dance. This explicit emphasis upon waka is not found in Zeami, but it constitutes one of the major themes of Zenchiku's treatises.

The largest section of the *Kabu zuinō ki* is a collection of notes on forty-seven plays. The titles are grouped into four categories: the Three Roles of Zeami (old man, warrior, and woman) and a miscellaneous group. One of Zeami's Nine Ranks (*kyūi*) is attributed to each play, a few brief remarks are appended, and one or more waka (and occasionally a couplet from a Chinese poem) is recorded. The poems seldom appear within the text of the play itself; rather, they are meant to express the poetic essence of the play. For example, the entry for the play now known as *Matsukaze* reads as follows:

"Matsukaze and Murasame." Style of the Flower of Profundity (*chōshinka fū*).

The heart and appearance of this piece is like dusk in autumn.

Moshio kumu	Could this be the sign
ama no tomaya no	of a brine-dipping
shirube ka wa	fisher-girl's hut?
uramite zo fuku	Blowing bitterly,
aki no hatsukaze	the first autumn wind.

(*Zoku kokka taikan* 10822, Fujiwara Teika)

The heart of this [piece] might also be called "demon-quelling."

Kamukaze ya	Crushing reeds
Ise no hamaogi	on the beach at Ise
orishikite	of the divine wind,
tabine ya suran	does he take his traveler's sleep
araki hamabe ni	on that rough shore?

(variant of *Man'yōshū* 500, wife of Go no Dan'ochi; *SKKS* 911, anonymous)

Kindly given, His Majesty's robe is now here.
I hold it high each day, revering the lingering scent.

(from *Kanke kōshū* 482, Sugawara Michizane)

These two roles are indeed the highest realization of the true meaning of noh. They are hovering visages that become drifting clouds in the morning and driving rain in the evening. The quality of yūgen deepens still more: an emotion of surpassing profundity. In sum, one could call it the appearance of women in tranquil repose, unable to rise. Thinking of the elegance of matchless palace women and gentlemen, [the two protagonists] themselves become elegant. What is more, they long for those days [of old], and so they also feel the impermanence of things. At the spring dawn, in the autumn evening, [the effect] is superlative. (*KKSS*, 128–29)

The prose section of this entry is somewhat longer than the norm, but the structure is typical. Note that neither the waka nor the Chinese poem appears in the text of the play itself. The first poem is from Teika's private collection, the *Shūi gusō*, and the next two verses appear in the *Sango ki* as examples of the "demon-quelling style" (*rakki-tei*). An apocryphal treatise traditionally attributed to Teika, the *Sango ki* is the source for most of the styles of waka discussed by Zenchiku, their definitions, and the accompanying example poems. Most of the later entries in the *Kabu zuinō ki* are categorized both as one of Zeami's Nine Ranks (in this case, the "style of profundity"), and as one of the poetry styles of the *Sango ki*.

The next section discusses the performances of such illustrious actors as Zenchiku's grandfather Komparu Gon-no-kami, Kannami, Zeami, and Dōami. Again, waka are used to illustrate qualities of their performance styles. Zenchiku concludes with a discussion of poems that he admires, pointing out examples of yūgen in both conception and diction.

3. *Go'on jittei*. This is a short work, perhaps composed for the edification of the powerful *daimyō* of Yamaguchi, Ōuchi Masahiro. There are more copies in existence than for any other Zenchiku-attributed treatise. After a brief introduction, similar in content to that of the *Kabu zuinō ki*, the Five Sounds are defined and illustrated with poems, some of which are the examples presented by Zeami in his *Go-ongyoku jōjō*. Next, "ten styles of waka" are presented, each illustrated by a play title and poem, but five of these are simply the *go'on* repeated; for this reason, Omote questions the authenticity of the Zenchiku attribution. On the other hand, most of the poems are also found in the *Kabu zuinō ki*, and the overall content corresponds with Zenchiku's output of the period (1456).

4. *Go'on sangyoku shū*. This work, dated 1460, opens with an introduction that cites both the Great Preface from the *Book of Songs* and the Kana Preface to the *Kokinshū*. The first half of the work presents examples of the Ten Styles (actually sixteen, in an arrangement taken from the *Sango ki*); these are grouped into subcategories of the Five Sounds.

Remarks concerning the use of the breath and other technical matters follow. Many of these passages are relevant to the rokurin ichiro treatises and have been cited in the current study. Perhaps most important of all is a passage that discusses Primal Water (*issui*), the formless, flavorless essence of song and dance. This passage concludes with brief remarks concerning the symbolism of the circle and dewdrop featured in the rokurin ichiro treatises. See chapter 6 for a translation and analysis.

5. *Shidō yōshō*. This work was recorded after the rokurin ichiro treatises. The manuscript, a Zenchiku holograph, is in the possession of Hōzan-ji (see chapter 1). It is difficult to date precisely, but on the basis of internal evidence Omote concludes that it was composed during the period surrounding Zenchiku's retreat at the Fushimi Inari Shrine in the year 1467 (see no. 21).

This work represents a major shift in Zenchiku's writings. He expands the Five Sounds into Eight:

1. *shūgen-on*   congratulatory sound
2. *shūgen-kyoku*   congratulatory pieces

3. *yūkyoku*	playful pieces
4. *yūgen-on*	sound of yūgen
5. *renbo*	love
6. *aishō*	sorrow
7. *rangyoku*	sublime pieces
8. *kankyoku*	tranquil pieces

Each is described rather than illustrated with waka. The new categories are 1, 3, and 8. *Shūgen-on* represents "the rank in which voices sound naturally in accordance with their individual natures. For example, in the case of wind and string instruments, there is an initial sound of the bamboo flute when it is blown, and the sound of a string when plucked. Proceeding from this [first] tone, the sound gradually enters the style of the piece, and thus music that expresses various feelings is produced." Here Zenchiku seems to differentiate between style (*kyoku*, as in "congratulatory pieces") and an essential, primal tone (*on*); in some respects, the description is reminiscent of the Circle of Longevity. Significantly, the yūgen category also acquires the suffix "*on*," and Zenchiku goes on to explicitly equate yūgen with Buddha Nature for the first time in his writings. Since all things possess Buddha Nature, all roles—even fearsome demons—can exhibit yūgen when performed with the requisite lightness and "penetration."

Yūkyoku represents "roles of playful disorder; murmuring softly, the willows and cherries flutter in the breeze . . ." This category seems to be have been devised to distinguish the gentle, graceful variety of yūgen from the more profound variety represented by *yūgen-on*. (The graph "play" replaces "faint.") Finally, *kankyoku* is the art of "grace and tranquility. This rank is like looking at rain falling gently upon flowers in bloom on the sparse, moss-covered branches of the famous ancient trees of Yoshino, Ōhara, and Oshio." In some ways, the final two categories—*rangyoku* and *kankyoku*—resemble the Circle of Breaking and Circle of Emptiness, respectively.

The final section of *Shidō yōshō* establishes various correspondences among body, speech, and mind, the first three circles, the Buddhist tripartite practice of precepts, meditation, and wisdom, and so forth. Also notable are prohibitions against impure behavior similar to those in number 12.

6. *Rokurin ichiro no ki*. See chapter 1.

7. *Rokurin ichiro no ki chū*. See chapter 1.

8. *Nika ichirin*. This is a brief text; it appears in the Hachiemon manuscript without a title (in such cases Omote or earlier editors have coined a meaningful title, based on the work's content). It contains two diagrams. The first shows all six circles, as well as an upright sword, superimposed;

this is said to indicate that "each and every thing in existence exhibits these principles." The second shows six small circles, labeled, arranged within one large circle; see fig. 2-8. This is said to represent the Mirror-like Wisdom that embraces all things, echoing a similar statement in the *Kichū*. It also contains the "Masukagami" poem found in the *Kichū*. The "two flowers" in Omote's title allude to the Essential Flower (*shōka*) and Functional Flower (*yōka*) discussed in the final paragraph. For a discussion of this terminology, see chapter 3.

9. *Rokurin ichiro dai'i*. This is a Hōzan-ji manuscript written in Zenchiku's hand; again, it originally had no title. Omote believes it was written after number 8, ca. 1458. It is simply an outline, containing many labels attached to each of the seven diagrams (one for each stage, roughly equivalent to the *Ki* illustrations). Many new Buddhist concepts not found in Shigyoku's commentary are introduced here. Among these are the Threefold Truth (santai: *kū*, *ke*, and *chū*) of Tendai thought, and the Three Minds of the Pure Land sects: sincerity (*shiseishin*), profundity (*shinjin*), and resolve (*ekō hatsugan shin*); and citations from various sutras. However, the final effect is chaotic; the categories seem tentative and unconvincing. The "eight mirrors" motif of the *Kichū* reappears here.

10. *Rokurin kyokumi*. This is a short, untitled work appended to the Hachiemon manuscript. It is primarily a list of practical meanings for the seven stages. Most of these correspondences appear in number 7.

11. *Rokurin ichiro gaishō*. This is a brief text that summarizes the progression of the seven stages. Most notable is the statement that "the One Dewdrop is the essential sword that exists before the Circle of Longevity appears." This is the only passage in any of the rokurin ichiro texts that associates these two categories in this fashion (usually the *kūrin* and ichiro are grouped together; see discussions in chapters 3 and 5).

12. *Rokurin kanjō hiki*. This manuscript is in the Komparu School collection, written by Zenchiku on the back of number 13. Much of the text is illegible. Most notable is the inclusion of Ten Prohibitions (*jikkai*) against coarse behavior, which Omote identifies to be of Shinto origin. These prohibitions are applied against inelegant styles of performance.

13. *Rokurin ichiro hichū (Kanshō bon)*. This is a Zenchiku holograph manuscript, dated Kanshō 6 (1465), in the Komparu School collection. This and number 14 are major restatements of the rokurin ichiro system. They incorporate the major themes of the *Kichū*, together with some of the additional Buddhist material from number 9.

The most important feature of the *Hichū* texts is the inclusion of the waka styles enumerated in numbers 1–5. Each of the *Sango ki* styles is assigned to a particular circle (and also to the final ichiro), and example poems are included; these are for the most part repeated from number 2. Also, Zeami's Nine Ranks are apportioned to the six circles. The manuscript contains many emendations and is messy in appearance. It can be seen as a first draft for number 14, although it contains some elements not found in the later work.

Although Zenchiku's application of waka theory to the rokurin ichiro symbols has not been examined in the current study, here are example poems—most of them well-known in the tradition—for each of his seven categories:

Circle of Longevity—of the yūgen style:

Wabinureba	Beckoned by the channel buoys
imahata onaji	at Naniwa,
Naniwa naru	now I would throw myself in!
mi o tsukushite mo	I suffer in pain,
awamu to zo omou	longing to meet with you.

(*Gosenshū* 961, *Shūishū* 766; Prince Motoyoshi)

Circle of Height—of the lofty (*taketakaki*) style:

Omou koto	Why is there no one
nado tou hito no	here to ask
nakaru ramu	of my feelings?
aogeba sora ni	As I gaze up in the sky
tsuki zo sayakeki	the moon is cold and clear.

(*SKKS* 1780, Jien)

Circle of Abiding—of the style of deep feeling (*ushin*):

Tsu no kuni no	Was the spring at Naniwa
Naniwa no haru wa	in the province of Tsu
yume nare ya	but a dream?
ashi no kareha ni	Across the withered reeds,
kaze wataru nari	the winter wind blows.

(*SKKS* 625, Saigyō)

Circle of Forms—of the balanced (*uruwashiki*) style:

Honobono to	Dimly, dimly,
Akashi no ura no	as dawn breaks in the morning mist
asagiri ni	at Akashi Bay,
shimagakureyuku	how I long for that boat
fune o shi zo omou	as it departs, island-hidden.

(*KKS* 409, anonymous; traditionally attributed to Kakinomoto Hitomaro)

Circle of Breaking—of the style that portrays the past (*shako*):

Musashino ya	Though I travel
yukedomo aki no	the Musashi plain,
hate zo naki	there is no end to its autumn sights;
ika naru kaze no	what sort of wind
sue ni fuku ran	might blow to its boundaries?

(*SKKS* 378, Minamoto Michimitsu; in *Kanshō-bon* only)

Circle of Emptiness—of the interesting (*omoshiroki*) style:

Yamazato ni	Oh, for a friend
ukiyo itowamu	in this mountain village
tomo mo gana	who too despises the sad world—
kuyashiku suginishi	we would talk of the past
mukashi kataramu	gone by with such regret.

(*SKKS* 1657, Saigyō; assigned to Circle of Breaking in *Bunshō bon*)

One Dewdrop—of the demon-quelling (*rakki*) style:

Nurete hosu	Wet, then dry,
tamagushi no ha no	the jewelled prayer wand:
tsuyujimo ni	how many ages
ama teru hikari	has light shone through the heavens
ikuyo henu ran	on the dew and frost of its leaves?

(*SKKS* 737, Fujiwara Yoshitsune)

14. *Rokurin ichiro hichū (Bunshō bon)*. This manuscript, in the possession of Hōzan-ji, is dated Bunshō 1 (1466) and again is in Zenchiku's hand. In comparison to number 13, the text is more carefully written. I had the opportunity to view this manuscript in person, and its appearance is extraordinary (it has been restored): the calligraphy is elegant, and the diagrams are finely drawn with accents in gold ink.

One significant difference with the earlier version is the apportioning of the waka to the seven categories. Most of the kūrin examples in the Kanshō version (including the poem given above) are now reassigned to the harin, and many of the ichiro examples are now grouped with the kūrin. This phenomenon indicates the tentative nature of Zenchiku's poetic correspondences.

The *Hichū* texts are perhaps the fullest expression of the rokurin ichiro teachings. They act as a repository for almost all of the elements that appear in the earlier drafts. For this reason, they are sometimes disjointed and difficult to understand without reference to these prior works.

15. *Yūgen sanrin*. This is another brief work, a Hachiemon manuscript. Again it summarizes the rokurin ichiro system; most notable is an emphasis upon the first three circles as the essence of yūgen, which is equated with Buddha Nature. An excerpt is translated in chapter 3.

16. *Meishuku shū*. This major work was published for the first time in 1969, the result of the recent discovery of a Zenchiku holograph in the Komparu School collection. The theme of this long and rambling treatise is the nature of Okina, the god who appears in the form of an old man in the congratulatory play of the same name. Zenchiku explains the significance of the *okina* mask and the pseudohistorical origins of the *okina* rituals. He then attempts to explain how various deities connected to the sarugaku tradition and to the Hata clan are all manifestations of Okina. Such diverse figures as Kōkatsu, Sugawara Michizane, the bodhisattvas Jizō and Kannon, and Amida Buddha are discussed in this light; each has certain attributes that, in Zenchiku's mind, form associations with Okina. The character *shuku* in the title refers to the deity Shukujin, an elusive figure who appears to have been worshipped as a guardian of the performing arts. In the case of sarugaku, which has strong ritual ties to Kasuga Shrine, he is associated with Kasuga-myōjin. Within Zenchiku's framework, Shukujin is another name for Okina.

This work is of limited interest in the study of nōgakuron or aesthetics, but it provides a wealth of fascinating, although often obscure, material for scholars of ethnology and Japanese religion.

17. *Emai-za keizu*. This is an abbreviated chart illustrating the Hata lineage of performers as understood by Zenchiku. Another holograph manuscript in the possession of Hōzan-ji, it has the appearance of a hastily composed outline, with many comments scrawled in almost illegible characters.

18. *Sarugaku engi*. The first half of this brief document quotes verbatim from Kaneyoshi's account of the origin of sarugaku in the *Ki* (no. 6). Zenchiku continues with a summary of the Hata lineage. This work is signed in Zenchiku's own hand as follows:

> [At] the mountain residence of Takigi in Yamashiro, the Tafuku-an; Ōnin 2, season of the third month, twenty-fourth day;
> wise old man Zenchiku, 64 years

This is the document used by scholars to determine Zenchiku's date of birth.

19. *Emai-za kabegaki*. This work details the annual festival performances and obligations of the Emai troupe. There is considerable disagreement about its dating and authorship.

20. *Bunshō gannen waka*. A collection of fourteen waka composed by Zenchiku, followed by a fragment of *kanbun* verse in praise of the Bud-

dhist deity Fudō-myōō. The latter is attributed to an unidentifiable source, "Kaku Taishi." This is a Hachiemon manuscript, dated Bunshō 1 (1466).

21. *Inariyama sanrō ki*. This is the diary of a retreat taken by Zenchiku and his wife at the Fushimi Inari Shrine, dated the sixth month of Ōnin 1 (1467). It records in detail prayers offered to the various shrines within the compound, providing a sense of the many Buddhist deities worshipped there, a practice eradicated in the Meiji period. It also contains accounts of supernatural dreams experienced by both Zenchiku and his wife during the retreat. This is a fascinating document that reveals details of Zenchiku's personal faith in the many deities of the Buddhist-Shinto pantheon.

22. *Jōdo-kyō hihan*. This is a critique of the "other power" (*tariki*) doctrine of the Pure Land sects. Its logic is somewhat hard to follow, but it concludes with an affirmation of the "self power" (*jiriki*) style of the *nembutsu*, in which recitation and concentration is continued day and night until a breakthrough occurs. Zenchiku's knowledge of the relevant Pure Land texts is notable. Again, this work reveals Zenchiku's personal interest in spiritual and doctrinal matters for their own sake, outside the context of nōgakuron.

23. *Sazen nikki*. This brief work opens with a personal account of an enlightenment experience: "How thankful! Having realized that my own body is [actually] True Suchness, from this day forward bad karma and deluded desires are no longer impediments." Zenchiku continues with a list of his monthly devotions to the deities of Ise, Kasuga, and so forth. As the provisional title suggests, this reads as an informal diary.

Glossary

Ai　哀

aishō　哀傷

A-ji　阿字

A-ji kan　阿字観

ama no iwa(ya)to　天の岩 (屋) 戸

Amanouzume-no-mikoto　天鈿女命

Amaterasu-ōkami　天照大神

Amenokoyane-no-mikoto
　天児屋根命

Amenominakanushi-no-kami
　天御中主神

Amida-nyorai　阿弥陀如来

anjū　安住

Ano Renshi　阿野廉子

arawaru　露る

ashikabi　葦牙

Ashikaga Yoshihisa　足利義尚

Ashikaga Yoshimasa　足利義政

Ashikaga Yoshimitsu　足利義満

Ashikaga Yoshinori　足利義教

aya　文

banpō　万法

banshō　万像

Bashō　芭蕉

Bishamonten　毘沙門天

Bishaō Gon-no-kami　毘沙王権守

Bishaō-jirō　毘沙王次郎

Bokusai　墨斎

bonnō　煩悩

Bunnan　文安

bushō ikon　舞声爲根

busshō　仏性

byōdōshō chi　平等性智

chadō　茶道

chang　長

Chan-jan　湛然

chen　貞

Cheng　鄭

ch'eng　誠

Cheng-hsüan　鄭玄

Ch'eng I　程伊

Ch'eng-kuan　澄觀

chen-ju　眞如

chen-ju sui-yüan　眞如隨綠

chi (wisdom)　智

chi (good fortune)　吉

ch'i　氣

Ch'ien　乾

chih　智

Chih-i　智顗

chih-ts'ang　知藏

Chikurinshō　竹林抄

Ch'in　秦

ching (stillness)　靜

ching (seminal essence)　精

Ch'ing-liang　清涼

Chin Niu　金牛

Chin-ssu lu　近思錄

Chinul　知訥

chisui　智水

Chōroku　長祿

chōshinka fū　籠深花風

Chou Lien-ch'i　周濂溪

Chou Tun-i　周敦頤

Chōwa　長和

Chu Hsi　朱熹

chūkyoku　中曲

Ch'un-ch'iu wei　春秋緯

chung　忠

daienkyō chi　大円鏡智

Daigen-gū　大元宮

Daijō-in　大乗院

Daijōin jisha zōjiki
　大乗院寺社雑事記

Dainichi-nyorai　大日如来

Deai (troupe)　出合の座

demono no tei　出物の体

dō　道

dōsei ichigen　動静一元

Eguchi　江口

Eikyō　永享

ekō hatsugan shin　廻向発願心

Emai- (or Enmai-) za　円満井座
engi　縁起
enjōshō　円成性
Enman-in　円満院
ensō　円相
etashō　依他性
Fa-hsiang　法相
Fa-tsang　法藏
Fu　復
Fu Daishi　傅大士
Fu Hsi (originator of the trigrams)
　伏羲
Fudō-myōō　不動明王
Fugan-ji　補厳寺
Fugen　普賢
fuhen　不変
Fu-hsi (Liang Dynasty)　傅翕
Fu'ichi Kokushi　普一国師
Fujiwara Kintō　藤原公任
Fujiwara Shunzei　藤原俊成
Fujiwara Teika　藤原定家
Fujiwara Yoshitsune　藤原良経
fūrin　風輪
Fushimi Inari　伏見稲荷
gagaku　雅楽
gaken　我見
gei'i　芸位
genki　元気
genmetsu (or genmechi)　還滅
Gen'on　玄音
Genpin　玄賓
gigaku　伎楽
Ginkaku-ji　銀閣寺
giri　義理
Giyō (or Kiyō) Hōshū　岐陽方秀
goi　五位
gogyō　五行
gomi　五味
Go-Murakami　後村上
Go no Dan'ochi　碁檀越
go'on　五音
gorin tō　五輪塔
gōsai fū　強細風
Gosenshū　後選集
gōso fū　強鹿風
Go-Tsuchimikado　後土御門
gozan　五山

gozō　五藏
Gyoan sanjin　漁庵散人
Gyōgi　行基
Gyōnen　凝然
Hachiemon　八佐衛門
hakai no bōzu　破戒の坊主
hakaku　破格
hana　花
hangyō　判教
harin　破輪
Hase-dera　長谷寺
Hasshū kōyō　八宗綱要
Hata no Kōkatsu (or Kawakatsu)
　秦河勝
Hata no Ujiyasu　秦氏安
Hatsuse　泊瀬
heng　享
hengeshō　遍計性
(Bishop) Henjō　遍昭
hi　皮
hie　冷え
hienobori　冷え上り
hietaru kyoku　冷えたる曲
Higashiyama　東山
Hino Tomiko　日野富子
Hirano　平野
hito　人
hōi　法位
hokkai taishō chi　法界体性智
hon　本
Hōnen　法然
hongaku　本覚
honji　本地
honji-suijaku　本地垂迹
honpushō　本不生
Ho Shan　禾山
hosshin seppō　法身説法
Hossō　法相
Hōzan-ji　宝山寺
hsiang　相
Hsien-shou　賢首
hsing　性
hsing ch'i　性起
hsiung　兇
hsün-hsi　薫習
Hsü-t'ang　虚堂
Hua-yen　華嚴

Hu Hung　胡宏
hun-t'un　混沌
Hu Wu-feng　胡五峰
i (differentiate)　異
i (justice)　義
i-ch'i　一氣
ichigen no ki　一元之気
Ichijō Fuyuyoshi (or Fuyura)
　一条多良
Ichijō Kaneyoshi (or Kanera)
　一条兼良
Ichijō Norifusa　一条教房
Ichijō Tsunemichi　一条経通
Ichijō Tsunesuke　一条経輔
Ichijō Tsunetsugu　一条経嗣
ichinen sanzen　一念三千
ichiro　一露
ifū　位風
i-hsin　一心
ikken　一剣
ikki　一気
ikki no gensui　一気の元水
Ikkyō (or Ikkei) Unshō　一慶雲章
Ikkyū Sōjun　一休宗純
Ikoma　生駒
i-kuan　一貫
inochi　命
Ise Shintō　伊勢神道
isshin　一心
issui　一水
issui no hajime　一水の初
issui no toku　一水の徳
itchō-niki-sansei　一調二機三声
itteki no tsuyu　一滴の露
itten tsuketaru toki　一点付たる時
i-yüan chih ch'i　一元之氣
jakusei tei　若声体
jen　仁
ji　事
Jien　慈円
Jihen　慈遍
ji hokkai　事法界
jiji muge　事事無碍
jikkai　十戒
jin　塵
Jinnō shōtō ki　神皇正統記
Jinson　尋尊

jiriki　自力
jirin　地輪
jittei　十体
Jizō　地藏
jo-ha-kyū　序破急
jōju　成就
jōjū fumetsu　常住不滅
jōsanrin　上三輪
jōsosa chi　成所作智
jū　住
Jūjūshin ron　十住心論
Ju-lai hsing-ch'i　如來性起
jurin　寿輪
jūrin　住輪
Kachō yozei　花鳥余情
kadō　華道
kagura　神楽
Kaidan-in　戒壇院
Kakinomoto Hitomaro　柿本人麻呂
kaku　格
Kaku Taishi　覚大師
Kamo　加茂
k'an　坎
K'ang-chieh　康節
kanka fū　閑花風
kankyoku　閑曲
Kannami Kiyotsugu　観阿弥清次
Kannon　観音
kanpaku　関白
kanro　甘露
Kanshi　貫氏
Kantan　邯鄲
Kanze Hisao　観世寿夫
Kanzeon　観世音
karin　火輪
karon　歌論
Kasuga　春日
Kasuga-myōjin　春日明神
Kasuga-taisha　春日大社
Kegon　華厳
Keikaku　経覚
Kemmu　建武
ken　見
ki (arising)　起
ki (pneuma)　気
ki (vessel)　器
kikai　器界

Ki no Turayuki　紀貫之

Kinkaku-ji　金閣寺

Kinmei　欽明

kinpa　金波

Kitabatake Chikafusa　北畠親房

Kitano　北野

Kōben　高弁

Kōfuku-ji　興福寺

kogaku　古学

kōjō tai　高情体

kōko kyakurai　向去却来

kokoro　心

kokoro no waza　心の態

kokoro-zuke　心付

kokugaku　国学

Komparu Anshō　金春安照

Komparu-dayū　金春大夫

Komparu Gon-no-kami　金春権守

Komparu Hachiemon Anki
　金春八佐衛門安喜

Komparu Yasaburō　金春弥三郎

Komparu Zenchiku　金春禅竹

komu haru　来む春

kō nari, na togetaru kurai
　功成り, 名遂げたる位

Kongō Gon-no-kami　金剛権守

konton　混沌

Kōryū-ji　広隆寺

Kōshō　康正

kōshō fū　広精風

kotan　枯淡

koto, fue no michi　琴, 笛の道

kotoba　詞

kotoba-zuke　詞付

kotsu　骨

Kōzan-ji　高山寺

Kuan-wu wai-p'ien　觀物外篇

kua-tz'u　卦辭

Kuei-feng　圭峰

kuge　公家

Kūkai　空海

K'ung An-kuo　孔安國

Kuninotokotachi-no-mikoto
　国常立尊

kūrin　空輪

kyakurai fū　却来風

kyogaku　虚楽

kyōgen kigo　狂言騎語

kyoku　曲

kyū, shō　宮, 商

kyūi　九位

Kyūji hongi gengi　旧事本紀玄義

li (advantage)　利

li (principle)　理

li (propriety)　禮

li (fire, the clinging)　離

Lieh Tzu　列子

Li T'ung-hsüan　李通玄

Lu Hsiang-shan　陸象山

mappō　末法

Matsumushi　松虫

meiri　名利

metsu　滅

mi no furumai　身の振舞い

Mibu no Tadamine　壬生忠岑

michi　道

michi no hito　道の人

Miketsu-kami　御食津神, 御饌津神

mikkyō　密教

mikoshi　御輿

Minamoto Michimitsu　源通光

Mitsutarō　光太郎

Miwa　三輪

mizu　水

mo　末

mokuzen shingo　目前心後

mon (aural effect)　聞

mon (pattern)　文

Monju　文殊

monomane　物眞似

mono no aware　物の哀

Motomasa　元雅

Motoori Norinaga　本居宣長

Motoshige　元重

Motouji　元氏

Motoyoshi　元能

(Prince) Motoyoshi　元良親王

mubutsu　無物

mufū　無風

mukyoku　無極

mumon　無文

Murakami　村上

mushiki　無色

mushin　無心

mushu　無主
Musō Soseki　夢窓疏石
myō　妙
Myōe Shōnin　明恵上人
myōka fū　妙花風
myōkan zatchi　妙観察智
naishi kuyō　内四供養
Nankō Sōgen (or Shūgen, Sōgan)
　南江宗沅
Nanzen-ji　南禅寺
Nara　奈良
nembutsu　念仏
(Lady to Gofukakusa-in,) Nijō
　後深草院二条
Nijō Yoshimoto　二条良基
niku　肉
nikyoku　二曲
ninjō　人情
nochi-jite　後仕手
nōgakuron　能楽論
Nonomiya　野宮
Nyorai juryō bon　如来寿量品
nyoraizō　如来蔵
ō　横
Obasute　姨捨
Ōjin　応神
ōke　応化
Okina　翁
Ōmi sarugaku　近江申楽
omizutori　御水取
omoshiro　面白
on　音
Ōnin　応仁
Onnami　音阿弥
ō no hana　王の鼻
ō no mai　王舞
Oshio　小塩
Ōuchi Masahiro　大内正弘
p'an-chiao　判教
pen　本
pen-hsüeh　本覧
Po (or Pai) Chü-i　白居易
P'u-i　普一
pu-pien　不變
rakki (or onihishigi) tei　拉鬼体
rakkyo　落居
ran'i　闌位

rangyoku　闌曲
renbo　恋慕
ri hokkai　理法界
riji muge　理事無碍
riken no ken　離見の見
rikidō fū　力動風
rikugi　六義
Rin'e (or Rinkai)　林懐
Rinzai　臨済
rinzō　輪蔵
Ritsu　律
ritsuryō　律令
rokkon shōjō　六根清浄
rokudai　六大
rokurin (or rikurin) ichiro　六輪一露
ruten　流転
ryo, ritsu　呂，律
Ryōbu Shintō　両部神道
Saburō　三郎
Sado　佐渡
Sagano　嵯峨野
Saichō　最澄
saidō fū　細動風
Saigyō　西行
Saigyō-zakura　西行桜
samaya-gyō　三昧耶形
Sandō　三道
sangaku　散楽
sankyō itchi　三教一致
sanrin shōjō　三輪清浄
santai (rō jo gun)　三体 (老女軍)
santai (kū ge chū)　三諦 (空仮中)
Sarudahiko　猿田彦
sarugaku　申楽
Sarugaku ennen no ki　申楽延年の記
Sarume　猿女
Sasamegoto　ささめごと
seiki　精気
seishin　精神
senbon　千品
sen-luo wan-hsiang　森羅萬象
senmon fū　浅文風
Sentoku　千徳
shako　写古
shaku　迹
Shao Yung　邵雍
shen　神

sheng-mieh　生滅
Shigekatsu　重勝
Shigyoku　志玉
shih-i　十翼
shihokkai　四法界
shih-shih wu-ai　事事無礙
shijū　始終
Shikisanba　式三番
shikō　四劫
Shin　秦
shin　心
shinbutsu shūgō　神仏集合
Shingon　眞言
Shingyokushū　眞玉集
shinjin　深心
Shinkei　心敬
Shinki　眞機
shinku　親句
shin no mihashira　眞の御柱
shinnyo　眞如
shinnyo zuien　眞如隨緣
shinra banshō　森羅万象
Shinshiki kon'an　新式今案
Shintō gobusho　神道五部書
Shirō　四郎
shiseishin　至誠心
shishi　私詞
Shishinden　紫辰殿
shisō　四相
shite　仕手
shitoku　四德
shō　生
shodō　書道
shōi　性位
shōka　性花
shōka fū　正花風
shōki　性起
Shōkō　称光
shōmyō　声明
Shōtetsu　正徹
Shōtoku Taishi　聖德太子
shou　収
shu (height)　竪
shu (altruism)　恕
Shūbun　周文
shūdō　習道
shūgen　祝言

shūgen-on　祝言音
Shūishū　拾遺集
Shukujin　宿神
Shun　舜
shunigatsu'e　修二月会
Shūon-an　酬恩庵
shurin (or ryūrin)　竪輪
shushi　呪師
Sōchō　宗長
soen fū　鹿鉛風
Sōgi　宗祇
Sōin　宗筠
soku　疏句
Sōtō　曹洞
Sotoba Komachi　卒都婆小町
ssu-fu　四府
ssu-te　四德
sugata　姿
Sugawara Michizane　菅原道眞
Suinin　垂仁
suirin　水輪
Sumidagawa　隅田川
Ta chuan　大傳
Tachibana-dera　橘寺
tachinoboru ten　立ち上ぼる点
T'aehyŏn　太賢
Tafuku-an　多福庵
Ta-hsüeh　大學
t'ai-chi　太極
taikyoku　太極
Takeda-za　竹田座
taketakaki　長高き
taketaru　闌けたる
Takigi　薪
takigi nō　薪能
Tamba　丹波
Tao　道
tariki　他力
Tayū　大夫
Teika　定家
tenchi kaibyaku　天地開闢
Tendai Daishi　天台大師
Tendai myōshaku　天台妙釈
tenpen　轉変
Tenri　天理
t'i　體
t'ien-li　天理

T'ien-t'ai　天台
Tōdai-ji　東大寺
Tōfuku-ji　東福寺
Toganoo　栂尾
tōjiroki tei　遠白き体
toki no chōshi　時の調子
Tosa　土佐
Towazugatari　とはずがたり
Toyo'uke (or Toyuke)-no-ōkami
　　豊受 (止由気) 大神
ts'ang　藏
Tsao-po　棗柏
Tseng Hsi　曾晳
Tseng Tzu　曾子
Tsung-mi　宗密
tung (motion)　動
t'ung (penetrate)　通
tung-ching i-yüan　動靜一元
Ugetsu　雨月
Ujikatsu　氏勝
Ujinobu　氏信
Urabe Kanehiro　卜部兼熈
Urabe (or Yoshida) Kenkō
　　卜部 (吉田) 兼好
uruwashiki　麗しき
ushin tei　有心体
Uzumasa　太秦
wabi　侘
wagō no shiki　和合識
waka　和歌
Waka kuhon　和歌九品
Wakamiya　若宮
wakan　和漢
Wakatai jisshu　和歌体十種
waki　脇
Wang Pi　王弼
Watarai Ieyuki　度会家行
Watari (Higaki) Tsuneaki
　　度会 (檜垣) 常昌
waza　態
wei-shih　唯識
Wen-yen chuan　言文傳
wu-chi　無極

Wu-chiao chang　五教章
wu-hsing　五行
Wu-t'ai shan　五臺山
wu-te　五德
Yamamba　山姥
Yamashiro　山城
Yamato　大和
yao-tzu　爻辭
Yasaburō　八三郎
yase　痩せ
yata no kagami　八手の鏡
yin-yang　陰陽
yōka　用花
Yōkihi　楊貴妃
Yoshida　吉田
Yoshida Bunko　吉田文庫
Yoshida (Urabe) Kanenobu
　　吉田兼信
Yoshida Kanetomu　吉田兼倶
Yoshida Kenkō　*see Urabe Kenkō*
Yoshida Tōgo　吉田東五
Yoshino Saigyō　吉野西行
yüan　元
yüan-ch'i (dependent origination)　緣起
yüan-ch'i (primal pneuma)　元氣
Yüan-ming pao　元命苞
yūgen　幽玄
yūgen-on　幽玄音
Yuiitsu Shintō　唯一神道
Yuiitsu Shintō myōbō yōshū
　　唯一神道名法要集
yuishiki　唯識
yūjō no gentei　幽情の玄底
yūkyoku　遊曲
Yume no ki　夢の記
yung　用
Yūryaku　雄略
Zeami Motokiyo　世阿弥元清
Zen　禅
Zenni Daitoku　禅爾大德
zenpa　全波
zōrin　像輪

Bibliography

PRIMARY SOURCES AND TEXTS

Zenchiku and Zeami Editions Used

Hisamatsu Sen'ichi 久松潜一 and Nishio Minoru 西尾実, eds. *Karon shū, nōgakuron shū* 歌論集, 能楽論集. *NKBT*, vol. 65. Tokyo: Iwanami shoten, 1961.

Ijichi Tetsuo 伊地知鉄男, Omote Akira 表章, and Kuriyama Ri'ichi 栗山理一, eds. *Rengaron shū, nōgakuron shū, hairon shū* 連歌論集, 能楽論集, 俳論集. Nihon koten bungaku zenshū, vol. 51. Tokyo: Shōgakkan, 1973.

Konishi Jin'ichi 小西甚一, ed. *Zeami shū* 世阿弥集. Nihon no shisō, vol. 8. Tokyo: Chikuma shobō, 1970.

Omote Akira 表章 and Itō Masayoshi 伊藤正義, eds. *Komparu kodensho shūsei* 金春古伝書集成. Tokyo: Wan'ya shoten, 1969.

Omote Akira and Katō Shūichi 加藤周一, eds. *Zeami, Zenchiku* 世阿弥, 禅竹. *NST*, vol. 24. Tokyo: Iwanami shoten, 1974.

Saigusa Hiroto 三枝博音, ed. *Geijutsu ron* 芸術論. Nihon tetsugaku zensho, vol. 11. Tokyo: Dai'ichi shobō, 1936.

Tanaka Yutaka 田中裕, ed. *Zeami geijutsu ronshū* 世阿弥芸術論集. Shinchō Nihon koten shūsei, vol. 4. Tokyo: Shinchōsha, 1976.

Zenchiku Works (all found in KKSS, and in ZZ where noted)

Bunshō gannen waka 文正元年和歌 (Poems composed in the first year of the Bunshō era [1466]).

Emai-za kabegaki 円満井座壁書 (Wall-scribblings concerning the Emai troupe).

Emai-za keizu 円満井座系図 (Lineage chart of the Emai troupe).

Go'on jittei 五音十体 (The five sounds and ten styles).

Go'on no shidai 五音之次第 (Progression of the five sounds).

Go'on sangyoku shū 五音三曲集 (Collection of the five sounds and three skills). *ZZ*.

Inariyama sanrō ki 稲荷山参籠記 (Record of a retreat at Inari Shrine).

Jōdo-kyō hihan 浄土教批判 (Critique of the Pure Land teachings).

Kabu zuinō ki 歌舞髄脳記 (Record of the essentials of song and dance). *ZZ*.

Meishuku shū 明宿集 (Collection illuminating [the nature of the deity] Shukujin). *ZZ*.

Nika ichirin 二花一輪 (Two flowers, one circle).

Rokurin ichiro dai'i 六輪一露大意 (The gist of six circles, one dewdrop).

Rokurin ichiro gaishō 六輪一露概抄 (Outline of six circles, one dewdrop).

Rokurin ichiro hichū (Bunshō bon) 六輪一露秘注 (文正本) (Secret commentary on six circles, one dewdrop—Bunshō era version). *ZZ*.

Rokurin ichiro hichū (Kanshō bon) 六輪一露秘注 (寛正本) (Secret commentary on six circles, one dewdrop—Kanshō era version). *ZZ*.

Rokurin ichiro no ki 六輪一露之記 (A record of six circles, one dewdrop). *ZZ*.

Rokurin ichiro no kichū 六輪一露之記注 (Commentary to "A record of six circles, one dewdrop"). *ZZ*.

Rokurin kanjō hiki 六輪潅頂秘記 (Secret record of the initiation to the six circles).

Rokurin kyokumi 六輪曲味 (Flavor of the six circles in performance).

Sarugaku engi 申楽縁起 (The origin of sarugaku).

Sazen nikki 作善日記 (Diary of good works).

Shidō yōshō 至道要抄 (The essentials of attaining the way). *ZZ*.

Yūgen sanrin 幽玄三輪 (Three circles of yūgen). *ZZ*.

Zeami Works (all found in ZZ)

Fūgyoku shū 風曲集 (Collection of singing styles).

Fūshi kaden 風姿花伝 (Transmission of style and the flower).

Goi 五位 (Five ranks).

Go'on 五音 (Five sounds).

Go'ongyoku jōjō 五音曲条々 (Details of the five sounds).

Kakyō 花鏡 (The flower in the mirror).

Kyakuraika 却来花 (The flower of return).

Kyūi shidai 九位次第 (The progression of the nine ranks).

Nikyoku santai ningyō zu 二曲三体人形図 (Illustrated figures of the two skills and three roles).

Rikugi 六義 (Six principles).

Sarugaku dangi 申楽談儀 (Talks on sarugaku), as told to Motoyoshi 元能.

Shikadō 至花道 (The way of attaining the flower).

Shūgyoku tokka 拾玉得花 (Gathering jewels, acquiring the flower).

Yūgaku shūdō fūken 遊楽習道風見 (Views on enjoying performance and learning the way).

Other (Non-Buddhist) Japanese Works

Genji monogatari 原氏物語 (The tale of Genji), by Murasaki Shikibu 紫式部. *NKBT*, vols. 14–18.

Hitorigoto 独り言 (Private utterances), by Shinkei 心敬. *NST*, vol. 23.

Ikkyū Oshō nenpu 一休和尚年譜 (Chronological record of the priest Ikkyū), by Bokusai 墨齋. Zoku gunsho ruijū, vol. 9, pt. 2.

Jinnō jitsuroku 神皇実録 (Authentic account of divine sovereigns). Zokuzoku gunsho ruijū, vol. 1.

Kanke kōshū 菅家後集 (Later collection of the Sugawara family). *NKBT*, vol. 72.

Kasuga gongen kenki 春日権現検記 (Record of miracles of the Kasuga deity). Gunsho ruijū, vol. 2.

Kogo shūi 古語拾遺 (Gleanings from ancient stories), by Inbe no Hironari 斎部広成. Gunshō ruijū, vol. 16.

Kokin wakashū 古今和歌集 (Collection of Japanese poems, ancient and modern). *NKBT*, vol. 8.

Man'yōshū 万葉集 (Collection of the myriad leaves). *NKBT*, vols. 4–7.

Nihon shoki 日本書紀 (Chronicle of Japan). *NKBT*, vols. 67–68.

Nihon shoki sanso 日本書紀纂疏 (Compiled notes on the Chronicle of Japan), by Ichijō Kaneyoshi 一条兼良. Kokumin seishin bunka kenkyūjo, ed.

Ruijū jingi hongen 類聚神祇本源 (Fundamental origins of the deities, assembled), by Watarai Ieyuki 度会家行. Zokuzoku gunsho ruijū, vol. 1; *NST*, vol. 19.

Ryōgū gyōmon shinshaku 両宮形文深釈 (Profound commentary on the symbols of the two shrines [of Ise]), trad. attrib. to Kūkai 空海. Kōbō Daishi zenshū, vol. 5; Zokuzoku gunsho ruijū, vol. 1.

Saigyō Shōnin danshō 西行上人談抄 (Talks with the priest Saigyō), by Ren'a 連阿. Nihon kagaku taikei, vol. 2.

Sango ki 三五記 (Record of the night of the full moon), trad. attrib. to Fujiwara Teika 藤原定家. Gunsho ruijū, vol. 16.

Sarugaku kōshōki 申楽後証記 (Later authentic record of sarugaku), by Ichijō Kaneyoshi 一条兼良. *KKSS*.

Sasamegoto ささめごと (Murmurings), by Shinkei 心敬. Nihon koten bungaku zenshū, vol. 51.

Shaku Nihongi 釈日本紀 (Annotated "Chronicle of Japan"), by Urabe Kanekata 卜部懐賢. Kokushi taikei, vol. 8.

Shinkokin wakashū 新古今和歌集 (New collection of Japanese poems ancient and modern). *NKBT*, vol. 28.

Shū'i gusō 拾遺愚草 (Gleaned fragments), by Fujiwara Teika 藤原定家. Tsukamoto Tetsuzō, ed.

Tenchi reiki ki 天地麗気記 (Record of the refined pneuma of heaven and earth), trad. attrib. to Kūkai 空海. Kōbō Daishi zenshū, vol. 5.

Towazugatari とはずがたり (An unrequested tale), by Lady Nijō 後深草院二条. Nihon koten zensho, vol. 105.

Toyoashihara shinpū waki 豊葦原紳風和記 (Harmonious record of the divine wind of the eternal reed-plain), by Jihen 慈遍. Zokuzoku gunsho ruijū, vol. 1.

Yamato Katsuragi hōzan ki 大和葛城宝山記 (Record of the sacred Mount Katsuragi in Yamato), trad. attrib. to Gyōgi 行基. *NST*, vol. 19.

Buddhist Works

Ch'eng wei-shih lun 成唯識論 (Treatise on the establishment of "consciousness only"), by Vasubandhu. *T* 1585.

Chin-kang pei 金剛錍 (Adamantine monument), by Chan-jan 湛然. *T* 1932.

Daibiroshana jōbutsu shinpen kaji kyō 大毗盧遮那成仏神変加持経 (Mahāvairocana sutra). *T* 848.

Daihōkōbutsu kegon-gyō 大方広仏華厳経 (Garland sutra). *T* 279.

Daiju kinnaraō shomon kyō 大樹緊那羅王所問経 (Sutra requested by the Kiṃnara king). *T* 625.

Gokyōshō kenmon 五教章見聞 (Views on "Treatise of the five teachings"), by Shigyoku 志玉, recorded by Gen'on 玄音. Edo period edition in collection of Ryūkoku University.

Hizō hōyaku 秘藏宝鑰 (The precious key to the secret treasury), by Kūkai 空海. Kōbō Daishi zenshū, vol. 1; Kōbō Daishi chosaku zenshū, vol. 1.

Hsiu hua-yen ao-chih wang-chin huan-yüan kuan 修華嚴奧旨妄盡還源觀 (Contemplation on practicing the profound principles of Hua-yen, exhausting delusion, and returning to the source), by Fa-tsang 法藏. *T* 1876.

Jigyō ryakki 自行略記 (Abbreviated record for one's own practice), by Genshin 源信. Eshin sōzu zenshū, vol. 3.

Muchū mondō 夢中問答 (Dialogues within a dream), by Musō Soseki 夢窓疎石. Nihon no shisō, vol. 10.

Myōhō renge kyō 妙法蓮華経 (Lotus sutra). *T* 261.

Pi-yen lu 碧巖錄 (Blue cliff record), by Yüan-wu 圓悟. Hekigan shū teihon.

Pǒmmang-gyǒng kojǒkki 梵綱經古迹記 (Record of ancient traces of the Brahma's net sutra), by T'aehyǒn 太賢. *T* 1815.

Sokushin jōbutsu gi 即身成仏義 (On becoming a buddha in this very body), by Kūkai 空海. Kōbō Daishi zenshū, vol. 1.

Ta-fang-kuang-fo hua-yen-ching shu 大方廣佛華嚴經疏 (Notes on the garland sutra), by Ch'eng-kuan 澄觀. *T* 1735.

Ta-fang-kuang-fo hua-yen-ching sui-shu yen-i ch'ao 大方廣佛華嚴經隨疏 (An embellishment of "Notes on the garland sutra"), by Ch'eng-kuan 澄觀. *T* 1736.

Ta-fang-kuang yüan-chüeh hsiu-to-lo liao-i ching lüeh-shu 大方廣圓覺修多羅了義經略疏 (Abbreviated notes on the "Perfect enlightenment sutra"), by Tsung-mi 宗密. *T* 1795.

Ta-sheng ch'i-hsin lun 大乘起心論 (The awakening of faith in the Mahayana), attrib. to Aśvaghosa. *T* 1666.

Ta-sheng ch'i-hsin lun i-chi 大乘起心論義記 (Principles of "The awakening of faith in the Mahayana"), by Fa-tsang 法藏. *T* 1846.

Wondon sǒngbullon 圓頓成佛論 (Treatise on the complete and sudden attainment of buddhahood), by Chinul 知訥. Shim Chae-yǒl, ed., *Pojo pǒbǒ*.

(Non-Buddhist) Chinese Works

Chih-yen 知言 (Knowing words), by Hu-hung 胡宏. Ssu-k'u ch'üan-shu.

Chin-ssu lu 近思錄 (Record of thoughts on things at hand), by Chu Hsi 朱熹. Shinshaku kanbun taikei, vol. 37.

Chou-i pen-i 周易本義 (Original meaning of the "Book of change"), by Chu Hsi 朱熹. Ssu-k'u ch'üan-shu.

Chuang Tzu 莊子. Shinshaku kanbun taikei, vols. 7–8.

Chung-yung 中庸 (Doctrine of the mean), attrib. to Tzu-ssu 子思. Chūgoku koten sen, vol. 4, edited by Shimada Kenji.

Han Fei Tzu 韓非子. Shinshaku kanbun taikei, vols. 11–12.

Hsiao ching 孝經 (Classic of filial piety), attrib. to Tseng Tzu 曾子. *Kōkyō*, edited by Hayashi Taisuke.

Hsün Tzu 荀子. Shinshaku kanbun taikei, vols. 5–6.

Huai-nan Tzu 准南子. Shinshaku kanbun taikei, vols. 54–56.

Huang-chi ching-shih shu 皇極經世書 (Supreme principles that regulate the world), by Shao Yung 邵雍. Ssu-k'u ch'üan-shu.

I ching 易經 (Book of change). Zenshaku kanbun taikei, vol. 9.

I chuan 易傳 (Commentary on the "Book of change"), by Ch'eng I 程伊. Erh-

Ch'eng ch'üan-shu.

K'ung Tzu chia-yü. 孔子家語 (Account of the school of Confucius), attrib. to Wang Su 王肅. Zenshaku kanbun taikei, vol. 20.

Lun-yü 論語 (Analects), by K'ung Tzu 孔子 (Confucius). James Legge, *The Chinese Classics*, vol. 1.

Mao shih ch'u 毛詩注 (Commentary to the "Book of songs") by Cheng-hsüan 鄭玄. Shih-san ching ch'u.

Meng Tzu 孟子 (Mencius). James Legge, *The Chinese Classics*, vol. 4.

Shih ching 詩經 (Book of songs). James Legge, *The Chinese Classics*, vol. 4.

Shih-shuo hsin-yü 世說新語 (A new account of tales of the world), by Liu I-ch'ing 劉義慶. Shinshaku kanbun taikei, vols. 67–68.

Shu ching 書經 (Book of history). James Legge, *The Chinese Classics*, vol. 3.

T'ai-chi-t'u shuo 太極圖說 (Explanation of the diagram of the Great Ultimate), by Chou Tun-i 周敦頤. Chou Tzu ch'üan-shu.

Tao-te ching 道德經 (The Way and its power), by Lao Tzu 老子. Zenshaku kanbun taikei, vol. 15.

Tso chuan 左傳 (Tso's commentary [to the "Spring and autumn annals"]). James Legge, *The Chinese Classics*, vol. 5.

SECONDARY SOURCES

Araki Kengo 荒木見悟. *Bukkyō to jukyō* 仏教と儒教. Kyoto: Heiraku-ji shoten, 1963.

Aston, W. G., trans. *Nihongi*. Rutland, Vt.: Tuttle Books, 1972.

Birdwhistell, Anne D. *Transition to Neo-Confucianism: Shao Yung on Knowledge and Symbols of Reality*. Stanford: Stanford University Press, 1989.

Brazell, Karen, trans. *The Confessions of Lady Nijō*. Stanford: Stanford University Press, 1976.

Buswell, Robert E., Jr., trans. *The Collected Works of Chinul*. Honolulu: University of Hawaii Press, 1983.

Carter, Steven D. *The Road to Komatsubara*. Cambridge, Mass: Council on East Asian Studies, Harvard University, 1987.

Chan, Wing-tsit. *A Source Book in Chinese Philosophy*. Princeton: Princeton University Press, 1967.

———, trans. *Reflections on Things at Hand*. New York: Columbia University Press, 1967.

Ch'en, Kenneth K. S. *Buddhism in China*. Princeton: Princeton University Press, 1964.

———. *The Chinese Transformation of Buddhism*. Princeton: Princeton University Press, 1973.

Chiu Hansheng. "Zhu Xi's Doctrine of Principle." In *Chu Hsi and Neo-Confucianism*, edited by Wing-tsit Chan. Honolulu: University of Hawaii Press, 1986, 116–37.

Cleary, Thomas, trans. *Entry into the Inconceivable*. Honolulu: Hawaii University Press, 1963.

Cleary, Thomas and J. C., trans. *The Blue Cliff Record*, vols. 2–3. Boulder: Shambala, 1977.

Conze, Edward. *Buddhist Thought in India*. Ann Arbor: University of Michigan Press, 1967.

DeBary, Wm. Theodore, and Irene Bloom, eds. *Principle and Practicality*. New York: Columbia University Press, 1979.

Dōmoto Masaki 堂本正樹. *Zeami* 世阿弥. Geki shobō, 1986.

Feng Yu-lan. *A History of Chinese Philosophy*, vol. 2. Princeton: Princeton University Press, 1952.

Foucault, Michel. *The Archaeology of Knowledge*, translated by A. M. Sheridan Smith. New York: Harper Colophon Books, 1976.

Fukui Kyūzō 福井久藏. *Ichijō Kanera* 一条兼良. Tokyo: Kōseikaku, 1943.

Gimello, Robert M. "Li T'ung-hsüan and the Practical Dimensions of Hua-yen." In *Studies in Ch'an and Hua-yen*, edited by Robert M. Gimello and Peter N. Gregory. Honolulu: University of Hawaii Press, 1983, 321–87.

Giradot, N. J. *Myth and Meaning in Early Taoism*. Berkeley: University of California Press, 1983.

Graham, A. C. *Disputers of the Tao: Philosophical Argument in Ancient China*. La Salle, Ill.: Open Court, 1989.

Haga Kōshirō 芳賀幸四郎. *Chūsei zenrin no gakumon oyobi bungaku ni kansuru kenkyū* 中世禅林の学問及び文学に関する研究. Kyoto: Shibunkaku shuppan, 1981.

———. *Higashiyama bunka no kenkyū* 東山文化の研究. Kyoto: Shibunkaku shuppan, 1981.

Hare, Thomas Blenman. *Zeami's Style: The Noh Plays of Zeami Motokiyo*. Stanford: Stanford University Press, 1987.

Hakeda, Yoshito S., trans. *The Awakening of Faith*. New York: Columbia University Press, 1967.

———. *Kūkai: Major Works*. New York: Columbia University Press, 1972.

Harich-Schneider, Eta. *A History of Japanese Music*. London: Oxford University Press, 1973.

Hirose Tamahiro 広瀬瑞弘. *Nō to Komparu* 能と金春. Kyoto: Hatsune shobō, 1969.

Hisamatsu Shin'ichi. *Zen and the Fine Arts*, translated by Tokiwa Gishin. Tokyo: Kodansha International, 1971.

Imai Kei'ichi 今井啓一. *Hata no Kōkatsu* 秦河勝. Kyoto: Sōgeisha, 1968.

Imai Usaburō 今井宇三郎. *Sōdai ekigaku no kenkyū* 宋代易学の研究. Tokyo: Meiji shoin, 1958.

Itō Masayoshi 伊藤正義. *Komparu Zenchiku no kenkyū* 金春禅竹の研究. Kyoto: Akao shōbundō, 1970.

———. "Kaidai 解題" (of the play *Nonomiya* 野宮). In *Yōkyoku shū* 謡曲集, vol. 3, edited by Itō Masayoshi. Tokyo: Shinchōsha, 1988, 450–53.

Katō Bunnō, et al., trans. *The Threefold Lotus Sutra*. New York: Weatherhill, 1975.

Katō Genchi and Hoshino Hikoshirō, trans. *Kogoshūi: Gleanings from Ancient Stories*. London: Curzon Press, 1972.

Keene, Donald. "The Comic Tradition in Renga." In *Japan in the Muromachi Age*, edited by John Whitney Hall and Toyoda Takeshi. Berkeley: University of California Press, 1977, 241–77.

Kitagawa Tadahiko 北川忠彦. *Zeami* 世阿弥. Tokyo: Chūō kōron, 1972.

Kiyota, Minoru. *Shingon Buddhism: Theory and Practice*. Tokyo: Buddhist Book International, 1978.

Kobayashi Shizuo 小林静雄. *Nōgaku shi kenkyū* 能楽史研究. Tokyo: Yūzankaku, 1945.

Kokumin seishin bunka kenkyūjo 国民精神文化研究所, ed. *Nihon shoki sanso* 日本書紀纂疏. Tokyo: Meguro shoten, 1935.

Konishi Jin'ichi 小西甚一. "Hie to yase 冷えと痩せ." *Bungaku, gogaku* 文学語学 10 (November 1957), 12–29.

――――. "Michi and Medieval Writing." In *Principles of Classical Japanese Literature*, edited by Earl Miner. Princeton: Princeton University Press, 1985, 181–208.

――――. *Michi: Chūsei no rinen* 道: 中世の理念. Tokyo: Kōdansha, 1975.

――――. *Nōgakuron kenkyū* 能楽論研究. Tokyo: Hanawa shobō, 1961.

Kōsai Tsutomu 香西精. *Zeami shinkō* 世阿弥新考. Tokyo: Wan'ya shoten, 1962.

Kubota Osamu 久保田修. *Chūsei Shintō no kenkyū* 中世神道の研究. Kyoto: Shintōshi gakkai, 1959.

Kuroda Masao 黒田正男. *Zeami nōgakuron no kenkyū* 世阿弥能楽論の研究. Tokyo: Ōbaisha, 1979.

LaFleur, William R. *The Karma of Words: Buddhism and the Literary Arts in Medieval Japan*. Berkeley: University of California Press, 1983.

Lai, Whalen Wai-lun. "*The Awakening of Faith in the Mahayana*: A Study of the Unfolding of Sinitic Mahayana Motifs." Ph.D. dissertation, Harvard University, 1975.

McCullough, Helen, trans. *Kokin Wakashū*. Stanford: Stanford University Press, 1985.

Mather, Richard B., trans. *Shih-shuo Hsin-yü: A New Account of Tales of the World*. Minneapolis: University of Minnesota Press, 1976.

Matsunaga, Alicia. *The Buddhist Philosophy of Assimilation*. Tokyo: Sophia University, 1969.

Merwin, W. S., and Sōiku Shigematsu, trans. *Sun at Midnight*. San Francisco: North Point Press, 1989.

Mezaki Tokue, "Aesthete-Recluses during the Transition from Ancient to Medieval Japan." In *Principles of Classical Japanese Literature*, edited by Earl Miner. Princeton: Princeton University Press, 1985, 151–80.

Munro, Donald J. "The Family Network, the Stream of Water, and the Plant: Picturing Persons in Sung Confucianism." In *Individualism and Holism: Studies in Confucian and Taoist Values*, edited by Donald J. Munro. Ann Arbor: Center for Chinese Studies, University of Michigan, 1985.

Nagashima Fukutarō 永鳥福太郎. *Ichijō Kanera* 一条兼良. Tokyo: Yoshikawa kōbunkan, 1950.

Nearman, Mark J., trans. "Kakyō." *Monumenta Nipponica* 37:3 (Autumn 1982), 333–74; 37:4 (Winter 1982), 461–96; 38:1 (Spring 1983), 51–71.

――――, trans. "*Kyakuraika*, Zeami's Final Legacy for the Master Actor." *Monumenta Nipponica* 35:2 (Summer 1980), 153–97.

――――, trans. "Zeami's *Kyūi*: A Pedagogical Guide for Teachers of Acting." *Monumenta Nipponica* 33:3 (Autumn 1978), 299–332.

Nishi Kazuyoshi 西一祥. *Zeami: hito to geijutsu* 世阿弥: 人と芸術. Tokyo: Ōbaisha, 1985.

Nishida Nagao 西田長男. *Nihon Shintō shi kenkyū* 日本神道史研究, vol. 5. Tokyo: Kōdansha, 1979.

Nishio Minoru 西尾実. *Dōgen to Zeami* 道元と世阿弥. Tokyo: Iwanami shoten, 1965.

————. *Zeami no nōgeiron* 世阿弥の能芸論. Tokyo: Iwanami shoten, 1974.

Nose Asaji 能勢朝次. "Komparu Zenchiku no suimi ni tsuite 金春禅竹の水味に付いて." *Bungaku* 文学, August 1934.

————. *Nōgaku genryū kō* 能楽源流孝. Tokyo: Iwanami shoten, 1938.

————. *Yūgen ron* 幽玄論. Tokyo: Kawade shobō, 1944.

Odin, Steve. *Process Metaphysics and Hua-yen Buddhism*. Albany: SUNY Press, 1982.

Okada Takehiko. "Chu Hsi and Wisdom as Hidden and Stored." In *Chu Hsi and Neo-Confucianism*, edited by Wing-tsit Chan. Honolulu: University of Hawaii Press, 1986, 197–211.

Omote Akira 表章 and Itō Masayoshi 伊藤正義, eds. *Komparu kodensho shūsei* 金春古伝書集成. Tokyo: Wan'ya shoten, 1969.

Omote Akira 表章 and Oda Sachiko 小田辛子, eds. *Komparu Anshō densho* 金春安照伝書. Tokyo: Wan'ya shoten, 1978.

O'Neill, P. G. *Early Nō Drama*. London: Lund Humphries, 1958.

Ooms, Herman. *Tokugawa Ideology*. Princeton: Princeton University Press, 1985.

Ōsumi Kazuo 大隅和男, ed. *Chūsei Shintō ron* 中世神道論. *NST*, vol. 19. Tokyo: Iwanami shoten, 1977.

Peterson, Willard J. "Making Connections: 'Commentary on the Attached Verbalizations' of the Book of Change." *Harvard Journal of Asiatic Studies* 42:1 (June 1982), 67–116.

Pilgrim, Richard B. "Zeami and the Way of Nō." *History of Religions* 12:2 (November 1972), 136–48.

Plaks, Andrew H. *Archetype and Allegory in the Dream of the Red Chamber*. Princeton: Princeton University Press, 1976.

Pollack, David, trans. *Zen Poems of the Five Mountains*. Decatur, Ga: Scholar's Press, 1985.

————. *The Fracture of Meaning: Japan's Synthesis of China from the Eighth through the Eighteenth Centuries*. Princeton: Princeton University Press, 1986.

Porkert, Manfred. *Chinese Medicine*. New York: William Morrow, 1988.

Rawlinson, Andrew. "The Position of the Astasāhasrikā Prajñāpāramitā in the Development of Early Mahayana." In *Prajñāpāramitā and Related Systems*, edited by Lewis Lancaster. Berkeley: Berkeley Buddhist Studies Series, 1977, 3–34.

Rimer, Thomas J., and Yamazaki Masakazu, trans. *On the Art of the Nō Drama: The Major Treatises of Zeami*. Princeton: Princeton University Press, 1984.

Rosenfield, John M. "The Unity of the Three Creeds: A Theme in Japanese Ink Painting of the Fifteenth Century." In *Japan in the Muromachi Age*, edited by John Whitney Hall and Toyoda Takeshi. Berkeley: University of California Press, 1977, 205–25.

Sanford, James H. *Zen-Man Ikkyū*. Chico, Calif.: Scholars Press, 1980.

Schafer, Edward H. *Pacing the Void: T'ang Approaches to the Stars*. Berkeley: University of California Press, 1977.

Schirokauer, Conrad. "Chu Hsi and Hu Hung." In *Chu Hsi and Neo-Confucianism*, edited by Wing-tsit Chan. Honolulu: University of Hawaii Press, 1986, 480–502.

Seidensticker, Edward G., trans. *The Tale of Genji*. New York: Alfred Knopf, 1975.

Shchutskii, Iulian K. *Researches on the I Ching*, translated by William L. MacDonald and Hasegawa Tsuyoshi, with Hellmut Wilhelm. Princeton: Princeton University Press, 1979.

Shiban 師蛮. *Honchō kōsō den* 本朝高僧伝. Dainihon bukkyō zensho, vol. 102.

Shimada Kenji 鳥田虔次. *Shushigaku to yōmeigaku* 朱子学と陽明学. Tokyo: Iwanami shoten, 1967.

Smith, Kidder, Peter K. Bol, Joseph A. Adler, and Don J. Wyatt. *Sung Dynasty Uses of the I Ching*. Princeton: Princeton University Press, 1990.

Takamine Ryōshū 高峰了州. *Kegon shisō shi* 華厳思想史. 2d ed. Kyoto: Hyakkaen, 1963.

Tamaki Kōshirō 玉城康四郎. "Kegon no shōki ni tsuite 華厳思の性起について." In *Indo tetsugaku to Bukkyō no shomondai* 印度哲学と仏教の諸問題, edited by Miyamoto Shōson 宮本正尊. Tokyo: Iwanami shoten, 1951. 281–309.

Taylor, Rodney L. *The Confucian Way of Contemplation*. Columbia: University of South Carolina Press, 1988.

Thornhill, Arthur H., III. "The Goddess Emerges: Shinto Paradigms in the Aesthetics of Zeami and Zenchiku." *Journal of the Association of Teachers of Japanese* 24:1 (April 1990), 49–59.

———. "Typology in Traditional Japanese Poetics: The Reception of Chinese Buddhist Models." In *Comparative Literature East and West: Topics and Trends*, vol. 1, edited by Cornelia N. Moore and Raymond A. Moody. Honolulu: University of Hawaii Press, 1989, 177–83.

———. "*Yūgen* after Zeami." Forthcoming.

Tillman, Hoyt Cleveland. "Consciousness of T'ien in Chu Hsi's Thought." *Harvard Journal of Asiatic Studies* 47:1 (June, 1987), 31–50.

Toita Michizō 戸井田道三. *Kannami to Zeami* 観阿弥と世阿弥. Tokyo: Iwanami shoten, 1969.

———. *Nō: kami to kojiki no geijutsu* 能: 神と乞食の芸術. Tokyo: Serika shobō, 1973.

Tomoeda Ryūtarō 友枝龍太郎. *Shushi no shisō keisei* 朱子の思想形成. Tokyo: Shunjūsha, 1969.

———. "The System of Chu Hsi's Philosophy." In *Chu Hsi and Neo-Confucianism*, edited by Wing-tsit Chan. Honolulu: University of Hawaii Press, 1986, 158–68.

Tu Wei-ming. *Centrality and Commonality*. 2d ed. Albany: SUNY Press, 1989.

———. *Humanity and Self-Cultivation*. Berkeley: Asian Humanities Press, 1979.

———. "The Idea of the Human in Mencian Thought: An Approach to Chinese Aesthetics." In *Theories of the Arts in China*, edited by Susan Bush and Christian Murck. Princeton: Princeton University Press, 1983, 57–73.

Tyler, Royall. *The Miracles of the Kasuga Deity*. New York, Columbia Unversity Press, 1990.

Ueda, Makoto. *Literary and Art Theories of Japan*. Cleveland: Case-Western Reserve, 1967.

Wajima Yoshio 和鳥芳男. *Chūsei no jugaku* 中世の儒学. Tokyo: Yoshikawa kōbunkan, 1965.

Waley, Arthur, trans. *The Analects of Confucius*. New York: Vintage Books, 1968.

———. *The Book of Songs*. New York: Grove Weidenfeld, 1987.

Watson, Burton, trans. *The Complete Works of Chuang Tzu*. New York: Columbia University Press, 1968.

Wayman, Alex and Hideko. *The Lion's Roar of Queen Śrīmālā*. New York: Columbia University Press, 1974.

White, Douglass. "Interpretations of the Central Concept of the *I Ching* during the Han, Sung, and Ming Dynasties." Ph.D. dissertation, Harvard University, 1976.

Wilhelm, Richard, and Cary F. Baynes, trans. *The I Ching or Book of Changes*. Princeton: Princeton University Press, 1967.

Wixted, John Timothy. "The Nature of Evaluation in the *Shih-p'in* (Gradings of Poets) by Chung Hung (A.D. 469–518)." In *Theories of the Arts in China*, edited by Susan Bush and Christian Murck. Princeton: Princeton University Press, 1983, 225–64.

Yamanoi, Yu. "The Great Ultimate and Heaven in Chu Hsi's Philosophy." In *Chu Hsi and Neo-Confucianism*, edited by Wing-tsit Chan. Honolulu: University of Hawaii Press, 1986, 79–92.

Yasura Okakō 安良岡康. *Chūseiteki bungaku no tankyū* 中世的文学の探求. Tokyo: Yūseidō, 1970.

Yü Ying-shih. "Morality and Knowledge in Chu Hsi's Philosophical System." In *Chu Hsi and Neo-Confucianism*, edited by Wing-tsit Chan. Honolulu: University of Hawaii Press, 1986, 228–54.

Yuasa Yasuo 湯浅泰雄. *Kodaijin no seishin sekai* 古代人の精神世界. Kyoto: Minerva shobō, 1980.

Yusa, Michiko. "*Riken no ken*: Zeami's Theory of Acting and Theatrical Appreciation." *Monumenta Nipponica* 42:3 (Autumn 1987), 331–45.

Index